Judith Brett is emeritus professor of politics at La Trobe University in Melbourne, where she taught from 1989 until her retirement in 2012. She was the third editor of the literary journal *Meanjin*, from 1982 to 1986. She has written extensively on Australia's political history as well as on contemporary politics, and contributes regularly to the *Monthly* magazine.

ALSO BY JUDITH BRETT

Robert Menzies' Forgotten People (1992 and 2007; winner of a Victorian Premier's Literary Award, a NSW Premier's Literary Award and the Ernest Scott Prize for History)

Australian Liberals and the Moral Middle Class: From Alfred Deakin to John Howard (2004; winner of the Ernest Scott Prize for History)

'Relaxed and Comfortable: The Liberal Party's Australia', *Quarterly Essay* 19 (2005)

Ordinary People's Politics: Australians Talk about Life, Politics and the Future of Their Country (with Anthony Moran; 2006)

'Exit Right: The Unravelling of John Howard', *Quarterly Essay* 28 (2007)

'Fair Share: Country and City in Australia', *Quarterly Essay* 42 (2011)

The Enigmatic Mr Deakin (2017; winner of the National Biography Award)

From Secret Ballot to Democracy Sausage: How Australia Got Compulsory Voting (2019)

'The Coal Curse: Resources, Climate and Australia's Future', *Quarterly Essay* 78 (2020)

Doing
Politics

WRITING ON
PUBLIC LIFE

Judith Brett

TEXT PUBLISHING MELBOURNE AUSTRALIA

The Text Publishing Company acknowledges the Traditional Owners of the country on which we work, the Wurundjeri people of the Kulin Nation, and pays respect to their Elders past and present.

textpublishing.com.au

The Text Publishing Company
Wurundjeri Country, Level 6, Royal Bank Chambers, 287 Collins Street, Melbourne Victoria 3000 Australia

The author and publisher gratefully acknowledge the publications in which earlier versions of these pieces appeared.

Published by The Text Publishing Company, 2021

Cover design by Chong W.H.
Page design by Rachel Aitken
Typeset by J&M Typesetting

Printed and bound in Australia by Griffin Press, part of Ovato, an accredited ISO/ NZS 14001:2004 Environmental Management System printer.

ISBN: 9781922330987 (paperback)
ISBN: 9781922459220 (ebook)

A catalogue record for this book is available from the National Library of Australia.

CONTENTS

Introduction
Going Public

It's been a dismal decade, or more. When did it start, this sense that Australia has lost direction? In 1996, when Pauline Hanson brought her mean-spirited grievances into the national parliament? In 2001, when John Howard refused to let the captain of the *Tampa* land desperate refugees rescued from drowning? In 2008 and 2009, when Kevin Rudd was so intent on wedging Malcolm Turnbull that he destroyed the possibility of a bipartisan energy policy? Or was it the next year, when the ALP's bovver boys convinced Julia Gillard to challenge Rudd for the leadership; or 2013, when Tony Abbott was elected on a series of lies about his plans for the budget, and became Australia's worst prime minister ever?

There are so many low points and not many highs. But there are a few, and we should acknowledge them: avoiding the worst of the global financial crisis, the bipartisan introduction of the National Disability Insurance Scheme, and the hugely successful management of the first year of the coronavirus pandemic by the combined efforts of the state and federal governments (though the second year has been a different story). As well, since Scott Morrison became prime minister, politics has become more civil than in the preceding years. This is not much, though, to balance the ledger.

All the time the planet has been heating, the natural environment continuing to degrade. China has been reshaping the international order, and our trading strengths in fossil fuels and international tourism and education have been evaporating. Only iron ore has reliable staying power, backed up by a basket of farm exports. There are plenty of ideas about how to diversify our export income using our natural advantages in renewable-energy sources, and some action in the private sector, but nothing yet that looks like national leadership from our politicians. They barely seem aware of how vulnerable our economy has become.

Leadership theory distinguishes between transactional and trans-formational leaders. Transactional leadership is an adaptation by management theory of Max Weber's rational-legal authority, where authority derives from adherence to established rules rather than from either tradition or from personal power, which Weber called charisma. The transactional leader offers competence with a focus on proper process within established structures, and elicits followers' compliance through systems of rewards and sanctions. The big drawback of transactional leaders is their difficulty in dealing with change.

Transformative leaders, by contrast, are all about change, reshaping people's values and perceptions and the way things get done, using their skills in communication to build trust and shared goals. When people criticise leaders for lacking vision and failing to provide 'real leadership', it is transformative leadership they long for. Transformational leaders inspire; transactional leaders reassure. Generally a lot more people crave reassurance than inspiration, particularly when we are talking about prime ministers and electorates, and anxiety trumps hope.

Most of Australia's successful prime ministers have been transactional leaders, offering competence and an incremental, pragmatic approach to change. It fits well with the Liberal Party's core mission of keeping Labor and its dangerous new ideas from the treasury benches. Robert Menzies and John Howard are the standouts, though Howard had more policy ambitions than Menzies. He succeeded in introducing a consumption tax but failed in his attempts to radically reform the industrial-relations system. Menzies was not so much interested in policy reform as in shoring up existing structures and institutions against Labor's socialist threats. In this he was remarkably successful. His failures too were characteristic of transactional leadership, as he clung to race-based policies in immigration and Indigenous affairs. After he retired, the Coalition governments of Harold Holt and John Gorton were freed to embark on reform.

The only Liberal leader who might be regarded as transformational was Alfred Deakin, though more so as a leader of the federation movement than as prime minister. During the 1890s Deakin's silver-tongued oratory imbued the cause of federation with spiritual meaning as he urged people to transcend their parochial colonial identities in the birth of new nation. Once federation was achieved, however, as the Commonwealth's first attorney-general and three times its prime minister, Deakin shifted his focus to building the institutional structures for the new level of government.

Our current prime minister, Scott Morrison, is clearly transactional, with a focus on practical outcomes and a reliance on process to manage political problems. He doesn't like being taken by surprise, or rushed into a response to unexpected events. 'We're looking into it,' he'll say. 'The government is taking advice.' Or he'll establish an inquiry. In response to Brittany Higgins' public allegation that she was raped in Parliament House by a fellow Liberal Party staffer, he established five. This can seem like playing for time till the heat dies down, rather than a genuine attempt to find real-world solutions. The crunch comes when the reports come in, if people are still paying attention. Then the government needs to take some responsibility for fixing and not just recognising problems.

Our last transformational prime minister was Paul Keating. As treasurer he opened up Australia's highly protected economy. As prime minister from 1993 to 1996 he tried to shift the culture: to convince Australians to become a republic, to embrace our location on the edge of Asia and to be generous in our acknowledgement of Indigenous rights. But he failed. The culture wars had already broken out over the recognition of frontier violence against Aboriginal people and the continuing injustice of their treatment by governments. John Howard took them up to Keating and won the 1996 election with the slogan 'For all of us'.

Around 2000, as pressure mounted for Australia to reduce its greenhouse-gas emissions, the culture wars were joined by the climate wars. Together these have diminished Australian public life, too often reducing it to sterile adversarialism which prioritises anger and indignation over sympathy and compassion, and leaves little room for doubt and the compromises on which successful democracies are built.

Complex policy problems have many stakeholders. Stable solutions require give and take, with major players prepared to live with what, to them, are less-than-perfect outcomes and to share the credit. Although adversarialism is baked into our parliament, there are plenty of opportunities for compromise: coalition and minority governments, upper houses not controlled by the government of the day, free and conscience votes, co-operation on parliamentary committees, the handling of preferences at election time. The capacity to compromise is evidence of strength, of respect for other interests and values and a common interest in enduring solutions, just as often as it is evidence of weakness and indecision.

One of the more depressing sights of the past few years was Prime Minister Morrison sitting with his back to Anthony Albanese during Question Time in June 2020. He did it again to Tanya Plibersek in October that year. We know Morrison doesn't like answering questions, especially when they come from women, but it showed an ignorant disrespect for our parliamentary traditions. The term His Majesty's Loyal Opposition, which dates from the early nineteenth century, was a major advance in the development of parliamentary government: one could oppose the government of the day without being accused of treason. Robert Menzies would never have done it.

Although Morrison is temperamentally adversarial, he is not a culture warrior like Howard, Abbott and the News Corp cheer squad. Focussed on winning elections, he is not very interested in ideas. Instinctively he responds to problems in terms of their electoral logic rather than their national importance; but decades of culture and climate wars have turned the party of Menzies from a champion of high culture and universities—traditionally the wellspring of ideas—into one at best sceptical of their value, if not hostile to them.

Contemporary Liberals still mine Menzies's 1942 speech to 'The Forgotten People' for images and arguments. It is where Joe Hockey's speechwriter found 'leaners and lifters'. But Menzies' Forgotten People were not just economically independent; they were also custodians of 'the intellectual life...which finds room for literature, for the arts, for science, for medicine and the law'. Menzies instigated the great expansion of Australia's universities during the 1960s and 1970s. Ironically for today's Liberal Party, the higher one's education, the less likely one is to vote Liberal, so the arts and the nation's cultural institutions are chronically underfunded compared with sport; and when COVID-19 hit, the universities were refused support. One has to draw the line somewhere, said the treasurer, Josh Frydenberg. But why there? It looks like an electoral calculation, for surely it cannot be in the national interest to weaken Australian universities' capacities to teach and do research, which is what has happened.

•

I have been lucky in my university and intellectual life. I was an undergraduate in the late 1960s when an Arts honours degree (I did politics and philosophy) was far more intensive and demanding than today's degree. Today, Arts students are offered far less than we were, and they have to pay much more for it. The current state of humanities and social-sciences teaching in Australia fills me with despair, as do the difficulties facing academics who want to write for the public.

I did my PhD at the University of Melbourne in the second half of the 1970s with Alan 'Foo' Davies, a professor of politics with a deep and long-standing interest in the light psychoanalytic ideas could cast on politics. He had gathered similarly interested academics and postgraduates around himself, including Graham Little, who used interview-based case studies to explore the relationship between individual experience and broader social themes. From time to time Foo would invite various Melbourne psychoanalysts to his room at the university for a seminar with interested academics and postgraduates. These were regularised into the Melbourne Psychosocial Group, which ran for a little over ten years from the late 1970s. It grew as like-minded people joined, including around 1980 an influx of Lacanians from Buenos Aires. As well, each year Douglas Kirsner and Max Charlesworth from Deakin University would organise a weekend Freud conference, which is still going.

The Melbourne Psychosocial Group had no formal organisational structure or letterhead, no purpose other than to discuss psycho-analysis and its possible applications, and little role in anyone's career plans beyond enriching their thinking and writing. Discussions were exploratory and open-ended: 'Have you thought of...' and 'I wonder if...' These were not the battles of ideas so beloved of cultural warriors, as if ideas already exist and all they need are champions, but the trusting to and fro of friendship and conversation which creates ideas: the spark of insight or the bringing-into-focus of half-formed thoughts and intuitions.

Such groups, which are the yeast of cultural and intellectual life, once found a congenial home in Australian universities, as did small magazines like *Meanjin*, where I honed my writing skills as its third editor (from 1982 to 1986). *Meanjin* was not an academic journal contributing to the development of a discipline, but a little magazine committed to shaping and informing public debate and contributing to Australia's literary culture. It was one among other little magazines such as *Overland*, *Quadrant*, *Arena*, *Thesis 11* and *Australian Book Review*, and dedicated literary journals like *Scripsi*, *Southerly*, *Westerly* and *Australian Literary Studies*. As well, from 1980 to 1989 the *Age Monthly Review* published long pieces of cultural and literary analysis, as did the *Australian's Review of Books* from 1996 to 2000. Although some publications, like *Meanjin*, were housed in universities, and most were edited by employed academics, the sources of their energy were outside the academy, in both progressive and conservative politics, in the social movements, and in commitment to Australian writing and culture. All participated in what the German sociologist Jürgen Habermas called the Public Sphere, the place where citizens in liberal democracies converse about the problems of the day, their meanings and their solutions.

The 1980s were an intellectually exciting decade, as wave after wave of theoretical innovation swept across the humanities and social sciences: cultural Marxism, psychoanalysis, structuralism and deconstruction. It was heady stuff, arcane and full of technical language which was jargon to outsiders, but with powerful new insights about the way language and culture embodied and maintained constellations of power, distorting and suppressing some stories and experiences, valorising others.

After I left *Meanjin* I took my developing editorial and writing skills to Arena, a Melbourne based new-left co-operative which published and printed a quarterly magazine, and held seminars and conferences. It was more political and more radical than *Meanjin*, and its intellectual remit was wider. In the early 1990s, with Guy Rundle, I edited and wrote for the new bimonthly *Arena Magazine*, as well as working on my book on Menzies. I had started a lecturing position at La Trobe, and the work with *Arena Magazine* was mostly after-hours, but it never occurred to me that I might need to justify it. It was engaged intellectual work and that was what I was paid to do, as well as to teach undergraduates about Australian politics.

The term 'public intellectual' then had some currency. For a time in the 1990s and early 2000s newspapers would publish lists of them, and many were academics like myself who were as committed to engaging in public debate as to participating in their academic disciplines, often more so. It was easier to imagine a public then than it is now, when opinion and debate has been fragmented by social media, although there are still places to publish engaged analytic writing, as I have found when writing *Quarterly Essays* and for the *Monthly*.

It was much easier, too, for academics to write for the public. University research audits now impose costs on academics who write for the public. Books are often scored the same as five articles in a refereed journal, though many books take much, much longer to research and write. I would not have been able to write my biography of Alfred Deakin had I still been employed at a university. It had to wait till I retired.

The research audits pose particular challenges for people writing about Australia. Local academic journals and publishers are rarely as prestigious as international ones. One option is to publish on Australian matters with international journals and publishers, but this risks forfeiting local readers. When I began the research for my Deakin biography one of my colleagues at La Trobe and a good friend, Robin Jeffrey, said to me, 'There would have been dozens of young men like Deakin in the British empire. Why not do a group biography?' Robin works on India and this was an interesting suggestion. The transnational British empire is his historical frame of reference, and as a Canadian living in Australia he is interested in parallels. But who would read it, I thought. Deakin has a particular place in the political history of Australia which would be of little interest to Canadians or New Zealanders or South Africans, with their very different policy and party histories. And they would get little readerly pleasure from my recreations of nineteenth- and early twentieth-century Melbourne.

In 'The Bureaucratisation of Writing', which I wrote in the early 1990s, I claimed that there were two preconditions for good writing: a fully imagined reader and something interesting to say. Neither of these is easy to achieve but for most of today's academics they are all but impossible, as casualisation and repeated restructures erode collegiality and as research audits push them towards purely academic writing. I was lucky. As a postgraduate pursuing my interest in psychoanalysis with a group of like-minded friends and colleagues, I built the skills and knowledge that later gave me things to say about public life; and as an employed academic I learned to write for the public.

The essays collected here were written under particular economic and social conditions which have changed markedly since I started writing in the early 1980s. The bureaucratisation of writing by universities has gone far further than I then imagined. Neoliberalism and its bedfellow, the new public management, assume a particular form of human subjectivity, the rational, opportunity-maximising, self-interested individual of market liberalism who is primarily motivated by competition in their working and public life. Universities have followed suit, placing great faith in competitive self-interest to motivate their staff.

Once, when I was discussing the problem of where to publish with a prominent academic, he replied, 'I don't care if no one reads my work—I publish for the points to get the next grant.' He was a very competitive, confident man who may still be able to think and write well in this frame of mind, but most such instrumental work is cautious and uninteresting, producing no new ideas, as attention focusses on what 'they' want and will reward rather than on the object of thought. Theorists of creativity have described the way the boundaries of the self blur during creative endeavour. As one thinks hard, the outer world falls away. But it is difficult to lose oneself in thought in today's universities, especially if one is employed casually, or anxious that one's subject area may not survive a hostile dean.

If universities are no longer conducive to engaged and creative intellectual work, people will find other contexts, as many always have. People with things to say will find places to say them and people who want to listen. I hope the essays in this book will find some of these writers and readers, and that they will continue the conversations here about how we do politics in Australia.

PART I

Prime Ministers 1

Prime Ministers I

1 Alfred Deakin and Minority Government

Edited version of the inaugural Alfred Deakin Oration, Queen's Hall, Victorian Parliament House, Melbourne, 23 August 2016.

I am extremely honoured to have been invited to deliver this inaugural Deakin Oration—to celebrate the 160th anniversary of the opening of this parliament, and the birth of Alfred Deakin to immigrant parents in a small cottage not two kilometres from here, in George Street, Fitzroy. My brief is to draw links between Deakin's time in Australian politics and the contemporary political situation. What was his legacy and what lessons does it hold for us today? It is, I will argue, the benefits of minority government.

But first I want to go back to the afternoon of Tuesday, 8 July 1879, when a nervous young Alfred Deakin was waiting to be sworn in as the newly elected member for West Bourke. A month short of his twenty-third birthday, he was tall, handsome and conspicuously young among the grey-bearded parliamentarians of the gold-rush generation. Coincidentally, his first day in parliament was also the day the beautiful Queen's Hall and the building's imposing vestibule were first opened to the public. Victoria's parliament house was built in stages, and the hall and vestibule filled in the middle of the U made by the two chambers built in 1856, later joined by a library on the eastern end.

Parliamentary ceremonies were occasions for grand spectacle in nineteenth-century Melbourne, and the opening of this parliamentary session drew a bigger-than-usual crowd to view the splendid new interiors as well as the new governor in his new state carriage. The vestibule, hall and galleries were so full of spectators that the invited guests and the parliamentarians themselves had difficulty making their way through the crowd, let alone finding seats. Deakin was to be sworn in when the Assembly met later that afternoon. Pattie Browne, who would become his wife, was in the Strangers Gallery, as I'm sure were his proud parents and only sister, all looking down on the scene where Alfred was to make his dramatic entrance into Victoria's parliamentary life.

Deakin had contested the seat of West Bourke, which ran from Hobson's Bay north between the Maribyrnong and Werribee rivers to the foothills of the Great Divide, after the powerful editor of the *Age*, David Syme, suggested him as a candidate to West Bourke's Liberal electors. He was, he later wrote, 'suddenly whirled into politics to wage a desperate and hopeless conflict against an adversary of exceptional ability and claims upon this most difficult seat'. This is a rather hyperbolic description of what was in fact a minor by-election, but it captures the sense of urgency and the focussed energy Deakin was to bring to the many points of crisis in his political life.

Against all expectations Syme's rookie recruit won the seat, but there was a hitch. The polling booth at Newham had run out of ballot papers early and ten men had been unable to vote. The losing side called for a re-run and there was much indignation in the press about the 'Newham Blunder'. Deakin had won by more than ten votes, but he found whole situation 'vexatious beyond belief' and tried to resign. As he had not yet been sworn in, he was told that this was not possible.

Sitting in the Assembly Chamber that Tuesday afternoon in July, Deakin had to listen as the Opposition attacked the validity of his election. He was to deliver the address in reply to the governor's speech, an honour reserved for new members, and fidgeted nervously as the session dragged on through the preliminaries and then through tea. When the Speaker finally called him, he spoke so rapidly that the parliamentary reporters could barely keep up. He remembered that 'Always highly nervous no matter how small the gathering to which I spoke, on this occasion my condition was so agonizing as to threaten mental paralysis.' But Deakin could always rely on his performative self, so he carried on, 'with little or no indication of the tremors that thrilled me, dried my palate and robbed me of control of my voice and knowledge of my movements'.

He had taken great pains with the speech and was very proud of it. Quoting Herbert Spencer, John Stuart Mill, William Gladstone and a few lines of the poet laureate Alfred Tennyson, after whom he'd been named, he rehearsed the core beliefs of Victoria's colonial liberalism: the radical possibilities of the new nation compared with the old world, where only incremental reforms were possible; the superior qualities of Victoria's colonists; the absence of class in the colony compared with Great Britain; the sacredness of the ballot box; and the key issue of the day, the need to reform the powers of the Legislative Council, which was regularly rejecting the legislation of the popularly elected Assembly.

His commitment to an active state and an emerging nation was already evident:

With our boundless wealth and the opportunities of the illimitable
future, it would be strange if the young Victoria did not look
forward to something more than a mere aggregation of individuals
gathered by accident or avarice—if we did not seek to establish
a great people moved by large national aspirations, governed by
wide national sympathies, and actuated by proudly loyal devotion
to the State.

Then, suddenly, he changed tack, shifting to the more personal matter
of the difficulties of taking his seat. After some explanations of the
various moves he had made to resolve the issue before today, words
tumbling from his mouth, he announced his intention to resign: in
fact, he had the resignation letter ready in his pocket.

In retrospect, he judged the speech poor, too doctrinaire and
dogmatic. Nevertheless the House applauded wildly, 'for its manner,
its fire and its conclusion'. Deakin always took great delight in
recounting his capacity to win over an audience. Twenty years
later, when Deakin wrote an account of these events in *The Crisis in
Victorian Politics*, their dramatic intensity for him was still palpable:
a minor electoral irregularity had thrust him into the centre of the
colony's politics; all eyes were on him as he made his maiden speech
with its explosive climax; the situation was 'one of the most dramatic
witnessed in the house', and so on. Just a few years earlier young
Deakin had wondered if his future lay on the stage; in the chamber
of the Victorian Legislative Assembly he had found the theatre
which suited his talents.

This chamber was to be Deakin's theatre for the next thirty-two
years, twenty as a member of the Victorian parliament and twelve
as the member for Ballarat in the federal parliament. He became
master of its procedures and its star performer. All his parliamentary

career was in this building, where the federal parliament sat until
it moved to Canberra in 1927. It is thus very fitting that it is in this
building that his legacy is being remembered and celebrated with
the inauguration of an annual oration.

When I was invited to give this oration, the 2016 election campaign
was underway and I was writing about Deakin's second period as
prime minister, when he led a minority government with the support
of the Labor Party. There was some prospect that the forthcoming
election on 2 July would deliver minority government, as did the 2010
election. Minority governments are new territory for contemporary
Australia—for politicians, the media and the public. So I thought
I would talk about how Deakin handled the very considerable
challenges of minority government in the first decade of the new
Commonwealth.

We have become so used to stable majority governments in
Australia that minority governments are treated as disastrous
aberrations and sure signs of political dysfunction, but for the
Commonwealth's first decade they were the norm. There were seven
changes of prime minister after Edmund Barton was sworn in as the
first prime minister, and only the last of these was the result of the
government losing an election—in 1910, when Andrew Fisher led
Labor to an absolute majority and a clean sweep in the Senate. The
first change was when Barton resigned to go to the High Court and
Alfred Deakin became prime minister for the first time. The other
five changes were the result of the government of the day losing a
no-confidence motion in parliament.

The first federal parliament, elected in 1901 with Barton as
prime minister, had three party groupings: the Liberal Protectionists,
the Free Traders and the Labor Party, and none had a majority in
their own right. The Liberal Protectionists, led by Barton, formed a

minority government. Labor was generally supportive; so on occasion were the Free Traders. Barton's government had to negotiate a different majority for each piece of legislation, often by accepting amendments from the other parties or relying on the votes of loosely aligned members. Many bills were dropped when agreement proved impossible.

Deakin was prime minister at the time of the second federal election, in 1903, which returned three parties of almost equal strength. The convention in these circumstances is that the prime minister remains prime minister until parliament meets, when his control of the House is tested. So Deakin went straight on, remaining as prime minister, with Labor's support. But the situation was inherently unstable—even untenable. Famously he asked, 'What kind of a game of cricket…could they play if they had three elevens instead of two—one team playing sometimes with one side, sometimes with the other and sometimes for itself.' Deakin was not a cricket fan, but he was a superb political communicator. The third Test was in full swing in one of the early classic Ashes series, with Australia's Victor Trumper putting on virtuosic displays of batting, so cricket was a timely analogy for the difficulties facing the federal parliament. In 1907 the situation in parliament became even more complex when a fourth grouping formed: of conservative Liberal Protectionists who moved to the cross benches because they thought Deakin was too close to Labor.

I have used the term 'party groupings' here. In the early years of last century, the Labor Party already looked like a modern party. Labor parliamentarians voted as a disciplined block on all issues except trade policy, and they were supported by a well-organised party outside the parliament, which set policy and controlled preselections. Non-Labor parties were much looser affairs. Members generally voted together, especially on confidence motions, but not always. And on other matters, many retained their independence of judgement, or split along state lines. External party organisations were weak and intermittent. Leagues sprang to life to support members at election time, but died away between and had no direct role in policy making. In the first-past-the-post electoral system then in place, vote splitting was a constant problem for non-Labor groupings, which could not exercise the same control over election candidates as the Labor Party.

At an electoral level, the story of the first decade is of the rise and consolidation of the Labor Party's electoral support, from 14 per cent of the vote in 1901 to 50 per cent in 1910, which delivered Labor forty-three seats in a seventy-five-seat house. This would be like the Greens going from third-party status in 1990 to majority government in 2000. It was a major electoral upheaval, and in 1909 it forced the two non-Labor elevens to bury their differences and form the Fusion party. These two events, Fusion and Labor's 1910 election victory, established the Labor–anti-Labor structure of our party system, which is still roughly in place and which, until very recently, mostly delivered clear majority governments in our federal parliament.

But as the last few elections have shown, our two main parties of Labor and Liberal have both been bleeding support, Labor to the Greens and the Liberals to minor parties of the right and centre. We have more independents, and we have discontented members of the Coalition flexing their muscles with threats to cross the floor and destroy the government's wafer-thin majority—not on confidence motions, but certainly on legislation. As well, whichever party wins a majority in the lower house is very unlikely to control the Senate. This bleeding of support has complex causes, but one of them is the blurring of clear ideological differences since the bipartisan embrace

of neoliberalism in the 1980s; another is the much more complex
and diverse society that the parties have to represent.

Whatever the causes, parliament is no longer a rubber stamp for
decisions made out of the public eye in cabinet or the party room but
has returned to the centre of our political life. I am not pessimistic
about this. I do not agree with those who see wafer-thin majorities
and an unwieldy Senate as dooming governments to unproductive
conflict, weak authority and legislative failure. Rather, these provide
opportunities to negotiate and build consensus, for goodwill and
good manners to return to our politics and for Australia's political
centre to be revived and strengthened. But if this is to happen,
today's parliamentarians need to learn how to be less partisan, and
here Alfred Deakin has much to teach them.

Deakin was attorney-general in Barton's cabinet and prime
minister three times during the Commonwealth's first decade, twice
with the support of the Labor Party and once as leader of the Fusion
government, which did have a majority but also a great deal of
internal tension. Deakin's governments did not achieve all their
legislation, but they did achieve a good deal: establishing a tariff
to protect Australian industries; determining the site for the new
capital, Canberra, after much political jockeying; implementing a
uniform immigration policy; establishing a Commonwealth literary
fund and beginning Australian support for Antarctic exploration;
expanding the High Court from three to five judges; regulating
contract immigrant labour; beginning the transcontinental railway;
and passing the Surplus Revenue Act, which made possible the first
Commonwealth welfare measure—the old-age and invalid pension.
His governments laid the foundation of Australia's system of naval
defence; assumed Commonwealth control of the former British New
Guinea; began the transfer of the Northern Territory from South

Australia to the Commonwealth; and established a pro-rata system for the dispersal of Commonwealth funds to the states.

Not all of this legislation was finalised when his government lost office to Labor in 1910, but Labor did not repudiate it and start again, as so often happens today. Labor had supported much of it in its initial stages and completed it within the already-established broad outlines. What I am interested in is not the content of the legislation, some of which we would not agree with today—such as the racially restrictive immigration policy or the extent of the protective tariffs. Rather, I want to ask: how did Deakin achieve so much as the leader of a minority government in a fractious parliament? What lessons do his methods of working hold for us today? I will put forward two answers. The first is that Deakin's focus was always on policy rather than party. The second is his style of leadership.

Policy Before Party

Let's return to the Tuesday in July 1879 when Deakin dramatically resigned from his newly won seat. That night he happened to ride home on the same omnibus as the premier, Graeme Berry, who said: 'It is all very well for you, it puts you on a pinnacle. But what of the party if you lose the seat at this juncture?' Berry had put his finger on an enduring aspect of Deakin's political outlook. He was never an entirely committed party man. Already a young and inexperienced Deakin was putting his personal integrity and sense of honour above party loyalty, and he was not at all sure that politics was for him. In later years, when his political career was well established, his commitment to policy repeatedly trumped his concern with party. He recognised that parties were necessary to organise the vote inside and outside the parliament, and as party leader he felt it was his responsibility to work as hard as he could to secure the re-election of his colleagues, but for him the party was only ever a means to an end, and that end was progressive, practical policy in the national interest.

Deakin spent the 1890s on the backbench in the Victorian parliament. He had been Victoria's chief minister in the latter part of the 1880s, when Marvellous Melbourne was at its height, and was deeply disillusioned by the financial and banking scandals which engulfed the colony in the early 1890s. For a time he considered leaving politics altogether, but he was held there by the prospect of federation and the creation of an Australian nation. This was not a party matter, but a national cause and the focus of his political energies in the 1890s. He was a member of the conventions that drew up the constitution, a key organiser and advocate in the Victorian campaign, and one of the three Australians who accompanied the constitution to Britain in 1900 for its passage through the British parliament.

Deakin is best remembered for his virtuosic political oratory which was crucial in achieving federation, particularly his speech to the Australian Natives' Association in Bendigo, when the cause was floundering and it looked like the referendum on the constitution might be lost. He told the association that its hour had come and 'that if we fail in the hour of crisis, we may never be able to recall our lost national opportunities'.

It was the supreme oratorical feat of Deakin's life, but it also shows us something from which today's leaders could learn. Deakin always had a sharp sense of the transience of moments of political opportunity—of how fleeting they were, how easily they could be lost and that they might not come again. He brought a sense of drama to political campaigns which at times seemed melodramatic but which focussed the minds of the political class—and his own—on what was at stake if the challenge was flinched. If Malcolm Turnbull were more like Deakin, Australia might already be a republic; and if Kevin

Rudd were we might already have an emissions-trading scheme.

During the federation campaign Deakin always argued for the broad national view against the parochial and sectional, and when the constitution was finally law and the Commonwealth inaugurated, Deakin saw it as the duty of those who had argued for federation to make it work. The constitution provided a framework for the government of the nation—but that was all. Federal institutions had to be built and federal laws passed for areas of federal responsibility, and federal sentiment and a wide federal perspective had to be nurtured among the people. Regularly in his speeches after federation, Deakin conjured up the map of Australia, reminding his audience that they were no longer just Victorians or South Australians or Tasmanians, they were now also Australians. This was Deakin's great mission in the federal parliament—to make real the promise of a nation carried in the constitution—and he brought all his gifts and his capacity for unstinting work to the task. This was the goal which parties should serve.

When the first Commonwealth parliament was elected, Deakin thought state loyalties and regional jealousies would be the main lines of conflict and division which the new nation needed to transcend. But another line of conflict was already present and shaping quickly, as the new Labor Party built its strength and two of his governments depended on Labor's support.

Here we come to the nub of the first lesson Deakin can teach today's political leaders as they manage minority and near-minority governments. Deakin argued that his dependence on Labor to pass legislation, and sometimes on members of the official opposition or on independents, was a good thing; that it had strengthened rather than weakened his achievements, for it made his government's legislation not just the achievement of one party, but 'organic Australian policy'.

The hundred or so acts passed since federation, he said, do not belong to any one party because since 1901 no one has had a majority. Passing them has always required the co-operation of two. This achievement did not belong to the Liberal Party alone, he said, but rather was a national achievement, the fruit of wide Australian experience. Deakin assumed a consensual centre which already existed and which it was the job of politicians to realise in institutions and legislation. For Deakin the centre was the place where politics connected with Australian lived experience and with the nation's needs—for defence, development, population, workable institutions of governance, civilised wages and working conditions. It was more like the nation's beating heart than a position on an ideological spectrum, and the Liberal Party which he led was only ever a means to express it. 'We have consistently put our policy in first place,' he said. 'It is for that policy we have politically lived.' And: 'The policy has made us and not we the policy.'

From the vantage point of today, Deakin's claim that his policies represented organic Australian policy seems well founded. Because they were developed with cross-party support, they lasted—some for more than three-quarters of a century, in what the journalist Paul Kelly called the Australian settlement.

Deakin had a clear focus on the policies and legislation he wanted to achieve. He would take support for these from wherever he could get it and compromise within limits to achieve outcomes he believed were in the long-term national interest. He did not think this privileging of policy over party made him weak, and if others criticised him for it, he didn't greatly care. Personal ambition for office barely figured. Deakin always claimed he had little personal ambition for himself, and after thinking about him hard for the past four years, I don't think he was dissembling.

Political Style

Deakin was sometimes called Affable Alfred. With bright eyes, a ready smile and a friendly quip, he was charming and unfailingly courteous to men from all parties. He got on well with many Labor men, especially with Labor's first parliamentary leader, Chris Watson, whom he liked a great deal. When Watson was the leader, they would sometimes discuss the parliamentary situation in a quiet chat over a cup of tea. Watson would be frank about the limits of Labor's co-operation, and Deakin could thus think through his options. He did have some personal antipathies, most notably towards the New South Wales Free Trader George Reid, but he hid them well, as he did much of his private thoughts and feelings. He was a good listener, who tried to find common ground. Kindly, considerate and modest, he never boasted and rarely took offence, even when it was given.

Deakin was a superb parliamentary debater and master of procedure. He could be trenchant in arguing for his legislation, but he also used his charm and his skills to keep parliament civil. One contemporary observer, Henry Gyles Turner, wrote that in parliament

> Mr Deakin had an exceptional faculty, not only for looking on the bright side of things himself, but for leading others to do the same. If the Labor Party regulated his proceedings, he invariably assumed they were following his directions...However much the galled jade might wince under the philippics of George Reid, Joseph Cook or Bruce Smith, his withers were unwrung. So deftly did he handle the situation that he often saved it from anarchic confusion by a few well-timed sentences, committing him to nothing but sufficing to divert a wrathful attack.

All of this is so unlike today's parliamentary behaviour. If Deakin were insulted, he pretended not to notice; if he had to compromise to achieve his ends, he acted as if this was what he had intended all along; if tempers were rising, he relieved the tension with a joke. Deakin did not meet fire with fire, did not stoke the conflict and animosities to harden lines of party division. Instead he met aggression with a quiet smile, disarmed opposition with a quip or self-deprecating remark, at all times trying to prevent the escalation of conflict so as to keep open possibilities of co-operation and agreement.

You might think that the parliament of the early twentieth century was a more civilised place than the bearpit of contemporary question times. Let me disabuse you. Long, rambling speeches were the order of the day. Sometimes this was deliberate stonewalling, as in one notorious speech which lasted for ten hours, and sometimes simply self-important windbaggery. Closure motions were very recent additions to parliamentary procedure and used sparingly. All-night sittings were common.

When Deakin walked into the House at the end of May 1909 as the leader of the newly fused Liberal Party, there was pandemonium. Everyone knew that a no-confidence motion against the Labor government was in the offing. William Lyne, who regarded the new party as a betrayal of the Liberal Protectionists' principles and history, repeatedly shouted, 'Judas, Judas.' Billy Hughes cupped his hands extravagantly to his ears as if listening to a far-off sound: 'I am waiting to hear the cock crow,' he said. The incident was omitted from Hansard.

Billy Hughes was Labor's guerrilla fighter and master of invective. He rained insults down on Deakin. To him, Deakin's inscrutable charm was a mask for his scheming ambition, and his professed commitment to principle and policy above party the cause of multiple betrayals of friends and associates. He was, said Hughes, the political mercenary of Australia, with 'an excuse and an explanation for everything' and 'a programme that changes to fit the bewildering circumstances of political warfare':

> There is surely some moral obliquity about a nature such as his. No act that he commits, no party that he betrays, no cause that he abandons, affects him at all. He regards himself as the selected and favoured agent of Providence. Everything that he does, he does for the very best. He does it because there is nothing else that can be done to conserve the welfare of the people and the interests of the nation. To realize this noble ideal he has assassinated Governments, abandoned friends to the wolves, deserted principles, and deceived the people.

The climax of weeks of disgraceful disorder and unrestrained invective came in the early hours of 23 July. Weary members had been sitting since three o'clock the previous afternoon. The ostensible object of debate was the Old Age Pension Bill, which Labor supported, but instead of debating the bill members were arguing about whether a sacred line had been crossed when the ever-angry Lyne refused to withdraw his comment that the father of a Queensland Liberal, Littleton Groom, would be turning in his grave to find his son sitting with the conservatives. The pointless rancour finally halted when the Speaker, who was being temporarily relieved in the chair, collapsed on the floor of the House crying, 'Dreadful! Dreadful!' Deakin told chastened members that his condition was grave, and he died some hours later.

Deakin's response to the attacks on him and his government was to sit and wait. He adopted what he described as 'Fabian tactics', after the Roman commander Fabius Maximus, who avoided pitched battles with the invading armies of Hannibal in favour of a war of attrition. 'By studied moderation of tone, refusal to resent insult and

by the strict suppression of my own speech and that of my friends
so far as I could influence them,' he let the storm rage 'until it died
of inanition while we meekly and patiently waited until their wrath
melted away'.

Deakin did not like conflict, and he did not see it as productive.
This is a view shared by many Australians today who long for our
federal parliamentarians to find ways to work together to develop
stable workable policies in the long-term national interest, rather
than the current churn of policies chiefly designed for short-term
party-political advantage.

The neoliberalism of the past few decades put competition at the
centre of our social and economic relations. Its ostensible primary
purpose was to release the creative energies of the market, but it
also elevated the hypercompetitive and the angry in our public life,
selecting people for politics who are energised by a good fight and
justify this by claiming that it is only through fighting that truth
emerges and progress is made. This reached its height under Tony
Abbott, who seemed to think that being an outstanding political
warrior was the greatest possible praise—no matter that the fight
achieved nothing lasting. Sometimes conflict can improve outcomes,
but not always. Anger can shout down truths as much as proclaim
them, and it can lead many who have much to contribute to abandon
the field. For, while some people enjoy a good fight, many do not.

One of the reasons Malcolm Turnbull was popular after his
successful challenge to Tony Abbott was that he promised a return
to calm and civility in our public life. He toned down the appeals to
fear, which is a close ally of anger, and he refrained from negative
personal campaigning during the 2016 election. Still, there were
many angry people elected in that election. There were also many
people elected who are calm and reasonable and willing to listen

to different views. In 2013, Cathy McGowan's defeat of Sophie Mirabella was a clear victory for civility and co-operation over anger and hyper-partisanship.

Deakin reminds us that one does not have to be good at anger to be good at politics. He also reminds us that there is scope for co-operation in our adversarial parliamentary institutions, but to utilise it one needs to focus on long-term policy outcomes and ignore chances to score short-term party advantages.

Since the election both the Opposition and the government have been talking about the need for co-operation and bipartisanship, saying that the public is tired of their reflex opposition to each other's policies and expects more bipartisanship—but they are doing this in a hyper-partisan way, effectively challenging the other side to be co-operative but giving nothing away themselves. So far we have not seen one genuinely co-operative gesture from either the government or the Opposition. Instead we have bullying and carping, done in public, through megaphones.

Deakin's legislative achievements depended on Labor's co-operation. This ended when Labor won majority government in its own right, but as we return to minority and near-minority governments both parties need to review their parliamentary strategies and learn to co-operate if we are to have stable policies in the long-term national interest. In the first decade of the twentieth century, co-operation between Deakin's Liberals, Labor and even at times the Conservatives created a set of policies and policy assumptions which lasted for three-quarters of a century. At the time, there was broad general agreement that these policies were in the national interest, and they had broad public and institutional support.

Let us not think that this achievement was easy or that it was inevitable. Parliament spent a good deal of its time brawling and stonewalling; there were mischievous amendments and plenty of personal invective. There was a real danger that if these early Commonwealth governments had failed, the new federation itself would have failed, that the new nation would have foundered on partisan differences, parochial jealousies and personal animosities. Deakin's leadership was critical to saving Australia from this fate.

The stability of the new federation is Deakin's greatest legacy, and this is not an achievement today's politicians can repeat. Most politicians are not given the opportunity to build a new nation. But they still face complex challenges to secure the nation's wellbeing. Deakin governed before Australia's party system had set into its current two-party form. Now, as this two-party form is breaking up, his handling of minority government has much to teach us.

2 Robert Menzies' Forgotten People

'Menzies' Forgotten People', Meanjin, *volume 43, number 2, 1984.*

Robert Gordon Menzies dominated Australian politics for almost two decades, yet while millions of words have been written on later prime ministers, particularly Gough Whitlam and Bob Hawke, he has attracted little interest. There are eulogies on the right, and polemics on the left, but the general understanding of the dynamics of his popular appeal, his personality and his political style remains superficial.

This is partly because Menzies retired from politics in 1966, before Australian political journalists began to write books in great numbers on campaigns and leaders; and it is partly because of the delay in the appearance of Menzies' official biography, which held up the release of his papers. But these are only partial answers. The unavailability of the papers may have hampered sustained biographical projects, but there has long been enough public material on which to base interpretive work on Menzies' political appeal and speculation on his place in the cultural imagination. His neglect must also be seen as part of Australian intellectuals' general lack of interest in conservatism. Where the labour movement and the various manifestations of radicalism have attracted interest and the advocates of social reform have seemed problematic, conservatives have been taken for granted. It is as if conservatism's advocacy of the given lures intellectuals into accepting it as given.

As a consequence, many on the left talk of 'conservative hegemony' as if they know what it means, and in some prima-facie sense they do. Central symbols of conservatism like the home, the family, the individual's rights and freedoms, are easy to spot. It is far harder to get inside these symbols and form some sense of the fears and anxieties being aroused and the real experiences being addressed. This requires sympathetic identification, which the left's understanding of ideology as either false consciousness or disguised self-interest has done little to encourage. The French Marxist Louis Althusser describes ideology as the imaginary representation of real experience. It is the way the experience is represented in language and image that is misleading, but it is nevertheless real experience which is being addressed.[1] If one wants to argue with these representations, and those who talk of conservative hegemony usually do, one has to grasp the real experiences that underlie them. Only then will one know what the argument is about.

So-called political rhetoric—the myths, symbols and metaphors of party conflict recited at election time and party meetings—is seldom taken very seriously by political commentators and historians. It is seen as a cliched, highly ritualised form of language incanted merely to arouse some already-existing party identification. Cliched and ritualised it may be, but this does not mean that this language does not bear complex and powerful meanings, providing people with ways of thinking and feeling about their social experience.

In a brilliant essay on ideology, Clifford Geertz argues that political symbolism is not just a response to social and political situations but is an important factor in shaping those situations;that just as different works of literature are more or less subtle, complex and convincing in formulating particular private emotional experiences, so different symbolic systems are more or less effective in crystallising particular social and political situations, and thus more or less effective in shaping the social and political world to their patterns. The theory of ideology, he argues, needs a theory of symbol formation, a theory of how private sentiment and experience is transformed into symbols of public significance, of how political symbolism is successful and how it fails. He thus suggests that theorists of ideology should look to those writers, mainly in literature and philosophy, who have been concerned to understand how symbols mediate meaning.[2]

Geertz draws on the work of Kenneth Burke, that elusive and difficult writer who has so suggestively turned his skills as a literary critic to the symbolic world at large. Burke has rescued the term 'rhetoric' from its rather limited use to dismiss language no longer felt, and revived its central meaning of the art of using language to persuade and influence the self or others to particular ways of seeing, feeling about and acting in the world. The central rhetorical device in such attempts to persuade is identification—the identification *of* things in such a way as to induce identification *with* them. Burke thus places the contest over definition and description firmly at the centre of our use of language.[3]

To begin to probe Australian conservatism and to develop some ideas about the basis of Menzies' popular appeal (and if we understood that, we might understand the dynamics of subsequent conservative prime ministers' popular appeal), I will take one of his more famous speeches, 'The Forgotten People', and draw out some of its themes by subjecting it to the sort of close scrutiny usually reserved for literary texts.

But if we are to talk of classes, then the time has come to say something of the forgotten class—*The Middle Class*—those people who are constantly in danger of being ground between the upper and the nether millstones of the false class war; the middle class who, properly regarded, represent the backbone of the country.

We don't have classes here as in England, and therefore the terms don't mean the same. It is necessary, therefore, that I should define what I mean when I use the expression 'the middle class'.

Let me first define it by exclusion: I exclude at one end of the scale the rich and powerful; those who control great funds and enterprises, and are as a rule able to protect themselves—though it must be said that in a political sense they have as a rule shown neither comprehension nor competence. But I exclude them because in most material difficulties the rich can look after themselves.

I exclude at the other end of the scale the mass of unskilled people, almost invariably well organised, and with their wages and conditions safeguarded by popular law. What I am excluding them from is my definition of the middle class. We cannot exclude them from the problem of social progress, for one of the prime objects of modem social and political policy is to give to them a proper measure of security, and provide the conditions which will enable them to acquire skill and knowledge and individuality.

These exclusions being made, I include the intervening range, the kind of people I myself represent in parliament—salary-earners, shop-keepers, skilled artisans, professional men and women, farmers, and so on. These are, in the political and economic sense, the middle class. They are for the most part un-organised and un-selfconscious. They are envied by those whose social benefits are largely obtained by taxing them. They are not rich enough to have individual power. They are taken for granted by each political party in turn. They are not sufficiently lacking in individualism to be organised for what in these days we call 'pressure politics'. And yet, as I have said, they are the backbone of the nation.

The above passage comes from a radio broadcast to 'The Forgotten People' made by Menzies in May 1942, three months after the fall of Singapore. This broadcast, which was subsequently published as a pamphlet and then as the lead essay in a book of the same title, has become something of a landmark in the regrouping of conservative interests that led to the formation of the Liberal Party of Australia in 1944, and its eventual winning of government in 1949. It was part of a weekly series in which, despite some inevitable discussion of wartime issues, the dominant theme was the sort of society that would be built after the war. In these broadcasts Menzies shaped and developed many of the political ideas he was to bring to the formation of the Liberal Party and later to the prime ministership. 'The Forgotten People' is the most famous of these. Conservatives look back to it as a classical statement of Australian liberal philosophy, radicals see it as foreshadowing the hegemony to come, and it is widely quoted in discussions both of Menzies and of Liberal Party ideology. Unconstrained by any considerations of policy or the need to communicate any information in it, Menzies' rhetorical skills are in full flight as he elaborates the type of people and values he sees excluded from power and influence by Labor, the people and values on which he was to build the Liberal Party's popular support.

Raewyn Connell and Terry Irving include excerpts from 'The Forgotten People' in their collection *Class Structure in Australian*

History under the heading 'a mass base for conservatism', and invite the reader to note Menzies' skilful identification of the social customs and prejudices of the groups he calls the middle class with the strategic interests of capitalism, and the role of the family in making the connection.[4] This is all they say, and it suggests that Menzies' skill was merely one of recognition, as if the patterns he drew accurately traced the patterns that existed; as if there were no other patterns that could be drawn; as if people did not have to be continually persuaded to certain ways of thinking and feeling rather than others. They take Menzies' words at face value and do not recognise that these words are attempting to effect political change. Yes, Menzies was identifying customs and prejudices, but this was far more than mere recognition; it was argument, carried out in image, metaphor, allusion and hyperbole, argument for one way of identifying oneself and one's interests rather than another—and one other in particular, which is attributed to the labour movement.

Labor and non-Labor are the two poles around which Australian political thought and action are organised, and each constructs an image of itself and what it stands for in contrast to the values attributed to the opponent. To understand the way in which Menzies was able to build a mass base for the Liberal Party we have to understand the patterns he was trying to draw and those he was trying to exclude. And as these patterns are created in language, it is to the language we must look. If we look closely at the language of 'The Forgotten People', noticing not just what Menzies says but how he says it, if we tease out its layers of association, its gaps and silences, we begin to reach through to the real fears, anxieties, achievements and experiences from which conservatism draws its mass support.

The title itself reveals Menzies' skill as a rhetorician, his gift for constructing evocative and complex symbols. The term 'forgotten people' does not in fact appear in the body of the text, where the address is to the 'forgotten class'—one of the traditional conservative ways of describing the middle class (which was also called the saviour, the average and the general class).[5] In 1933 John Latham, then attorney-general in Lyons' United Australia Party government, wrote:

> It seems to me that the middle class is too often left out of it in political matters; though it is one of the most valuable in the whole community. It is not rich, but it is not poor, and it is often forgotten. It includes very nearly all professional men, most farmers and rural producers, a tremendous number of shop-keepers, a large number of clerical employees, a considerable proportion of manual workers, especially the skilled and more particularly the highly skilled artisans, and all kinds of people working on their own account.[6]

It is generally claimed that such people are forgotten in the struggle between particular sections because they are not as selfish and pushing as the other parties: the very rich, and organised labour. In 1942 this claim was particularly apt, as the United Australia Party was a spent force, and it seemed that the interests and values it represented might well be forgotten.

But this speech is being made in the middle of a war, and Menzies is not just addressing the forgotten *class* but the forgotten *people*. At a time when patriotic symbols are unifying people to fight a war, when many people must feel that they have almost forgotten their private pre-war hopes and ambitions, Menzies is appealing to them to think about when the war is over and to rekindle their individual aspirations. The title nicely captures the speech's dominant tone of self-pity. To call people forgotten is to suggest that they have been forgotten, to arouse their anxiety and then to to soothe it by presenting oneself as someone who notices and remembers. In addressing the forgotten people Menzies is offering his reassuring recognition.

At the same time he is attempting to prevent himself from being forgotten. Menzies' political longevity and the stability and success of the Liberal Party under his leadership make it easy to forget how close to political oblivion he was in 1942, and in what disarray non-Labor was. Menzies had succeeded to the UAP prime ministership after Joseph Lyons' sudden death, a death which many felt had been hastened by certain actions of Menzies. Six months after he became prime minister, Europe was at war. The UAP–Country Party coalition barely scraped back into government in the election of 1940, and in 1941, after a long overseas trip during which dissatisfaction mounted against him, both in his own party and in the country at large, Menzies resigned from the prime ministership and the leadership of the party.

In 1942 he was on the backbenches of a depleted Opposition, led by the aged Billy Hughes, and a Labor government was managing the war effort. The series of broadcasts, of which this was one, was part of Menzies' strategy for keeping himself before the public eye when he lacked the public office from which to do so, and for declaring his ambition to lead the inevitable regrouping of conservative forces. Menzies identifies with the forgotten people he addresses. The following defence of the middle class from the speech is echoed again and again in his frequent self-pitying references to his own situation in various public statements at this time. He felt he had been the victim of envy, as he was telling them they were.

> To discourage ambition, to envy success, to hate achieved superiority,
> to distrust independent thought, to sneer at and impute false motives
> to public service, these are the maladies of modern democracy,
> and of Australian democracy in particular. Yet ambition, effort,

thinking, and readiness to serve are not only the design and
objectives of self-government but are the essential conditions of
its success.

The main point to notice about the title of the speech is the change of
the second word, 'class', to 'people'. In this transformation Menzies is
simply making explicit what has always been implicit in conservative
rhetoric—that the middle class is not a concept of class at all but
a moral category referring to desirable political values and social
attitudes.[7] Although there are occasional glimpses in 'The Forgotten
People' of the material advantages enjoyed by the middle class (there
are allusions to private schools and to the ability of the middle class to
afford university education for their children), there is no reference
at all to the traditional economic role of the bourgeoisie. There is
nothing in the speech on the importance of independent enterprise
for the economy, nothing on the importance of market freedoms,
and Menzies' list of groups composing the middle class does not even
include the group John Latham referred to as 'all kinds of people
working on their own account'.

Menzies' list begins with salary earners, who are distinguished
from wage earners not in terms of their contribution to the free-
enterprise system but by their form of payment and their degree of
incorporation into the views of management. Menzies claims that
the middle class is the dynamic class, but nowhere is this dynamism
given an economic role.

> The case for the middle class is the case for a dynamic democracy
> as against a stagnant one. Stagnant waters are level and in them the
> scum rises. Active waters are never level; they toss and tumble and
> have crests and troughs, but the scientists tell us that they purify
> themselves in a few hundred yards.

The closest Menzies comes to giving some substance to this dynamism is the claim that the middle class 'provides the intelligent ambition which is the motive power of human progress'. The spirit of enterprise has become the spirit of aspiration in a fairly stable status system in which education is the main means of advancement. Again and again Menzies emphasises the middle class's commitment to the education of their children; there is no role here for the self-taught, risk-taking entrepreneur.

> The Scottish ploughman walking behind his team cons ways and means of making his son a farmer, and so he sends him to the village school. The Scottish farmer ponders upon the future of his son, and sees it most assured not by the inheritance of money but by the acquisition of that knowledge which will give him power, and so the sons of many Scottish farmers find their way to Edinburgh and a university degree.
>
> The great question is: 'How can I qualify my son to help society?' and not, as we have so frequently thought: 'How can I qualify society to help my son?' If human homes are to fulfil their destiny, then we must have frugality and saving for education and progress.

That the middle class is a moral category and not an economic one is clearly seen in one of the speech's organising figures, the contrast between 'backbone' and 'spineless'. Early in the speech the middle class is described as 'the backbone of the country', and the listener (and later reader) is warned of the dangers of inflicting a 'fatal injury upon our own backbone'. That its members themselves have backbone is one of the class's chief virtues—they do not want to live 'spineless and effortless on the benevolence of an all-powerful state':

> Are you looking forward to a breed of men after the war who
> have become boneless wonders? Leaners grow flabby, lifters grow
> muscles.

One of the emotional paradoxes of the speech is that while people are
asked to identify with the strengths and independence suggested by
images such as backbone, Menzies is continually reminding them of
their insecurities and anxieties, centring these on the vulnerability of
their savings, a popular conservative theme. The image that comes
through passages like the following is not of confident inner strength,
of people of 'fierce independent spirit', but an almost pathetic timidity:

> The artist if he is to live, must have a buyer; the writer an audience.
> He finds them among frugal people to whom the margin above
> bare living means the chance to reach out towards that heaven
> which is just beyond our grasp.

Lacking a distinctive economic role, the middle class is defined in
terms of domestic symbols that have no fixed social boundaries. The
supreme value of the middle class comes from their 'stake in the
country', understood in terms of their 'responsibility for homes—
homes material, homes human and homes spiritual'. Associated
with 'homes material' are the virtues of frugality and patriotism;
with 'homes human', ambition for one's children (the absence of
any reference to family conviviality and tenderness is striking); with
'homes spiritual', independence (spiritual referring here to the spirit
of the plucky, not the devout). It is the value they put on the home
that defines the middle class:

> I do not believe that the real life of this nation is to be found in
> either great luxury hotels and the petty gossip of the so-called
> fashionable suburbs, or in the officialdom of the organised masses.

It is to be found in the homes of people who are nameless and unadvertised, and who, whatever their individual conviction or dogma, see in their children their greatest contribution to the immortality of the race.

The passage progresses from the great luxury hotels and fashionable suburbs to the homes of the nameless and unadvertised middle class, and to the officialdom of the organised masses. The working class is not given its own domestic space (not even rented rooms) but is defined in terms of the relations of the workplace. It is as if they do not have wives, homes and children. In contrast with the symbols of home and children with which most can identify, work is presented negatively. Organisation, mass, level and officialdom form a cluster of associations around work which represent it as an anonymous, dull and routine world in which the chances for individual satisfaction and achievement are few. Evoking the sense that one is no one at work, the suggestion is that one is someone at home and that the significance of individuals inheres in their domestic relations. This domestic space will later become the locus of an identity formed in leisure-time pursuits.

The ploy is obvious: to get people to identify their political interests and values with their private and domestic rather than their economic roles, and hence to create a space for a non-Labor party which can accommodate manual workers and factory managers, the owners of businesses and their clerical employees and, most importantly, the wives of them all. In this speech we see Menzies arguing for a view of politics which excludes all those images and issues which were so difficult in the 1930s, and includes all the benefits which post-war affluence was to bring. He is attempting to shift the terrain of politics away from the workplace and the conflicts of the economy towards the home and the consensual symbols of the domestic sphere.

•

The home has been a symbol of harmony, peace and stability since the middle of the nineteenth century, when to praise and protect it became one strategy for coping with the anxieties caused by rapid social change. Its virtues were championed in the face of an outside world which was threatening and impossible to understand or control. It is not surprising in a time of war that Menzies should elaborate the virtues of the home and evoke the sense of the home as refuge.

> ...one of the best instincts in us is that which induces us to have one little piece of earth with a house and garden which is ours, to which we can withdraw, in which we can be among friends, into which no stranger may come against our will.

But the sense of home as a refuge, while particularly poignant during a war, can always draw on the anxieties endemic to capitalism's relentless transformation of ways of life.

In understanding the role of the home in conservative ideology it is important not just to see it negatively as a refuge or retreat, but to recognise the positive values that are being evoked when the home is championed. While the home stands in general opposition to the outside world and so is a refuge in the face of a wide range of threats, including those posed by international events, it also stands in a more specific opposition to work, and by extension to the economy, politics and the law. One way of understanding modernisation is as increasing rationalisation. Different areas of human activity become organised according to impersonal criteria like profitability, efficiency, bureaucratic regulation or the law, and people's participation in these areas is understood in terms of abstractions like economic role or legal and bureaucratic status. In contrast to such rationalisation and abstraction the home stands for face-to-face relations, mediated by everyday language (rather than bureaucratic, legal or technical language) in which it is people's moral and personal qualities that matter.

At various points in the speech Menzies rejects an abstract understanding of social relations in favour of understanding in terms of individual motives and actions.

> We speak glibly of many things without pausing to consider what they signify. We speak of 'financial power', forgetting that the financial power of 1942 is based upon the savings of generations which have preceded it…We speak of 'man-power' as if it were a matter of arithmetic, as if it were made up of a multiplication of men and muscles without spirit.

And he rejects policy designed 'to weigh men according to their political organisation and power, as votes and not as human beings'. Here Menzies is contrasting the commonsense language of everyday understanding, which is the language of the home, with the abstract language of modern politics and economics, and rejecting the latter as diminishing the individual.

In the passage cited earlier (beginning 'I do not believe that the real life of this nation…') in which Menzies introduces the central role he is giving to the home in his account of the middle class, the home is contrasted on the one hand with the self-indulgent life of the rich and on the other with the officialdom of the organised masses. When first discussing this, I noted that the organised masses (the working class) are denied a home and defined only in terms of their work relations, which are presented as dull and routine. I want now to notice the way Menzies is attaching negative symbols of modernisation to the labour movement. 'Organisation', 'mass', 'level' and 'officialdom' all invoke the impersonal world of bureaucracy. Towards the end of the speech there is a hint of the production line, that supreme symbol of the fragmentation and alienation of modern life, when describing the dangers of an all-powerful State that 'will dole out bread and ideas with neatly regulated accuracy'.

Here production-line imagery describes the individual's relationship with the State, but the production line is unspoken, as is the bureaucracy of corporate capitalism. One of conservatism's key strategies is to deflect the anxieties engendered by modernisation onto the labour movement, and its championing of the welfare state. The labour movement, in embracing abstractions like class in order to understand the economic relations of people under capitalism, can be presented by conservatives as condoning those relations.

It is to the language in which Labor argues about politics that conservatives direct attention, not to the arguments. Their refusal to talk about politics in terms of class must be understood not just as a refusal to recognise conflicts of interest, but as a refusal of the abstractions involved. Of course such a refusal is convenient, enabling the avoidance of many political and moral problems, but it must be recognised that much of the moral conviction in conservatism's championing of the individual comes from this reluctance to see individuals in terms of their abstract social, economic or political positions. Labor and non-Labor thus construct images of each other which rarely meet.

The assembly-line imagery, the negative associations attached to union organisation and the welfare state to implicate them in the alienation of modern life, and the rejection of abstract terms like 'manpower', have their counterparts in Menzies' association of the middle class and the home with a simpler, pre-modern way of life.

His use of an archaism like describing the middle class as 'feeding the lamps of learning', his citing of Burns' 'The Cotter's Saturday Night' as best illustrating the values of homes spiritual, his reference cited earlier to the Scottish ploughman walking behind his plough, and his contrast between 'landless men [who] smell the vapours of the street corners', and 'landed men [who] smell the brown earth' place his construction of the middle class within the opposition between the city and the country, which Raymond Williams has shown is central to organising our thinking and feeling about industrialisation. The country or rural way of life is idealised as simpler, more authentic and more communal than the soulless city, and the changes associated with industrialisation are represented as the loss or despoiling of this rural way of life.[8] In invoking this opposition, Menzies is placing the home and the middle class in the place of the country, and the labour movement in the place of the city and of the losses associated with modernisation.

In Australia, non-Labor parties have been characterised by the juxtaposition of such conservative rhetoric with the pragmatic pursuit of progress and development. The more single-minded the pursuit of development in the guise of progress, the louder the values of home and the country seem to be proclaimed, as in the rhetoric of the Queensland premier Joh Bjelke-Petersen. This paradoxical relationship needs probing, but I suggest it partly has to do with who is being addressed, the public or the private business and financial interests, and partly with the way in which the structure of conservative thought is attached to the English (and Scottish) rural past and countryside, and so does not appear in immediate contradiction to a programme of development pursued in Australia.

•

Conservative parties have always, until recently, drawn more support from women than from men, and the oppositions between home and work, home and the modern-industrial bureaucratically regulated world, home and the labour movement, suggest some reasons for this. The tying of non-Labor to the experiencing of people as individuals speaks to women whose daily lives in the home are spent dealing with people as individuals, and who do not have to make decisions in terms of profitability, or class position and solidarity, or bureaucratic regulation. Women in the home deal with people face to face, equipped with moral and emotional concepts like selfishness, duty, hope and love. They understand people and society in ordinary language, and the more technical and abstract language which conservatives ascribe to the Labor Party thus appears to threaten the very basis of their daily lives. Women's often-remarked political individualism arises not just from their unorganised social existence and the consequent difficulty they have in forming a sense of collective political interests, but from their daily experiences of people as individuals. It is not just a cognitive weakness but a moral conviction.

Much of Menzies' speech seems particularly addressed to women, and in exploring this I think we uncover another central political change Menzies was attempting. Not only was he trying to shift the terrain of politics away from the workplace and the economy towards the home, he was drawing women's concerns and experiences into the centre of his account of the middle class. While a passage like the following no doubt speaks to many men whose working lives have brought them few satisfactions, it speaks primarily to women in their roles as homemakers and mothers:

The real life of the nation…is to be found in the homes of people
who are nameless and unadvertised, and who…see in their children
their greatest contribution to the immortality of the race.

Prima facie the forgotten people Menzies is addressing are the middle
class, but they are also the women whose particular interests and
problems have generally been forgotten by a politics organised
around the conflicts of the economy and the workplace. In 1942
Menzies was articulating conservative ideology in a way which
particularly addressed women. It is one of the cliches that passes
for knowledge in our understanding of Menzies that he appealed
to women, and this is generally glossed in terms of his paternalism
and their corresponding willingness to be patronised. Again this sort
of argument fails to take conservatism seriously, giving little credit
to those who feel themselves to be addressed by it. In elaborating
the virtues of the home as central to non-Labor values, Menzies was
elaborating the virtues of women's traditional social space. While
this can be seen as reinforcing women's traditional role, it is also
making it more likely that the needs of women in the home will be
articulated as political demands. The implicit appeal to women in
'The Forgotten People' becomes explicit after the Liberal Party is
formed in 1944, and in this explicit appeal we see one of Menzies'
central strategies in building the Liberal Party's political base. This
is worth exploring a little, for it shows just how successful Menzies
was in the rhetorical battle with the Labor Party.

Menzies' 1946 policy speech included a direct appeal to women:

May I say that this speech is addressed not only to men but to
women. Indeed, even more to women than to men! For, during
the war, even the most unimaginative of men must have become
acutely conscious of the incalculable importance of the work done

by women in industry, in the Services, and in the home. Upon our wives and mothers has fallen the main burden of the dreadful anxieties of war, of every civil restriction, of every shortage, of the standing in queues, of the cessation of the home delivery of goods, of the sharp reduction in domestic help, of the housing shortage, of gas and power rationing when strikes are on. Women, even more than men, have been responsible for the family saving that has done so much to fill our war loans. It is the women of Australia who most eagerly seek those policies which will build homes, will banish the fear of depression, will hold out the hope of advancement for husband or son or daughter; who want a better system of education; who know that lower taxes would brighten the future and bring more contented work and more goods and services.

While women's role in industry and the Services is mentioned, it is their role in the home that is elaborated and which is seen as carrying the main burden of the anxieties of war. Those virtues of frugality and aspiration for one's children, earlier ascribed to the middle class, are now explicitly ascribed to women; and to them a new one is added—the eager consumer of the future. Increased home ownership, the expansion of education, and the greater availability and increased range of consumer goods are some of the changes which were to occur in the 1950s, and we see them here being presented as issues which particularly concern women.

Menzies' 1949 policy speech has a supplementary statement on women's special problems, and if we compare this with Chifley's 'No Glittering Promises' speech of the same election, we can see just how much more conscious Liberal Party rhetoric then was of the need to speak to women's experiences.[10] One of Chifley's main strategies in his policy speech is to evoke the memories of the unemployment of the Depression, when the country had a non-Labor government, but in doing this he dwells only on men's experience during that time.

> So far as it can humanly contrive, never again will the dole queues be seen in this country. Never again will competent workmen stand idle for months and years while limitless work remains to be done. Never again will young men drift hopelessly from town to town and State to State, searching for the jobs which in all this wide land did not exist for them.

His images here of the dole queue and aimless young men and, elsewhere in the speech, of thousands of breadwinners ill-clad and underfed queueing at factory gates, his evocation of the fear of the sack and the right of every man to receive a fair return for his labour, enterprise and initiative, all speak primarily to men's experiences in the workplace. Men are asked to vote as workers and, although the term 'breadwinners' implies wives and children, the particular experiences of women during the Depression are not mentioned. If Menzies had wanted to remind the electorate of the Depression, he would have spoken of mothers living on tea to feed their children, shifting endlessly between rented rooms and seeing their children go ill-clad to school, and he would have evoked the suffering of wives watching helplessly as their husbands' spirits were broken by their futile search for work.

But Menzies does not want to talk of the Depression, and this is crucial. For in the Depression the key political issues were centred on the right to work, the control of employment possibilities: that is, on issues which could most easily be understood in terms of class. Menzies wants to shift people's perceptions of what politics is about, away from issues concerning the workplace and the economy and into the home; he wants to address voters as homemakers and owners and parents. Later, with increased affluence, they will be addressed as consumers. And it is Menzies' stroke of genius that in addressing voters in this way he makes a central place in Liberal Party rhetoric for women.

•

The emotions and experiences which 'The Forgotten People' addresses are paradoxical and contradictory. People are praised as independent while being subtly reminded of how dependent and vulnerable they are; the labour movement is presented as the villain of modernisation in a way which disguises capitalism's unremitting transformation of ways of life and makes it impossible to recognise Labor's humanist values; the praising of the home as a symbol of individualism makes it easier for a non-Labor party to recognise women's particular needs and interests. These paradoxes have an emotional and social logic, they are convenient in many ways, but it is too easy to dismiss them as evidence of hypocrisy or rationalisation. They are based on values that are held with conviction and seem to be confirmed in people's daily experience.

These values and experiences, however, could be contained in other symbolic frameworks. People can respond to different descriptions of themselves, can pay attention to different aspects of their experience. This is why the scrutiny of political language is so important, for it is in language that the descriptions of themselves on which people act are shaped, and the battle over such descriptions is one of the main sites of political conflict.

1   See 'Ideology and Ideological State Apparatuses', *Lenin and Philosophy and Other Essays*, Monthly Review Press, New York, 1971.

2   'Ideology as a Cultural System', in *The Interpretation of Culture*, Basic Books, New York, 1973.

3   Kenneth Burke, *A Rhetoric of Motives*, Part 1, University of California Press, Berkeley, 1969.

4   *Class Structure in Australian History: Documents, Narrative and Argument*, Longman Cheshire, Melbourne, 1980, p. 349.

5   Peter Loveday, 'The Liberals' Image of their Party', in *Australian Conservatism*, ed. Cameron Hazlehurst, Australian National University Press, Canberra, 1979, p. 243.

6   *United Australia Review*, 20 April 1933.

7   See Tim Rowse's *Australian Liberalism and National Character*, Kibble Books, Melbourne, 1978, pp. 197 ff.

8   Raymond Williams, *The Country and the City*, Chatto & Windus, London, 1973.

9   This was no doubt partly due to the fact that the powerful Australian Women's National League was one of the organisations from which the Liberal Party was formed, and expected some gains from the loss of its separate political identity.

10 Reprinted in Ben Chifley, *Things Worth Fighting For*, Melbourne University Press, 1952.

3 John Howard and the Australian Legend

From Australian Liberals and the Moral Middle Class: From Alfred Deakin to John Howard, *Cambridge University Press, Melbourne, 2003, chapter nine.*

John Howard is the most creative leader Australian Liberals have had since Robert Menzies remade the Liberal Party in the 1940s. When he became leader in 1995, after a nightmare twelve years for the party which involved no less than six changes of leadership, Howard faced the task of renewing the party as a plausible contender for national government. Since then he has tirelessly reworked the images, themes and arguments of Liberal Party philosophy to respond to both the social and economic changes in Australia since Menzies' retirement, and to a changed Labor Party.

Howard is steeped not just in Australian Liberal rhetoric, but in the experiences he speaks to: families and small businesses centred on work and neighbourhood, bounded by a relatively taken-for-granted nationalism. Howard's critics have mocked him as a suburban man pushing Australia back into the conformity of the 1950s.[1] This is grist for the satirist's mill, but it is not good history. Howard is not going back. Because Australian Liberals lack political memory, and because the party was re-formed in 1944, Menzies is seen as the originator of the values and arguments Howard espouses. He is not. Menzies too was adapting an inherited political language. Howard is Menzies' successor not because he mined his words and images to oversee a return to 1950s Australia, but because like him he has been able to adapt the language and thinking carried in his party's traditions to the circumstances of his political present.

When he became Liberal leader for the second time, in 1995, Howard faced the task of recreating a language of social unity and cohesion for the Liberals after their thirteen-year association with economic liberalism and the language of competitive, market-based individualism. The first detailed evidence we have of Howard's thinking is in the 1988 policy document *Future Directions*, produced during his first stint as leader. *Future Directions* mixed dry economic policies, such as the need for smaller government and deregulation of labour practices, with social policies based on support for families and an assimilationist nationalism. It pitched its appeal to a broad popular audience with the subtitle 'It's time for plain thinking'. In arguing that Australia needed to return to and strengthen traditional values, Howard understood that the Liberal Party needed more than economic policies to win government.

Future Directions' popular appeal was undercut by its cover image of a blond family in front of a white-picket fence with a large brick home and a new white car. This was an image not just of the Liberal Party's base in the affluent middle class, but of its nostalgia for the simpler world of two-parent Anglo (or at least Caucasian) families. Combined with the trouble Howard got himself into over Asian migration, it made him an easy target for accusations of being out of touch with the realities of contemporary Australia—of multiculturalism, single-parent families, and the struggles of the unemployed and the working poor.[2] But Howard's opponents were badly misled by the cover image. Inside were the arguments and images Howard has used to reconnect the Liberal Party with the contemporary Australian experience.

The cover image and the emphasis on traditional family values invited obvious comparison with the homes Menzies placed at the centre of national life in his Forgotten People speech. But there were big differences. In 1942 the home was a consensual symbol of domestic life and Menzies was using it to argue against Labor's construction of social and political identity in the relations of work and the economy. He was not defending the traditional home against other sorts of homes, inhabited by gay couples, single mothers or blended families. Nor was he presenting the home as fragile and threatened by family breakdown, crime, social decay. The homes of Menzies' middle class were solid castles of privacy and individual freedom whose only threat was too much government interference. In the 1980s championing the home was more fraught, when only about one-fifth of households were single-breadwinner, married couples with children. Homes and family life did not provide the same easy pickings for consensual politics in the 1980s and 1990s as they did in the 1940s and 1950s.

The second social theme of *Future Directions* was its assimilationist nationalism. Policies on multiculturalism and Indigenous Australians are brought together under the heading of 'Building One Australia':

> We want a united Australia proud of its distinctive identity and history in which all Australians, irrespective of social background, ethnic heritage, religion or nationality have an equal opportunity to achieve what they might want for themselves and their families.

Future Directions was launched to a theme song about a plain man, with a country beat and the repeated chorus 'Son, you're Australian / That's enough for anyone to be.'[3] The most significant aspect of this refrain is not its obvious appeal to nationalism but its dismissal of affiliations to social groups and identities larger than the family and smaller than the nation—class, religion, ethnicity, region, gender, race. Family and nation are enough for anyone. Other bases of social identity risk limiting individuals' freedoms and dividing the nation.

Throughout the 1980s Labor made minority issues work for it. It built on and renewed its alliance with the new middle class of the 1970s, which had taken up issues of sexual tolerance, gender equity, the environment, racial and ethnic diversity; and it strengthened the alliance with non-British Australians. Whether or not Indigenous issues ever worked for Labor at the electoral level is a moot point, but the party gave them attention as part of the progressive agenda inherited from Gough Whitlam. There is a continuity between the Labor Party's commitment to class politics and its embrace of the new issues of the 1970s in the attention to the social conditions which shape and limit people's life chances, and to the possibilities of state action for reforming these. Like class, differences in gender, sexuality, race and ethnic background create inequalities of power, resources and life chances which can be ameliorated by government action.

Just as Labor drew on its origins in responding to the demands of identity politics, so under John Howard has the Liberal Party. In the 1996 election campaign Howard turned the tables on Labor by presenting it as captive to minority interests and so out of touch with 'mainstream Australia'—the current name for the consensual centre of Australian life. From the beginning of the two-party system, when Alfred Deakin's Liberal Protectionists joined with George Reid's Free Traders turned anti-socialists, the Liberal Party has claimed to inhabit the consensual centre of Australian politics, to be the only party which is above sectional and special interests, a party of nation not of class. Here is Deakin addressing the inaugural meeting of the Commonwealth Liberal Party at the Melbourne Town Hall in 1909:

> This is not a policy aimed at the interests of any class. It is a national policy addressing itself in a practical manner to the practical needs of the people of Australia today.

And here is Howard ninety years later, in his 1996 Menzies Lecture:

> The Liberal Party has never been a party of privilege or sectional interest or narrow prejudice…Liberalism has focussed on national interests rather than sectional interests.

The party of the section, the part, the class is of course the Australian Labor Party. The trick for a successful Liberal leader is to give this opposition between consensual centre and illegitimate section new meaning and force by drawing on the events and experiences of the day. No matter how the whole is described—whether as the nation, the national interest, the Australian way of life, ordinary Australians, middle Australia, the mainstream—this is the Liberal Party's claimed political space.

When Howard became leader again in 1995, the Liberal Party had lost its grip on the consensual centre and no longer knew how to talk the language of unity. Its enthusiastic embrace of neoliberal economic policies had been accompanied by growing reliance on the language of choice and competitive individualism. The high point of this was the 1993 election, when John Hewson was out-politicked by Paul Keating into carrying all the electorate's anxieties about the preceding ten years of economic-rationalist reforms. Keating, who had been overseeing a process of tariff reduction that was decimating much of Australia's manufacturing sector, mocked Hewson's commitment to finish the job by calling him Captain Zero.

Hewson was an economist and merchant banker who had only been in the Liberal Party a few years before becoming its leader. He lacked the deep affinity with the party's political traditions which a leader needs to produce convincing political rhetoric under pressure. After the Liberals lost, the party undertook a public soul searching. How had they lost the unlosable election to a prime minister who was responsible for the worst recession since the war? There were the standard reasons based on the underhand tactics of Labor.[4] There was the GST and the associated complex package of taxation reform—it was always going to be hard to win government while promising a new tax. There were deficiencies in the campaign, Hewson was inexperienced, and so on.[5] But the most popular explanation was that the Liberals failed to convey to the electorate a vision of Australia's future. Former Liberal MP John Hyde believed that the party did have a social vision but that the leadership had failed to communicate it. They needed memorable expressions; he suggested they put away the economic textbooks for a while and read some good biographies and political speeches, some heroic poetry even.[6]

John Hewson himself was well aware of the difficulties. In his 1990 Menzies Lecture he had lamented that 'Our party has long suffered from want of an evocative phrase such as Chifley's splendid "light on the hill".'[7] Clearly he was not the one to produce it. Hewson was followed by Alexander Downer, whose one memorable phrase, 'the things that batter', was that of a silly schoolboy not a statesman. So when Howard became leader in 1995 he had to create a convincing consensual language for the Liberal Party, and by his third election victory in 2001 it was clear he had done this with astonishing success.

Howard's renewal of the Liberal Party's language has occurred in two stages. The first was to reinvigorate the attack on Labor as the party of the section or part, by continuing to represent it as the party of unions and the organised working class, with disparaging references to union battalions and union bosses, and a preoccupation with illegal union activities. Class and the union movement have now been joined as illegitimate sectional interests by a host of other groups—feminists, environmentalists, multiculturalists, republicans, gay activists, the Aboriginal industry—sometimes all lumped together as noisy minorities, sometimes as the elites of the chardonnay set. Here is Howard in his first Headland speech in 1995:

> There is a frustrated mainstream in Australia today which sees government decisions as increasingly driven by the self-interested claims of powerful vested interests with scant regard for the national interest...This bureaucracy of the new class is a world away from the myriad of spontaneous, community-based organisations which have been part of the Australian mainstream for decades.[8]

The Liberal Party's 1996 campaign slogan, 'For all of us', and Howard's explicit appeal to mainstream Australia was a reworking of the Liberals' standard move against Labor, with a sharpened edge of grievance after thirteen years of Labor governments. The campaign director, Andrew Robb, says it 'was aimed predominantly at middle Australia...to reach people who legitimately felt betrayed. What we were saying was that in governing, we would not just consider the wellbeing of a select few, but we would consider the broad national interest. We would govern not just for some, but *for all of us*.'[9]

The Liberals' 1996 campaign was also a response to perceived shifts in the patterns of social and economic advantage since 1983. In a reversal of the traditional patterns of party–class identification, Labor was represented as governing in the interests of the rich as its base now included 'the social-progressive, often highly educated, affluent end of middle Australia'.[10] As Barry Jones commented after the election defeat, Labor had been seen as cultivating 'the big end of town'.[11] The rich could be inserted as an elite minority interest for those who wished to hear it, and for Labor's traditional supporters it added to their sense of desertion.

The Liberals' campaign pitch was overwhelmingly successful. A Liberal exit poll identified a shift to the Coalition of a significant section of Labor's blue-collar male base. Robb gloated that this 'significantly broadened the Coalition's voting base within middle Australia. And this movement overwhelmingly comes from workers and their families—Howard's battlers.'[12] The term 'Howard's battlers' was quickly taken up by journalists and pundits to explain the election results. This was a decisive rhetorical victory for the Liberals. Howard had begun appealing to battlers in 1995.

> Powerful vested interests seem to win the day when it comes to duchessing the government and access to public funding. The losers have been the men and women of mainstream Australia whose political voice is too often muffled or ignored—the families battling to give their children a break, hardworking employees battling to get ahead, small businesses battling to survive, young Australians battling to get a decent start in their working lives, older Australians battling to preserve their dignity and security, community organisations battling the seemingly ever-expanding role of intrusive central government.[13]

Like the Forgotten People, battlers were unorganised individuals, their identity located in family and local community, their enemies well-organised interests and an intrusive central government. But there were subtle and important differences. They were more clearly identified with small business (Menzies' forgotten people included the professions), the sense of powerlessness and grievance was stronger, and they were explicitly identified as workers.

When I was working on the emotional and rhetorical patterns of 'The Forgotten People', I was struck by the absence of the symbol of work from the speech. This was surprising. Work, after all, was central to the middle class's belief in its own economic virtue. In place of work, Menzies gave inordinate emphasis to thrift and savings. The reason for this, I surmised, was the successful hold the labour movement then had on the symbol of work. Workers wore blue singlets, not grocers' aprons and certainly not suits. Since the 1940s, not only has the nature of work changed, but the Labor Party, in widening its base to include sections of the middle class, has given less emphasis to its labourist traditions. As Labor governments under Hawke and Keating restructured the national economy in the name of the long-term national interest, they destroyed thousands of jobs in the traditional protected manufacturing industries. The cry 'What about the workers?' ceased to be a rallying cry for Labor supporters and became an accusation of betrayal. Labor's central symbol of work was left to drift, vulnerable to a takeover by the other side.

Like Menzies' transformation of the forgotten class into the forgotten people, Howard's battlers transcend class identities and include both the employed and the self-employed as they struggle to raise a family and make ends meet.[14] With the widespread acceptance of the term 'Howard's battlers', Australian Liberals won a historic victory over Labor, from which—seven years later—Labor had not yet recovered. It not only claimed to represent the mainstream, or the whole, but did so in a way that directly challenged Labor's core historic identity. It also showed that class had all but disappeared as a basis of ordinary Australians' political identity and understanding.

There was a stronger sense in the 1996 campaign of what the
Liberal Party opposed than what it stood for. The contrast was
between a vaguely defined 'Us' and whatever minority most aggrieved
you. The consensual space Howard had opened up with the slogan
'For all of us' filled up with grievances about various 'Them' who
were preventing a self-declared mainstream 'Us' from receiving
their fair share of resources and recognition. Many more grievances
flooded into the centre than Howard had bargained for, and for the
first term he struggled to regain control of the political agenda from
Pauline Hanson and One Nation. But one cannot govern for long
on the basis of grievance and negativity. By his second term Howard
was ready to start on the next stage of providing the Liberals with
a workable language of unity—by raiding the Australian Legend.

•

The Australian Legend was a term coined by the radical historian
Russel Ward in the 1950s to describe a set of distinctive Australian
character traits forged from the nineteenth-century settlers' experience
of the land: egalitarianism, practical improvisation, scepticism towards
authority, larrikinism, loyalty to mates, generosity. Ward claimed
that the Australian tradition was inherently radical and that ordinary
Australians were naturally left-wing. The itinerant rural labourers who
formed the first Labor parties bore its virtues, as did the Australian
diggers of World War One, and it captured aspects of Australian
working-class culture and its collectivist political traditions.[15]

Until Howard, Australian Liberals had left the legend to Labor.
Labor was the party of 'mates', committed to egalitarianism, the fair
go and an assertive Australian nationalism. Liberals spoke a language
of respectability, deference to Britain and support for the institutions
of the state. Neither Menzies nor Fraser made any attempt to wield
the imagery of the legend, and Gorton's larrikinism made him unfit

to hold high office in the eyes of Liberal Party powerbrokers. But, as the historian John Hirst pointed out, the Australian Legend was never as inherently radical as Ward had argued, and had a conservative version, 'the Pioneer Legend' of land-holding rural Australia.[16]

During the 1980s the Australian Legend experienced a revival in Australian popular culture, as globalisation and growing international tourism focussed attention on the uniqueness of Australia's natural environment and on the people who lived outside the cities. This revival could be seen in the popularity of films such as *The Man from Snowy River*; the transformation of rural work clothes like Drizabones, Akubras and riding boots into fashion items; the confidence of Australian country music; and the explosion of domestic outback tourism.[17]

Labor benefited from aspects of this revival. Republican anti-Britishness was used against the Liberal and National parties' support for the monarchy. But its rural provenance presented Labor with difficulties: the men from Snowy River and the heroes of the outback were probably racists. And the Australian Legend clearly had stronger roots in Australian working-class than middle-class experience. Its revival thus added an overlay of obvious cultural difference to the tensions between the ALP's historic labourist working-class base and its new urban middle-class supporters excited by contemporary Australia's cosmopolitan possibilities. The legend seemed to be about Australia's past, with little to offer its multicultural present and future. So, as with the symbol of the worker, Labor in government loosened its grip on the egalitarian imagery of the Australian Legend and Howard claimed it to fill out his picture of the consensual mainstream of Australian life.

In his 1997 Australia Day speech Howard reflected on the sources of national identity:

The symbols we hold dear as Australians and the beliefs that we have about what it is to be an Australian are not things that can ever be imposed from above by political leaders of any persuasion. They are not things that can be generated by [a] self-appointed, cultural elite who seek to tell us what our identity ought to be. Rather they are feelings and attitudes that grow out of the spirit of the people.

Howard posited two sources for these: great traumatic events such as Gallipoli; and 'long usage and custom', such as our tradition of 'informal mateship and egalitarianism'. Howard was staking out the traditional symbols of Australian nationalism for the Liberal Party, and the speech continued with a list of a few of Howard's favourite things about Australians: their 'tremendous spirit and versatility', their 'adaptability', their 'tolerance and openness', their 'scepticism and irreverence'.[18]

Howard's speeches after 1997 were filled with characterisations of what he variously calls the Australian Way, Australian values, the Australian identity or the Australian character. A few examples:

Our society is underpinned by those uniquely Australian concepts of a fair go and practical mateship.[19]

Being Australian means doing the decent thing in a pragmatic and respectable society which lives up to its creed of practical mateship...Australians are a down-to-earth people. It is part of our virtue. Rooted deep in our psyche is a sense of fair play and a strong egalitarian streak.[20]

Being Australian embodies real notions of decency and pragmatism in a classless society which lives up to its creed of practical mateship.[21]

The openness and unpretentious character of Australians has

given us a well-deserved reputation for tolerance and hospitality.[22]

In speeches like these Howard reworked Australian Liberals' understanding of the virtues on which the nation is built. He didn't completely drop the older moral middle-class rhetoric of service and leadership but he attached it to the more broadly popular forms of the Australian Legend. Thus he praised the surgeon hero of Changi, Edward 'Weary' Dunlop, for his laconicism and his mateship, as well as for 'his commitment to his country and his selfless service to his men'.[23]

Like many Australian men, Howard is fascinated by the lessons of war, both for individuals and nations. Both his father and his grandfather fought in World War One, and as prime minister Howard has been able to visit the sites of their wartime experiences. In many speeches he has embraced the national myth of Gallipoli, 'where our nation's spirit was born'.[24] The death in 2002 of the last veteran of that campaign, Tasmanian Alec Campbell, became an occasion of national mourning, with Howard himself delivering a eulogy at the state funeral in which he presented Campbell's life as 'contain[ing] the richness of our nation's history'.[25] Campbell had spent six weeks at Gallipoli as an underage boy soldier. Most of his life he was a radical trade unionist and office bearer, and so to Liberal eyes a bearer of the various vices of militant unionism. Howard passes lightly over Campbell's radical politics as his life becomes an exemplar of the virtues of the legend.

The death of sporting hero Sir Donald Bradman, the previous year, provided Howard with another occasion to reflect on the history of Australia's national spirit. Bradman's phenomenal cricketing success in the Test matches against Britain in the 1930s and 1940s, claimed Howard, 'reinforced the national spirit, which was born out of the Australian sacrifice during World War One and helped to display the independence and self-reliance of a young nation barely decades old'.[26]

Bradman spent longer at the crease than Campbell did at the front, but he too had another life, as an Adelaide stockbroker and company director, and as a long-serving cricket administrator. Throwing the lives of these two men, the radical trade unionist and the stockbroker cricketer, into the powerful solvent of the Australian Legend, their class differences are dissolved and they are reborn as nation-building comrades in arms, decent Australians and equally plausible representatives of the consensual centre.

Howard has also raided the Australian Legend to restate Australian Liberals' long-standing belief that they are the party which best allows Australia's civic spirit to flourish. He has revived the concept of the volunteer to express the Liberals' foundational belief that society is based on the actions and qualities of individuals. In 1954 the Liberal Party asserted that 'We Believe in the spirit of the Volunteer…the greatest community efforts can be made only when voluntary co-operation and self-sacrifice come in aid of and lend character to the performance of legal duties.'[27] Howard now calls Australia 'the greatest volunteer society in the world'. With the language of citizenship now captured by statist meanings and ideas of entitlement, the concept of the volunteer reclaims active civic involvement as a core Liberal value. Describing volunteers as the people who 'when the chips are down hold our society and our community together' is a fresh and convincing restatement of the now rather cliched claim of the moral middle class to be the backbone of the nation.

Volunteering is a flexible description of people's engagement with civic activities, from fire brigades to helping out at the local football club or school to the great 'volunteer army' of World War One. In yet another brilliant move, Howard then links volunteering to the Australian Legend by describing it as an expression of mateship: 'The great Australian capacity to work together in adversity—I call it mateship.'[28] So citizens have become volunteers have become mates, and Howard has planted the Liberals' flag firmly in Labor's territory of vernacular egalitarianism.

Howard has been astonishingly successful in linking contemporary Australian Liberalism to the Australian Legend. It has given him a flexible language of social cohesion which is distinctively Australian and which enables him to generate convincing contemporary rhetoric. It enables him to talk to rural Australia, where aspects of the legend still inform people's daily lives, as well as to families in the suburbs, where it connects with a deeply held commitment to ordinariness. And it can be turned, for state occasions, into a modest national story. His moving of the volunteer from the relative invisibility of local community good works into the centre of national life has restored a meaningful civic identity to Liberal rhetoric.

Howard's opponents have been misled by his own description of himself as a social conservative and so missed his takeover of the symbolic repertoire of Australia's radical-nationalist past to reconnect Australian Liberalism with ordinary Australian experience. His critics, many of whom value skill with words, have been misled by his rhetorical dullness. Howard is not a great orator: his language is plain and repetitive. There are no striking metaphors, no rolling cadences, no flights of fancy. Once he has hit on a form of words—like 'practical mateship'—he repeats it, without embellishment, in speech after speech. This may be boring, but it does not mean Howard does not have a vision, or that he is unable to strike chords from aspects of Australian experience.

There are still obvious tensions between Howard's commitment to radical economic policies which bring change and anxiety into people's lives, and his professed social conservatism. After all, the trade unionists whose rights he attacks with industrial-relations reform, the small-business owners struggling to implement the GST or sent broke by extended trading hours, the young people working all hours in the deregulated service industry, also have families and want security. But there is nothing new in this. Politicians in capitalist democracies have always allowed big business and financial interests considerable room to move against people's established entitlements and ways of living. This was progress. The problem for the Liberals was that they had no plausible way of talking about anything other than economics. John Howard gave them one.

---

[1] For example, the brilliant portrayal of him by Max Gillies as Barry Humphries' Sandy Stone in Guy Rundle's *Your Dreaming* (2001).

[2] *Future Directions: It's Time for Plain Thinking*, Liberal and National Parties, December 1988;

for more extended discussion, see Judith Brett, 'Future Directions: New Conservatism's Manifesto', *Current Affairs Bulletin*, 96, June 1989, pp. 11–17.

[3] *Sydney Morning Herald*, 5 December 1988.

[4] See David Kemp, 'Defeated by Fear, Smear and Cynicism', *Australian*, 19 March 1993, p. 11.

[5] Gerard Henderson, *Menzies' Child: The Liberal Party of Australia 1944–94*, Allen & Unwin, Sydney, 1994, pp. 303–06.

[6] 'Liberals Must Have a Heart', *Australian*, 16 March 1993, p. 9.

[7] Hewson, 1990 Menzies Lecture, in A. Gregory (ed.), *The Menzies Lectures 1978–1998*, Sir Robert Menzies Lecture Trust, Melbourne, 1999, p. 211.

[8] Cited in Gerard Henderson, *A Howard Government? Inside the Coalition*, HarperCollins, Sydney, 1995, p. 29.

[9] Andrew Robb, 'The Liberal Party Campaign', in Bean et al., *The Politics of Retribution: The 1996 Federal Election*, Allen & Unwin, Sydney, 1997, p. 37. See also John Howard's address to the Queensland Division of the Liberal Party State Council, 22 September 1996, p. 4.

[10] Robb, 'The Liberal Party Campaign', in Bean et al., *The Politics of Retribution*, pp. 36–37.

[11] Barry Jones, 'Notes on the Labor Defeat', in Gary Jungwirth (ed.), *Labor Essays*, Pluto Press, Sydney, 1997, p. 5.

[12] Robb, 'The Liberal Party Campaign', p. 41.

[13] John Howard, 'The Australia I Believe In: The Values, Directions and Policy Priorities of a Coalition Government', Liberal Party of Australia, Canberra, 1995.

[14] Marilyn Lake, 'Howard's Battle Cry', *Age*, 29 October 1996.

[15] Russel Ward, *The Australian Legend*, Oxford University Press, Melbourne, 1958.

[16] John Hirst, 'The Pioneer Legend', *Historical Studies*, 18, 1978, pp. 316–37.

[17] Graeme Turner, *Making It National: Nationalism and Australian Popular Culture*, Allen & Unwin, Sydney, 1994, chapter 1.

[18] John Howard, Address to Australia Day Council's Australia Day Luncheon, Darling Harbour, Sydney, 24 January 1997. See also 'The Role of Government: A Modern Liberal Approach', 1995 National Lecture Series, Menzies Research Centre, 6 June 1995, for a less-developed formulation of the same position.

[19] Address to Federation of Ethnic Communities Council National Conference, Brisbane, 20 November 1998.

[20] Keynote Address to Australian Council of Social Services National Congress, Adelaide, 5 November 1998.

[21] 'The Australia I Know', in Constitutional Essays, website of Australians for a Constitutional Monarchy, 11 November 2002.

[22] New Year's Message, 31 December 1999.

[23] Fifth Annual Sir Edward 'Weary' Dunlop AsiaLink Lecture, Melbourne, 11 November 1997.

[24] Speech to the Dawn Service, Gallipoli, Turkey, 25 April 2000.

[25] Address at the State Funeral of Alec William Campbell, St David's Cathedral, Hobart, 24 May 2002.

[26] John Howard, 'Peerless Bradman an Inspiration Across Time', *Age*, 27 February 2001; see also Sir Donald Bradman Oration, Melbourne, 17 August 2000.

[27] 'We Believe', in Graeme Starr, *Liberal Party of Australia: A Documentary History*, Drummond/ Heinemann, Melbourne, 1980, p. 198.

[28] Volunteer Awards ceremony, Cronulla Leagues Club, Sydney, 14 August 2001.

4 John Howard's Blemish

Age, 26 September 1997.

Freud's phrase 'the return of the repressed' reminds that, however much we may wish it, the darker side of our imaginings and of our actions, the things we wished we'd never done or never thought, cannot be simply wished away, locked into a dark cupboard of the mind and left there. Because they won't stay locked up; they will find ways to creep unexpected into the daylight hours and allow us to entertain forbidden thoughts. So a campaigner against sexual immorality, denouncing in great detail the sins of others, can contemplate the pleasures he's determined to ban.

I've been thinking of this phrase a good deal lately in listening to the public debate on native title, and in particular to the Coalition's insistence of its goodwill towards Indigenous Australians. Even as this goodwill is insisted on, it seems to me one can hear the return of the repressed in the language being used, the return of many of the racist assumptions and practices of Australia's history.

The first phrase which alerted me to this was the common talk of 'blanket extinguishment' as one of the options in dealing with the High Court's inconvenient findings of the continuing existence of native title in its Mabo judgment. It's an unusual metaphor; a plainer term could have been used—'total' or 'wholesale', or 'complete'.

Blankets, as bearers of comfort and warmth, have played a duplicitous role in the history of British people's relations with Indigenous peoples. Not only were they given as symbols of goodwill in exchanges which were never equal, but sometimes they were deliberately infected with white men's diseases. Their metaphoric presence in the contemporary debate about native title seems to me to carry the memory of this duplicity, and the wish that it were all still so easy. If only the native tribes had indeed been tricked from their land with a few beads and blankets; if only the West's material superiority in the provision of bodily comforts had lured them to forget completely their traditional ways and give up their land willingly to us; if only the blankets had extinguished native title as we had thought, how much easier it all would be. Couldn't we find a way to return to the state we thought we had, when terra nullius prevailed, when there were no recognised native title rights? So we go back to the blanket box to see if that duplicitous item can serve us yet again, no longer as an item of exchange but this time to smother, like putting out an annoying grass fire.

Then there is John Howard's repeated and emphatic insistence that Aboriginal Australians are the most profoundly disadvantaged group in Australia. Whenever he wants to insist on his concern, as for example when opening the Reconciliation Convention in May this year, emphatic insistence that he recognises Indigenous disadvantage is the main way in which he chooses to display his concern. The problem with this is that while there is much truth in it in terms of

access to services, such as health, education and housing, it also repeats
the assumption of white Australia's past that Aboriginal culture and
society was impoverished, with nothing to offer; the assumption,
that is, that to be Aboriginal was to be deficient, that Aboriginality
itself was a disadvantage compared with all the manifold blessings
of being born white. If the stress on material disadvantage were
accompanied by some awareness of the strengths of Aboriginal
culture, then the impression he conveyed would be quite different.
But as it is, the implication is that the solution is what assimilationists
have always thought—to provide the opportunities for Aboriginal
people to 'catch up'.

Perhaps the most revealing of Howard's words is his use of
'blemish' to acknowledge that everything in Australia's past is not rosy.
Speaking to the Reconciliation Convention he defended Australia's
proud history of progress and achievement, as he has done many
times before, speaking on behalf of 'the overwhelming majority
of Australians who are proud of what this country has achieved,
although inevitably acknowledging the blemishes in its past history'.

Blemishes are superficial imperfections, having little to do with
underlying structures. A smooth, fair cheek can be blemished by a
small birthmark or a too-dark freckle; a reputation can be blemished
by a minor indiscretion or uncharacteristic lapse of judgement. But
is 'blemish' the right word to describe a whole historical relationship
between two races, one of which conquered and dispossessed the
other?

It does admit the role of skin colours in this history, but plays
it down, implying that racism was a mere surface matter, not a
foundational belief justifying to white people their dispossession of
another race.

But, deeper than this, it seems to me to express the wish that if only this country had been unoccupied and unpossessed, unblemished by the presence of another race, or if only the original inhabitants had disappeared as they were meant to do, then we wouldn't have been tempted into violence and injustices, and we wouldn't have to make excuses now for this blemish on our past; we would simply have taken possession of an uninhabited land and prospered.

So the blemish slips from us to them. Those with the touch of the tar brush are the stain spoiling our national story of goodness and progress, not the deeds and thoughts of the pastoralists and settlers who took the land; not the deeds and thoughts of the founding fathers who excluded them from the nation; not the deeds and thoughts of the administrators who broke up the families and took the children away. And certainly not the deeds and thoughts of those who are now working overtime to make the High Court's judgment on native title as empty as possible.

PART II

Prime Ministers 2

1 Kevin Rudd's Narcissism

'Rudd the Narcissist', Monthly, *October 2013.*

When Bob Hawke faced off against Malcolm Fraser in 1983, my late friend and colleague the political psychologist Graham Little, writing in *Meanjin*, saw it as a contest between personality and character.

> Character is organized, socially responsible, predictable; personality is fluid, radically individual, elusive. Character is repeated again and again so that it seems to be human nature itself; personality seems ephemeral because it is always in process and revealing new facets. Most importantly, personality is assigned to the outer surface where persons interact, while character refers to a solid hidden core; character is solid where personality is a kind of hidden chemistry between people.

Personality brings excitement to political life, and the hope of a better world; character offers reassurance that things don't need to change too much to stay the same.

In 1983 character was dominant: Margaret Thatcher in the United Kingdom, Ronald Reagan in the United States, and here in Australia we had just had eight years of 'Life wasn't meant to be easy' under Malcolm Fraser. But in Australia the pendulum had swung back to personality with the election of Hawke, a big, public figure, ambitious, vain, and enormously popular. Reaching out to people, he offered a politics of consensus after the combativeness of Fraser, and promised to bring Labor's spirit of reform back onto the government benches after the crash and burn of Whitlam's governments.

There is an obvious fit between personality and reforming parties. The politics of change needs the buzz, the extra energy that personality brings, to break through settled assumptions and give people the confidence to think differently. Max Weber called personality in politics charisma, the political authority that comes not from tradition, the way things have always been done, nor from a constitution, what is legal, but from the capacity of the individual to take others with them beyond the boundaries of the present to visions of possible futures. Australian leaders who have had charisma have mostly been of the left: Whitlam, Hawke, Keating for some. A case could be made for Alfred Deakin, but not for any other Liberal leaders. And not all of Labor's leaders have been charismatic, certainly not its most successful, John Curtin and Ben Chifley, who were both firmly grounded in Labor traditions.

For political leaders, both personality and character have their strengths and their dangers. The dangers of character are that in relying too much on the ways of the past, the leader will be unable to respond effectively to changed circumstances and the inevitable unpredictability of events; that they will approach new problems with the solutions that worked last time they were in government. This is what Fraser did, as if undoing Whitlam's agenda would be enough to restore Australia's prosperity. But the world economy had changed and it didn't work. And it is where John Howard was at the end of 2007 when he faced Kevin Rudd as Labor's new leader for his fifth election since winning in 1996.

Then, he offered reliable, predictable leadership so that we could all be 'relaxed and comfortable'. Eleven years later his predictability was looking more like inflexible, unproductive stubbornness as he refused, again and again, to sign the Kyoto Protocol on reducing carbon emissions or to say sorry to the Stolen Generations, and as he clung to the Liberal leadership instead of facilitating its orderly transition to his long-serving treasurer, Peter Costello. In fact his predictability had become a bit of a joke. When, like clockwork, he appeared for his morning powerwalk, he would be accosted by supporters with high-fives and red roses, but also by protestors angling for a spot on that night's news: an animal-rights activist dressed as a sheep; the John Howard Ladies' Auxiliary Club, in pink frocks and floral hats, offering iced yellowcake and a jar of xenophobia; the *Chaser* boys dressed as white rabbits to help him pull one of their brethren out of a hat. In his own electorate of Bennelong he was challenged by the charming ex-ABC television presenter Maxine McKew.

His biggest challenge, though, was Kevin Rudd, whose leadership had transformed Labor's electoral chances. Rudd was Mr Personality writ large, a consummate public communicator who promised to break through Howard's stubborn refusals by signing the Kyoto Protocol and apologising to the Stolen Generations. Labor won with a 5.74 per cent swing and Howard lost Bennelong to McKew. A new government had been elected and it seemed, at first, that the country could be changed, like it was in the watershed years of the Whitlam governments.

The first official act of the new government was to ratify the Kyoto Protocol, and Rudd opened his government's first parliamentary session with a gracious and intelligent speech of apology to Indigenous Australians on behalf of the Australian government for the trauma inflicted on them by the removal of children from their families. These two dramatic symbolic actions displayed the power of personality to effect change and its understanding of the importance of symbolism.

Rudd's greatest political strength was his capacity to communicate with electors, and to reawaken them to the possibilities of politics. He was keen to incorporate community consultation into government policy making, as it tackled the backlog of problems it inherited from Howard's governments. Since 1998, when they were introduced by Peter Beattie, the Queensland government had been holding so-called community cabinets in which the cabinet met with members of the public in day-long sessions to hear their opinions and answer questions, often in regional locations. Rudd took this up for the federal government and held twenty-four community cabinet meetings in his first period as prime minister. Just what they actually contributed to policy formation is unclear, but they signalled his desire for more open, responsive government, and they got cabinet ministers and their advisers out of Canberra.

In early 2008 he held a huge talkfest in Parliament House, the 2020 Summit, in which around a thousand invited participants talked through a weekend to come up with big ideas to shape the nation's future. Heady stuff. I was there, assigned to the stream of governance, but it was never clear where these big ideas would end up. There were no motions, and certainly no votes: just facilitators with butcher's paper, a host of scribes recording into computers, loud voices and held tongues, chair people with their own ideas, and a pretty mad scramble on the final Sunday-morning session to record the 'Top Ideas'. In the final session and after, many participants agitated about which ideas made the list and whether those that did were an accurate representation of their stream's deliberations. But this was to miss the point.

The summit was not a deliberative body but an exercise in consultation and communication with a cross-section of elite opinion, though a cross-section decidedly from the progressive side of the political spectrum. Its mood was optimistic as participants, much of the media and many members of the public embraced the opportunity to think about Australia's future and to connect with the new government in a spirit of co-operation and goodwill.

The optimism didn't last. During 2008 the government seemed still to be in consultation mode, with inquiries running across major policy areas. When would it start governing? Disillusion is an inevitable accompaniment of a leader who releases hope, but in Rudd's case there was more. His skill at public politics was not matched by the skills of backroom political work: doing deals, building consensus, managing the flow of paper, making decisions. With the support of Wayne Swan as treasurer and Ken Henry as treasury secretary he steered the country successfully through the global financial crisis at the end of 2008 and Australia avoided a recession. But when it came to legislating for what he had called 'the great moral challenge of our generation', he came a cropper.

The government could not get its emissions-trading scheme through the Senate, even though it had a sympathetic leader of the Opposition in Malcolm Turnbull and the Greens with the balance of power. Turnbull has written that Rudd was one of his biggest obstacles to his getting the legislation through the Coalition party room, as he refused to negotiate or discuss possible amendments.

Similarly, Rudd refused to meet with the Greens' Senate leaders, Bob Brown and Christine Milne. Sidelining Turnbull was an own goal if ever there was one. The Liberals' climate sceptics were emboldened to move against Turnbull, replacing him with Tony Abbott, who in 2009 told regional Victorians that 'the climate change argument is absolute crap'. Rudd dropped the legislation, even though it gave him the trigger for a double-dissolution election which he might well have won.

Personality is an ally of narcissism. Freud gave narcissism a bad name, associating it with the self-centeredness of infancy and a stage through which individuals pass on their development towards psychological maturity. But Freud also saw in the narcissistic character an unequalled potential for leadership, linking it to creativity and the capacity to inspire cultural change. But political change needs more mundane skills. In his failure to build support for his government's legislation Rudd was displaying the shortcomings of his politics of personality.

Philip Chubb in his book *Power Failure* quotes a senior government adviser: 'He would have to be the only person with the solution, and systematically disordered and re-ordered decision-making so that he could control its dynamics and dominate the outcome.' Rudd was manipulative and relentlessly focussed on himself as an individual in the decision-making process.

The next year, in May 2010, Rudd and Swan sprang a resource-rent tax on the mining industry without any prior consultation. Ambushing Australia's most powerful industry in an election year was about as smart as Chifley taking on the banks. Didn't Rudd remember that the Australian Mining Industry Council's advertising campaign had killed the Hawke government's commitment to national land-rights legislation in the 1980s? The big miners swung into action with a brutal campaign against the resource-rent proposal, claiming that mining had saved Australia from the worst effects of the global financial crisis. Rudd's popularity started to fall. With an election due at the end of the year, some in the parliamentary party panicked. Two months later, acting from a combination of incompetence and hubris, the parliamentary party deposed him and installed Julia Gillard as prime minister.

Although Rudd had begun began his maiden speech in 1998 with the words 'Politics is about power', it was becoming clear that he did not know how to exercise it. In his *Quarterly Essay* on Rudd, 'Power Trip', David Marr quotes a shrewd old bureaucrat who has worked with a few prime ministers and wonders if Rudd really understood the way power works at the top. 'He isn't afraid to pick a fight, but doesn't then behave like a prime minister: he involves himself so much; puts himself on the line so quickly; doesn't exercise authority by keeping at a distance.'

This is Rudd of 'the buck stops with me', who presented himself as the fixer of last resort of all the nation's problems and rushed in to take the blame for all the problems with his government's home-insulation scheme, whisking his notebook out of his top pocket to note down the names of worried insulators and reassuring them that there would be another phase of government largesse once the problems were sorted out. Why did he think he had to take all the blame? There were a few other candidates—like shonky small-business operators. No one really expects the prime minister to act as everyone's local member, sorting out their problems for them with this and that government scheme; but having promised something he then found he couldn't deliver, he had only himself to blame when he walked away and people were angry. There is a failure of judgement here as Rudd promises too much and delivers too little, both in small things like the promise to the insulators and in large policy reversals like the ETS.

Implicit in these failures of judgement is a fantasy of concentration of power in himself as prime minister. Bucks stop—or not—in many places in liberal parliamentary democracies like ours: in particular with individual ministers, with state premiers, and behind the scenes with senior public servants. By mid-2010 Rudd had become, in Marr's words, 'the choke point' in the government, just as he was in Wayne Goss's Queensland government when he ran the Cabinet Office. Rudd's micromanagement and need to be on top of every detail was also about owning all the outcomes of government as he treated senior public servants as underlings, patronised caucus, ignored advice, bypassed his ministers and hogged all the big announcements for himself.

Three years later, facing another election, Rudd challenged Gillard and was briefly prime minister again, supported by a caucus desperate to save the furniture from a looming landslide defeat. According to Pamela Williams in the *Australian Financial Review*, the Liberal Party campaign team used a personality diagnosis to guide its tactics in the psychological warfare of the 2013 campaign. A friendly psychiatrist had provided an informal diagnosis of Rudd as suffering from a destructive personality disorder known as 'grandiose narcissism'.

This drew people's attention to Rudd's sensitivity to criticism and to his absolute conviction of his intellectual superiority. Challenge that and it will rattle him, tempting him into ugly displays of ill-conceived retaliation, which will put off undecided electors. The Friday before the election, the epithet 'narcissistic megalomaniac' was flung at Rudd as he walked down a mall with supporters. Labor colleagues, journalists, pop-psychologists over dinner or drinks, all used 'narcissism' as a pejorative, an accusation, obvious proof of Rudd's unsuitability for high office.

But, as Williams points out, the Liberal Party's secret diagnosis of Rudd's narcissistic personality disorder presents a riddle: if the symptoms were all so obvious and the character flaws so marked, how was it that Labor chose Rudd not once but twice to lead the country? The answer is that narcissism is more than just a personality disorder.

The American psychoanalyst Heinz Kohut has a 1972 essay on narcissistic rage which may well have informed the diagnosis given to the Liberals. It identifies many of Rudd's personality traits: his perfectionism and micromanagement, his love of the limelight, his paranoia and need for revenge, his outbursts of temper, the politician with rage at his core who David Marr described in the conclusion of his *Quarterly Essay*. But Kohut also helps us to understand how narcissism can be creative and serve larger ends. The key is for the self-love, the grandiosity, the self's urgent need to revenge wrongs done to it, to be invested in a cause or an institution beyond the self which is strong enough to contain the narcissistic energies and harness them for general social use. Many politicians have had rage at their core, rage at the humiliations and injustices of their childhood and the burning desire to solve for others what they could not solve at the time for themselves.

Rudd's politics were forged in the hard years after his tenant farmer father died and the family lost their home. He joined the Labor Party to contribute to a fairer Australia in which the humiliations of his dispossessed widowed mother and her children would not be felt by others, in which bright kids from poor backgrounds would have the means to get on. His determination to make Australia a place in which kids didn't have to suffer like he had was accompanied by a determination to remake himself from a fussy little kid on the margins of other people's lives into someone who was both unassailable and at the centre of things. Ambition and ideals, self-love and love of others: these are the drivers of a political life but achieving a balance between them is difficult.

Rudd was not a monster. He had the capacity to connect people with the Labor Party and make them feel that it mattered which side won, something none of his successors have been able to do as effectively. Yes, his dysfunctional leadership was in large part a consequence of his narcissism, but the Labor Party must take a share of the blame. Because its sense of purpose beyond the winning of power had been eroded, with too much focus on the distribution of spoils and too many untalented time-servers—like the factional powerbrokers who led the move against him—it did not provide Rudd with enough examples to live up to and its ideals were too weak to contain his self-focussed ambition.

2 Julia Gillard's Speech

Combination of 'Gillard and the Misogynists', Monthly, November 2012, and contribution to 'Women and Power' panel, Noosa Long Weekend, June 2013.

Our political institutions are deeply gendered. Parliaments acquired the power to choose the government as part of a historical process lasting several centuries in which battles with words and votes replaced battles with swords, axes and battering rams as the only legitimate way of settling political differences and rival ambitions among groups of men competing for political control. Parliaments' origins were in male rivalry, male aggression, male valour, male physical strength and how to manage these. It was about men winning and losing, men challenging and emerging triumphant, men knowing how to accept defeat and learn from it, men knowing how to lead. Organised team sports emerged around the same period, as arenas for the exercise and display of masculine virtues.

Despite our parliaments still being something of a boys' club, women have been operating effectively in them for decades now, as local members and as cabinet ministers. But a woman prime minister was always going to be something else. The top job—the leader—is a focus for emotional identification and for assumptions about leadership in a way that being a local member or even a minister is not. When Julia Gillard became Australia's first female prime minister, deep assumptions about gender and political power were mobilised against her.

In her final speech in parliament as prime minister, on 26 June 2013, Gillard said that being the first female to hold the office did not explain everything about her prime ministership, but neither did 'it explain nothing': 'it explains some things, and it is for the nation to think in a sophisticated way about those shades of grey,' she said. Staring at us through these shades of grey are the leering faces of her public male antagonists: Tony Abbott, Alan Jones, Andrew Bolt, mobilising misogyny for political ends.

Gillard became Australia's first woman prime minister in June 2010 after she successfully challenged Kevin Rudd. He had led Labor to victory in 2007, but by 2010, with an election due, things were not going well for his government. With his popularity slipping in the polls, some inside the government made the fateful decision that Gillard should challenge him for the leadership. She won and immediately called an election, which delivered a hung parliament— so Gillard and Abbott competed for the support of one Green and five independents. Gillard's superior negotiating skills won the support of three of the independents and Labor formed government with a majority of two.

In November 2011 this increased to three after the Speaker resigned and was replaced by the Deputy Speaker, the Queensland Liberal National Peter Slipper, who resigned his party membership, following the precedent of Speakers in the British parliament. The Opposition was furious and soon Slipper was under investigation by the federal police for misuse of Cabcharge vouchers and for sexual harassment of a former staffer, James Ashby. He took leave of absence as Speaker in April 2012 and formally resigned in October. In the interim the Opposition's assault on him and on the government for not removing him was relentless. After the investigation revealed an obscene text message sent to Ashby, on 9 October Tony Abbott moved that Slipper be removed as unfit for office and accused Prime Minister Gillard of protecting a sexist and misogynist.

> …what this prime minister has done is shame this parliament. Should she now rise in this place to try to defend the Speaker, to say that she retains confidence in the Speaker, she will shame this parliament again. And every day the prime minister stands in this parliament to defend this Speaker will be another day of shame for this parliament and another day of shame for a government which should have already died of shame.

This was the catalyst for Gillard's famous misogyny speech. As she told Anne Summers a year later in an interview at the Sydney Opera House, 'The speech was a crack point. I thought after everything I have experienced, I have to listen to Tony Abbott lecture me about sexism. That gave me the emotional start to the speech and once I started, it took on a life of its own.'

> I will not be lectured about sexism and misogyny by this man. I will not. The government will not be lectured about sexism and misogyny by this man—not now, not ever. The leader of the Opposition says that people who hold sexist views and who are misogynists are not appropriate for high office. Well, I hope the leader of the Opposition has a piece of paper and he is writing out his resignation, because if he wants to know what misogyny looks

like in modern Australia he does not need a motion in the House
of Representatives; he needs a mirror. That is what he needs.

Indeed.

Since she became prime minister Gillard had been subject to
continual slurs about her gender and sexuality. A decorative bowl
in her kitchen was compared with her barren womb. Tony Abbott,
flanked by Bronwyn Bishop and Sophie Mirabella, stood in front
of 'Ditch the Witch' and 'Juliar: Bob Brown's Bitch' signs at an
anti–carbon tax rally. Her clothes and appearance were a constant
subject for commentary, including Germaine's Greer's notorious
comment on her 'big arse'. The ABC showed an appalling satirical
sitcom, *At Home with Julia*. One episode had her and her partner
lying naked post-coital under an Australian flag. It is hard to imagine
such liberties being taken with John Howard or Kevin Rudd or Scott
Morrison and their wives, and it licensed an obscene free-for-all
against her on social media. A Liberal Party fundraising dinner for
the Queensland Liberal Mal Brough had a menu item, Julia Gillard
Kentucky Fried Quail: 'small breasts, huge thighs and big red box.'
I first heard this obscene sequence years earlier, in a best man's
speech at a wedding, so it was not original. But it was disgusting,
and I hesitate even to repeat it, except that it shows how, under Tony
Abbott, obscene denigration of Julia Gillard had become standard
in the Opposition.

Peter Slipper's obscene text messages to a young man he was
flirting with were not of the same order. True, they revealed him
to have a misogynistic fear of women's sexuality—or at least to be
prepared to entertain such fears—but they were private, never meant
for public viewing. Men have been exchanging dirty jokes about
women's genitalia for centuries, and many men have unspeakable

fantasies about women's sexuality. Slipper's private failed come-on made public was not of the same order as obscenity against women mobilised for political ends. This is why the claim that Labor was inconsistent to attack Abbott for misogyny yet support Slipper as Speaker seemed weak to so many women. Abbott had it coming.

·

Abbott's trope of 'Juliar' took off, given oxygen by her confusing backflip over a carbon tax. The broadcaster Alan Jones, who had previously told his radio listeners that Gillard should be put in a chaff bag and thrown out to sea, said to the Sydney University Liberal Club shortly after the death of her father that 'Every person in the caucus of the Labor Party knows that Julia Gillard is a liar…The old man recently died a few weeks ago of shame. To think that he had a daughter who told lies every time she stood for parliament.' Perhaps Abbott's echoing of Jones's derogatory comment by repeating the word 'shame' in his parliamentary attack was the tipping point for Gillard, supplying the emotional charge that made her speech so electrifying.

Jones's comment was beyond appalling, breaching the social conventions that protect death and mourning from the intrusion of politics. The changes in attitudes to sex and gender since the 1960s have been the subject of political debate. Feminism as a political movement engendered counter movements from those defending traditional gender roles. Similarly, the increasing liberalisation of sexual practices has been the subject of political debate. But, apart from the debate about euthanasia, death has not been subject to partisan political differences, and the strength and swiftness of the public's reaction to Jones's comment show that most believe it should not be. John Gillard was not a public figure and his death should not have been used to score political points against his daughter.

And she, although a public figure, should have been allowed the privacy of her grief. Later, in the wake of Gillard's misogyny speech castigating Abbott, the Melbourne columnist Andrew Bolt claimed: 'Power is Julia Gillard's true passion as she plays the gender card, victim card and her father's death for advantage.'

Jones and Bolt put Gillard into a place beyond human feeling, where she was so motivated by power that ordinary human emotions, even grief for her beloved father, were nothing more than pretexts for cynical political manipulation in her determination to keep legitimate male aspirants from office. This is Lady Macbeth dashing the suckling child from her breast lest her maternal feelings soften her resolve to do what it takes to put her husband on the throne.

Julia Gillard as Lady Macbeth was already a well-established trope among her detractors. The day after Gillard replaced Rudd as prime minister, Andrew Bolt wrote in the *Herald Sun*: 'As deputy leader she said Yes to his every dud policy? But now "Lady Macbeth" washes her hands.'

The way Julia Gillard came to power permanently damaged her chances of being accepted as a legitimate prime minister. This is more than the argument that women are expected to behave better than men, and that if she'd been a man she would have got away with it. It is about our deeply gendered constructions of political power. After she became prime minister, Gillard was repeatedly attacked for her role in Kevin Rudd's removal, by Liberals, by the Rudd camp and by journalists. The message was clear: she became prime minister illegitimately. Then, when she became leader of a minority government through processes that are par for the course in a democracy, the claim was that she had lied her way there by negotiating on a carbon tax. Such vitriol is rarely directed at men who have defeated a rival or reneged on a core policy.

The most extended elaboration on the theme of Julia Gillard as Lady Macbeth was by the Liberal minister Christopher Pyne, who claimed in parliament that to compare Gillard to Lady Macbeth was unfair to Lady Macbeth as 'she only had one victim to her name; this prime minister has a list of victims longer than Richard III.' What exactly was the crime which elicited this comparison? Gillard's adviser had tipped off some protesters to comments Tony Abbott made about the tent embassy in Canberra and precipitated an unseemly security scuffle. To this Pyne added the dispatch of Rudd, the lie she told to win the election about never having a carbon tax, the demotion of Senator Kim Carr from cabinet, and a few other manoeuvres of the sort that are standard fare in day-to-day parliamentary politics. But none of this was the real crime, which was that she, a woman, had usurped a man, that she had become prime minister illegitimately, through deceit, betrayal and violence, on 'a dark, dark Canberra night'.

Lady Macbeth and her husband plot to kill the king, Duncan—a guest in their home—and to usurp his throne. When Macbeth has second thoughts, Lady Macbeth urges him on, making her famous speech in which she claims she would crush the skull of the babe at her breast rather than renege on the pact they have made. A figure of unbridled and frustrated female ambition, she must work through her man, using deceit and passion. Later, mad with guilt, she cannot wash the blood from her hands. We have to remember, though, that Lady Macbeth never actually killed anyone. It was Macbeth who wielded the dagger, and wielded it again and again. It was he who held the power. Focussing on her is a convenient way to excuse out-of-control male aggression.

When I was writing my book on Robert Menzies, I came across an essay he wrote on hatred as an instrument of war policy. The context

was the war against Japan and Menzies was discussing the emotions
one should feel towards a wartime enemy. He distinguished between
legitimate, manly, full-blooded aggression and hatred, which was
the mark of a small man. Menzies presents legitimate aggression
as aroused by situations of danger or conflict—and then it's over,
leaving the bearer unscathed, like the sportsmen who shake hands
at the end of a tough match. Hatred, by contrast, persists—and in
persisting it warps and damages the person who hates.

Menzies was deeply committed to British institutions of legitimate,
rule-bound conflict—parliament, the Bar, sport, all institutions which
harness male aggression for useful social ends—and he valorised
the manly virtues of ambition and competitiveness. All the negative
aspects of aggression—its destructiveness, its deceitfulness, its bitterness—he split off into hatred, as illegitimate aggression which operates
outside of the rules, pursing its nefarious aims by the back door and
in the dark.

For Menzies the paradigmatic perpetrators of illegitimate
aggression were the communists, and he put into their mouths
Lady Macbeth's advice to her husband as they prepare to welcome
the king, Duncan, to their castle, where they will murder him:
'Look like the innocent flower but be the serpent under it.' Lady
Jean Spender, the wife of one of Menzies' ministers, Percy Spender,
remembered that when Menzies suspected her husband of nursing
ambitions towards him, he said to her, 'Give me the dagger, Lady
Macbeth.' He did not confront her husband.

Lady Macbeth is a figure of female ambition, using underhand
and illegitimate means to dispatch men from power. The message in
the comparison between Gillard and Lady Macbeth is clear. Calling
her a witch points more crudely to the same archetype of an evil,
manipulative female power which threatens to emasculate and kill

men. It is this archetype that licensed repeated appalling obscene and misogynist attacks on her.

What can you do when daily the misogynist fantasies of so many men are being projected onto you? How do you remind people that you are an ordinary human being, when not even bereavement protects you? Julia Gillard bravely tried to ignore them, to not respond, to pretend not to notice. In the end she did perhaps the only thing she could do. She fought back, and her attack on Abbott for his misogyny is now one of Australia's most memorable speeches.

3 Tony Abbott's Climate Denial

'Comment: He Will Never Stop', Monthly, *August 2017, with an update.*

Again and again, first as leader of the Opposition, then as prime minister, and sulking on the backbench after he lost the job to Malcolm Turnbull, Tony Abbott wrecked the chances of Australia achieving a bipartisan policy on emissions reduction. When, at the end of 2009, he successfully challenged Malcolm Turnbull for leadership of the Liberal Party, the catalyst was Turnbull's co-operation with the Rudd government over the introduction of an emissions-trading scheme. Winning by one vote, Abbott immediately announced a secret ballot on whether the party should support Labor's legislation. The result, fifty-four against to twenty-nine for, spelled the end of the Opposition's co-operation with the government on its Carbon Pollution Reduction Scheme.

When the scheme reappeared in 2011 as a price on carbon under Prime Minister Julia Gillard and her climate-change minister, Greg Combet, Abbott made this 'great big new tax on everything' the centrepiece of his campaign to defeat the government at the next election. Abbott's then chief of staff, Peta Credlin, later boasted on Sky News about how easily she and Abbott had been able to bamboozle the public over Labor's carbon price.

> Along comes a carbon tax. It wasn't a carbon tax, as you know. It was many other things in nomenclature terms, but we made it a carbon tax. We made it a fight about the hip pocket and not about the environment. That was brutal retail politics and it took Abbott about six months to cut through and when he cut through, Gillard was gone.

When he won the election in 2013 he repealed the legislation. There were scenes of jubilation in the lower house as a scheme which took thousands of hours of work to establish and was already lowering Australia's carbon emissions was thrown away. It was a disgrace.

To be sure, others have also contributed to the long-running disaster of Australia's climate policies: the Greens under Bob Brown who, in a fit of self-indulgent high-mindedness, refused to support Labor's legislation in the Senate; Kevin Rudd, who walked away from the 'great moral challenge of our generation' when the going got tough; and Julia Gillard, with her culpable naivety in promising that there would be no carbon tax in a government she led, and then agreeing that the scheme her government introduced could be called a tax. But it is Abbott's belligerent prosecution of what Labor's long-serving shadow environment minister Mark Butler called the climate wars that tells the sorry tale. It was Abbott who gave focus and a voice to the motley collection of climate sceptics in the Coalition party room and kept alive the delusion that coal has a viable long-term future. For even if it were not the case that burning coal is contributing to global warming, the rapid development of renewables and their plummeting price were numbering its days. If one can make energy from the sun, wind and tides, why would anyone bother digging up and transporting coal?

In 2107, from the backbench, he was at it again. For a brief moment in early June, the Independent Review into the Future Security of the National Electricity Market, chaired by Australian Chief Scientist Dr Alan Finkel, held out the hope that Australian politics might reach a bipartisan consensus on a scheme both to reduce emissions and to increase energy supply, by providing the certainty the private sector needs to invest in new energy generation. Fearing Abbott and his troops, Prime Minister Turnbull had already ruled out an emissions-intensity scheme, even though it had widespread industry support. Finkel knew he couldn't consider it, even if it was a better option than the clean-energy target he eventually recommended.

The clean-energy target seemed like clever politics. As it was 'technology-neutral' it did not explicitly rule out coal. Labor promised to work with the government to hammer out a deal it could live with when it returned to government. Business welcomed the possibility, finally, of a bipartisan agreement that would provide the certainty needed for new investment in energy generation. The Business Council of Australia, the Australian Industry Group, the Energy Users Association of Australia, and energy retailers Origin, AGL and Energy Australia were all on board, and argued that the clean energy target would lower prices for consumers.

Not so, said Abbott, whose special contribution to the debate has been to reduce complicated, technical arguments to simple cut-through slogans with little connection to reality. The clean-energy target is a tax on coal, he declared. After the Finkel review was delivered, Abbott upped his profile and his attacks on the government.

Setting out his conservative manifesto to the Institute of Public Affairs at the end of June, he called for a moratorium on new wind farms, a freeze on the renewable energy target at its current level of 15 per cent, and the construction of another 'big coal-fired power station'. Contrary to the evidence in the Finkel review and the assertions of the energy providers, Abbott claimed that the renewable-energy target was causing people's increased power bills by making coal uneconomic, and that if private investors would not build a new coal-fired power station then the government should step in and make good this market failure 'as soon as possible'. Just why this last suggestion is either a liberal or a conservative one is hard to fathom. It sounds much more like an old-fashioned socialist argument for re-nationalisation of the power supply.

But consistency was never Abbott's strong point. His major preoccupation was always product differentiation, drawing up the battlelines between the Liberal Party and its major enemy the Labor Party and winning the fight. From this perspective the main problem with the proposed clean-energy target was that it was too similar to Labor's policy. Abbott believed, he told Paul Kelly in early July, that energy policy was 'the best hope for the government to win the next election'. Attacking the big fat carbon tax worked in 2013, so why wouldn't it work again?

In his address to the IPA, Abbott approvingly quoted John Howard: 'While compromise is necessary in politics, conviction is the foundation of success.' But all success meant for Abbott was knocking the other guy out of the ring. It did not mean achieving good and enduring policy outcomes for the nation. The problem for Australia's energy policy was that Abbott's addiction to the climate wars meant he always blew up bipartisan solutions, even though only bipartisan solutions can deliver the certainty needed for the new investment in energy generation, and only new investment will increase supply and bring energy prices down.

There was little point in Turnbull and his energy minister, Josh Frydenberg, trying to appease Abbott or his followers in the party room over any policy that took climate change seriously. Having claimed in 2009 that arguments for climate change were 'absolute crap', Abbott went on to subvert Australia's climate policy as a champion of coal. If coal didn't exist, he would have found something else. His arguments were only ever the path to a pre-determined position that there be no effective action on climate change. For Abbott, scepticism about climate change was not just a convenient point of difference from Labor: it was baked into his public identity and, as an identity issue, stubbornly resistant to argument and evidence.

There was also something else at play in Abbott's determination to wreck the clean-energy target, what the Romans called *dolor repulsae*—the pain of defeat—and it seemed unassuageable as the shame and humiliation of losing high office drove him on, with the thinnest of rationalisations for his actions. This was not the simple desire for revenge that we saw so clearly with Rudd as he undermined Gillard. It was more a desperate need still to be heard and taken seriously, to believe he had something to offer when he had been so soundly rejected, to numb the pain with manic activity. Continuing to deny that humanity needed to reduce carbon emissions ensured he would stay in the headlines.

In October 2017, two years after losing the top job, he gave a speech in London to the climate-sceptic Global Warming Foundation in which he likened advocates of global emissions reductions to 'primitive people once killing goats to appease the volcano gods'. In a mindboggling display of ignorance, he claimed that if it was in fact occurring, global warming was more likely to do good than harm. 'Far more people die in cold snaps than in heatwaves,' he said. Tell that to the Pacific Islanders whose homes are being washed away, or to victims of catastrophic bushfires. And he appeared oblivious to the risks of ecological devastation. It got him headlines, though, and he was there for the kill when Turnbull's National Energy Guarantee triggered an internal challenge against him, even when Turnbull bowed to the sceptics and took out its modest energy-emissions reduction, leaving only affordability and reliability.

In 2019 Abbott lost his seat of Warringah to the independent Zali Steggall, who challenged him on climate change, but this did not shut him up, and at the end of the year, with the fires already out of control in New South Wales, he was telling an interviewer on Israeli radio that the world was in the grip of a 'climate cult'.

Since he became prime minister, Scott Morrison has read the signs, both from the markets as capital deserts fossil fuels, and from the expected ramping up of international action under Joe Biden's presidency. So he has been quietly nudging his government towards a credible emissions-reduction policy. At the time of writing, he was not yet there. The National Party was still urging the government to invest in a new coal-fired power station, and assuring coal miners that their jobs were safe so long as Labor was kept from office, and Liberal climate deniers like Craig Kelly were still sounding off. Abbott has joined the IPA as a Distinguished Fellow and turned his contrarian attention to 'virus hysteria and health despotism' and the dangers of putting safety ahead of risk. In a long recorded speech for the IPA he warns against the usual suspects of woke fads and pandering to China, but he never once mentions climate.

As it became clear early in 2021 that Morrison was trying to shift the Coalition away from its ideological denialism, Abbott dug in, telling Paul Kelly in the *Australian* on 6 February that, 'We were elected in 2013 to do four things—to keep our borders secure, to repeal Labor's bad taxes, to keep the budget under control and to end Labor's emissions obsessions. The one thing you have to do is to keep faith with the electorate.' But the electorate has changed and Abbott is on the wrong side of atmospheric physics. He owes Australia an apology for its wasted decade. When will he say, 'I was wrong and I'm sorry'?

4 Malcolm Turnbull's Optimism

'Comment: Turnbull's Frolic', Monthly, June 2016 and review of Malcolm Turnbull's A Bigger Picture, Australian Book Review, number 422, June 2020.

2016

Since his return as Liberal leader Malcolm Turnbull has told us again and again that there has never been a more exciting time to be an Australian. Really? What about the gold rushes of the 1850s, when hopeful young immigrants flooded into Victoria; or the mid-1950s, when the long boom took off and ordinary people had more jobs and houses and whitegoods than their parents raising families in the 1920s and 1930s ever dreamed of; or the early 1970s, when the social movements were in full swing and the Whitlam government was just around the corner?

Of course, Turnbull's statement is not a historical proposition at all, but a claim about the mood best suited to the times we live in. 'We have to be optimists,' Turnbull told David Koch on *Sunrise* last year, and an optimist he is about the promises of agility, innovation, creativity and the rest of it.

It is no doubt a very exciting time to be Malcolm Turnbull, prime minister at last, with his final chance to shape the future. But what about the rest of us? Do Turnbull's excitement and optimism capture and enhance something in the public mood, or is he off on a frolic of his own?

There are two strong arguments for the frolic. The first is global warming, now a climate emergency as the world heats at the swifter end of climate scientists' predictions. At the Climate Code Red website David Spratt reports NASA's satellite data on this February's mind-blowing temperature spike, when the average global temperature spiked at 1.35 degrees Celsius above the global norm for the past fifty years and close to 2 degrees above the pre-industrial benchmark of the mid-eighteenth century. And the further north on the planet, the greater the increase from the norm, with February in Alaska, Scandinavia and much of Russia being 4 degrees above monthly averages, and a massive 6 degrees above average north of the 75-degree latitude line. Melting resulted in the lowest extent of Arctic sea ice ever recorded for February. On these figures, the goal of the Paris Agreement to keep the global average temperature increase to 1.5 degrees is already obsolete.

We are already seeing devastating impacts: the Great Barrier Reef dying from coral bleaching; a wildfire in Alberta raging through the boreal forests, and the northern-hemisphere fire season is just beginning; drought in the Mekong Delta, ruining rice farmers. How, in the face of such events, can one be optimistic? True, the politics of responding to climate change have improved a lot since Turnbull replaced his flat-earther predecessor, and deniers and sceptics have largely disappeared from public view. But Australia is still a laggard in global responses.

If we had enough time, the incremental politics of slow boring through hard boards would no doubt eventually reduce the world's carbon emissions to safe levels. But we don't. So where in all this is optimistic Malcolm Turnbull, who knows that climate change is real and dangerous, not to mention his mealy-mouthed minister for the environment, Greg Hunt? There was no mention of climate change in the budget, and they are running a scare campaign about power prices against Labor's policy of 50 per cent renewable energy by 2030.

Bill McKibben's 'Comment' in the February 2016 issue of the *Monthly* gives the most plausible explanation, which is that both are caught in the classic Augustinian trap: Oh Lord, make me chaste—but not yet; not until all the climate sceptics have been flushed out of the Coalition, not until the fossil-fuel and energy companies have had time to transition into renewables and maintain their dividends, not until a technological breakthrough by our agile and creative scientists has made renewables a lay-down misère. But this is magical thinking, not political leadership. Fear, not optimism, is the realistic government response to the climate emergency.

The second argument for Malcolm Turnbull's optimism being a frolic of his own with little purchase on the public mood is Australia's escalating generational inequality. Since Wordsworth's enthusiasm for the transformative possibilities of the French Revolution ('Bliss was it in that dawn to be alive, But to be young was very heaven!'), political optimism has been strongly associated with the young and their belief that their energies and ideas can make the world a better place. It was because Gough Whitlam tapped into the confident optimism of young baby boomers that his government is remembered for its transformation of the Australian political landscape rather than its bungled governing. But there is no such youthful spirit today to give wings to Turnbull's optimism.

Generations X and Y are generally finding it much harder to make their way than did their parents and grandparents. Jennifer Rayner makes the case in her book *Generation Less*. Soon to be thirty, she compares her life as a renter in insecure work with the lives of her parents at the same age: 'settled, prosperous parents of three. Homeowners; tenured workers tucking away super and long-service leave.' Those born after 1980 are more likely to be in casual, contract or insecure employment than their parents and grandparents were at the same age. They advance more slowly in their careers. And they are far, far less likely to be buying a house, and so are likely to be renting from one of Australia's growing number of landlords who negatively gear their investment property (or properties) and hope for capital gains as house prices rise even further beyond the purchasing power of aspiring young homebuyers.

It's hard to be optimistic when you're facing a lifetime of renting, as the government gives tax breaks to people to buy their sixth property but not to you for your first. There are many factors pushing up house prices, but negative gearing is one. With Labor's modest proposal to rein it in and the government's refusal to do anything about it, negative gearing has become a symbol of generational inequity at the heart of this election campaign, putting Turnbull on the side of the comfortable middle-aged trying to get ahead rather than the anxious young trying to get started.

Alfred Deakin, the most significant prime minister of the Commonwealth's first decade, was also an optimist. He regarded pessimism as a moral failing, describing it in an unpublished essay on 'Optimism' as 'a frost which threatens religious morality and society'. From when he first entered Victorian politics in 1879 as an idealistic twenty-two-year-old, Deakin abhorred the negative 'Obstructionists' who stood in the way of progress, and in 1906 he famously attacked the policies of George Reid as nothing but a 'necklace of negatives'.

In the 1880s, Deakin's optimism was in line with the general mood of the country, as the Australian colonies prospered from increased migration and plenty of British capital. When the economy crashed in the early 1890s, Deakin's optimism took a hit, and he almost put politics behind him for good. For the rest of the decade he refused ministerial office. But he stayed on, his optimism fed by the prospect of federation, for which he worked tirelessly. Federation was an optimistic, nation-building project, and once the Commonwealth was inaugurated Deakin committed himself to securing the legislative foundations of its key institutions and policies.

Deakin was prime minister three times during the Commonwealth's first decade, and never once did he lead a party with a majority in either the House of Representatives or the Senate. Minority government was the order of the day, with governments always hostage to the next no-confidence motion. After federation in 1901, there were five changes of government on the floor of the house before Labor won the 1910 election and became Australia's first government to lead with a majority in its own right. The politics were bitter and often personal, and there were long periods in which little legislation was passed.

Deakin's optimism and courtesy helped him navigate the turbid parliamentary waters, but his real lifeline was his unwavering policy commitments to building Australia's white population, protecting its infant industries and securing an independent defence capacity for Australia. He was also fuelled by a determination to pass a raft of practical legislation needed to get the Commonwealth up and running, from settling the site of the new capital to establishing an office of statistics. During his three periods as prime minister, party concerns for political survival were secondary to his determination to go 'straight on' while he had the power to achieve practical outcomes. His optimistic nature no doubt helped him in this, but it was grounded in a clear sense of legislative purpose. We may not now agree with all his policies, but that is not the point. He knew what he was in politics to achieve, and he tried to achieve it.

Malcolm Turnbull's public persona has some similarities to Alfred Deakin's: he is charming, courteous, never at a loss for a word, a good writer; and he promises to bring the Liberal Party back to the moderate centre of Australian politics that Deakin helped create. And both are self-proclaimed optimists. But where Deakin's optimism was steadied by his unwavering policy commitments, Turnbull's seems free-floating, like thought bubbles in the wind, anchored neither in the mood and urgent needs of the time nor in his own core beliefs.

2020

Malcolm Turnbull looks us straight in the eye from the cover of his handsome biography, *A Bigger Picture*. With just a hint of a smile, he looks calm, healthy and confident. If there are scars from his loss of the prime ministership in August 2018, they don't show. The book's voice is the engaging one we heard when he challenged Tony Abbott in July 2015 and promised a style of leadership that respects people's intelligence. It takes us from his childhood in a very unhappy marriage, through school and university, to his astonishing successes in media, business and the law, his entry into politics as the member for Wentworth, and his exit from parliament.

It is a Sydney story, full of the Sydney identities Turnbull worked with as he made his name and fortune: Kerry Packer, of course, but a host of others, and the politicians, like Neville Wran and Bob Carr, who were his friends. Like the young Paul Keating, he sat at the feet of Jack Lang. The stories of his successes, friendships and enmities before he entered politics are lively and well told, but they have a rehearsed feel, the jagged edges worn away. The book's energy is in his three years as prime minister, which occupy more than half the book.

The brutal twists and turns of the week when Peter Dutton challenged Turnbull make for compelling reading, not least because Turnbull is so frank in his character assessments of the key players. He was amazed that anyone, including Dutton, could seriously think he was a viable candidate for leader. He believed Greg Hunt was motivated solely by his desire to be foreign minister in Dutton's cabinet. He was hurt by what he saw as betrayal by Mathias Cormann, whom he had come to trust and thought was his friend.

Turnbull remains unsure exactly what role Scott Morrison and his supporters played in the events of that week, but he was relieved that it was he and not Dutton who became prime minister. Turnbull's take on Morrison is the only published close-up view we have so far of the man who is now our prime minister. He sees him as a purely political animal, with few policy convictions and widely distrusted by his colleagues. He also believes his compulsive leaking as treasurer derailed the government's policy options, such as on the GST and negative gearing.

There are detailed chapters on his government's major domestic and foreign-policy achievements. He is especially proud of the same-sex-marriage legislation's victory over the Coalition's right wing. Many of the staunchest advocates of 'traditional' marriage, he notes, were the keenest practitioners of traditional adultery, a comment he repeats when discussing the ban on sexual relations between ministers and their staff, which he introduced after the affair between Barnaby Joyce and his erstwhile media adviser became public. Turnbull had already had to speak to several ministers about this kind of thing, he writes, leaving us to wonder who.

Turnbull's singular failure was to achieve an energy policy that took seriously Australia's responsibility to lower its emissions. Turnbull's support for Kevin Rudd's emissions-trading scheme was the catalyst for his losing the Liberal Party leadership to Tony Abbott in 2009, and he trod softly on climate when he became leader a second time. After the first loss he went into a black depression, the first time this ebullient, gifted man had experienced serious mental illness, and he considered leaving politics for good. But he stayed, and believes that he emerged from the darkness a better, stronger and less self-absorbed person.

It was this better person, determined to consult widely and build consensus, who many of us found so frustrating. Why wouldn't he do a Gough, crash through or crash in a confrontation with the climate deniers? This book helps us understand why.

The prime minister Turnbull is most like is Whitlam, both brilliant, ambitious Sydney lawyers with big visions and big egos, but where Whitlam was able to ride a hunger for change in Australia, the times did not suit Turnbull. He was not a partisan warrior in a parliament that had become polarised, at least since Howard and toxically so under Abbott; and he was not sufficiently tribal for the Liberal right, who believed he was a Labor Trojan horse.

There have always been rumours that Turnbull tried to join Labor. However true these are, he concluded, rightly, that he belonged in the party committed to individualism and free enterprise, not the party of collectivism and the unions. He hoped he would be able to steer the Liberals back to the centre, closer to its liberal foundations, and as prime minister he worked hard to consult widely and build consensus. He eschewed captain's calls and restored proper processes of cabinet government after the Abbott debacle. But he didn't hate

Labor and was widely criticised by his side for not running a negative campaign in 2016. Nor did he heed the many warnings from his colleagues about who not to trust, which was pretty well everyone in the senior Coalition team. If he had, he writes, 'I would not have been able to work with any of them', or achieve anything.

Paul Keating said of Turnbull, 'brilliant, utterly fearless and no judgement'. This book give plenty of evidence to confirm all three qualities. The achievements of his early adulthood are astonishing, as he walks into the lives of the great and powerful and achieves extraordinary successes, like defeating the British government in the Spycatcher case, and making serious money. Other reviewers have criticised some of these accounts as a little self-serving, and no doubt they are. Most people are unreliable narrators of their own lives.

It was the lack of judgement I was most interested in when I read the book, and his buoyant unrealistic optimism. As a political leader he made two spectacular failures of judgement. The first was the Godwin Grech affair when, as leader of the Opposition, he accused Prime Minister Rudd of giving special treatment to a mate on the basis of emails Grech leaked to him. He liked and trusted Grech but the emails turned out to be fake and he was hugely embarrassed.

The second was his decision to take the country to a double-dissolution election in July 2016. It was a foolish decision, which I can only put down to an over-optimistic reading of his government's electoral chances. A normal election could have been held as soon as August, and the trigger was unconvincing—to pass the Building and Construction Industry bills. He thought it would deliver a more workable Senate. Instead the Coalition barely scraped home, and he destroyed a massive amount of political capital.

The book gives us clues to the origins of this his lack of judgement, in its first chapter on Turnbull's childhood. His parents, Coral and Bruce, were ill-suited, an ambitious, intellectual woman and a good-looking, knockabout guy. They married a year after Malcolm was born, but the marriage didn't last. When Malcolm was about eight his mother left for New Zealand with another man. He was sent to boarding school, where he was desperately unhappy, and Bruce brought him up. The story Bruce told his young son was that Coral had gone to study, and that she loved him more than anything else on earth. Maybe she did, but she had left him, and this truth only slowly became apparent to him as 'her absence crept up on me like a slow, cold chill around the heart.' By sheltering him from the truth, Bruce was protecting his son's self-esteem, but perhaps he also weakened his reality-testing capacities, leaving him vulnerable to unrealistic optimism and misplaced trust.

In one important life matter, though, Turnbull's judgement was impeccable. He wed his wife, Lucy, forty years ago this March, and together they have built a loving, supportive marriage of equals and raised two children. He told Leigh Sales that he had always had 'a stronger sense of Lucy and me than I do of me'.

Malcolm Turnbull lost the Liberal leadership twice because of his belief that climate change is real. In office he was unable to act effectively on this belief. Seeming to promise so much, he turned out to be a disappointment, as leaders so often do. For all the hopes we project onto them our political leaders are only people, trying to do their best with the circumstances—and the colleagues—fate gives them. I finished this book with a great deal of sympathy for Turnbull. He failed to defeat the climate deniers in his party, but at least he tried.

5 Scott Morrison's Quiet Australians

'Howard's Heir: On Scott Morrison and His Suburban Aspirations', Monthly, *September 2019, with an addendum in 2021.*

John Howard was the Liberal Party's first suburban man to become prime minister. With Scott Morrison's miracle win in 2019 we have another. Howard etched the groove, and Morrison has settled comfortably in. He is, he tells us, just a normal, average guy, living in the suburbs, paying off an average-sized mortgage on a typical three-bedroom family home, with two young kids and a supportive loving wife, Jenny. They met when they were sixteen, married at twenty-one, and still walk round holding hands. He was brought up by loving, community-minded parents, and he and Jenny are doing the same for their girls, just like millions of other families in Australia's sprawling suburbs. And he loves his local footy team, to boot. Nothing to see here.

No man who reaches the top in politics is ever just a normal, average guy. He will have above-average ambition, for starters, thicker skin and greater self-belief and will to power, as well as being much better paid than the average Joe. But compared with his immediate predecessors, Morrison does look normal. Tony Abbott was too weird and Malcolm Turnbull too rich to represent widely shared experiences. When Abbott told us how he and Margie would sit at the kitchen table to sort out the family budget, it just drew attention to how rarely we saw her, and we wondered how he fitted family life into his obsessive exercise regime. And we all knew there was no need to budget in the Turnbull household. Not only did he and Lucy have a Harbourside Mansion, but an apartment in Manhattan where they went to re-centre themselves after he lost the leadership to Morrison. Retreat to his place down the coast would have kept him within representative range, but a bolthole in New York?

Howard too was more ordinary than his immediate predecessors, Andrew Peacock and Alexander Downer. Both were private-school-educated. Peacock was elected to federal parliament at a by-election when Menzies retired, early in 1966. Downer's grandfather was premier of South Australia, a federation father and a senator in the first Commonwealth parliament. His father, also Alexander, was a member of Menzies' cabinet and ended his political career as Australia's high commissioner in London. Andrew and young Alex went into politics with high expectations of success, but neither became prime minister.

Howard's family was Liberal, but not Liberal royalty. His father ran a service station and he went to Canterbury Boys' High. Morrison's father was a policeman and he went to Sydney Boys' High. Both grew up in the Sydney suburbs, Howard in Earlwood and Morrison in Bronte, which was not quite the super-rich suburb that it is today when Morrison was growing up in the 1970s and 1980s. Still, Morrison's family was a notch above Howard's and more actively involved in the local community. His father rose to be a police commander and was a member of the Waverley Council for sixteen years, including a brief period as mayor.

Both men clearly enjoy public life and seem never to tire of meeting and greeting. Bob Hawke had the same quality. It makes a politician very attractive. Shorten tried, but he often looked as if he would rather be somewhere else. So did Turnbull. Extraverts have a natural advantage in political life, especially when they seem as comfortable in their own skin as Morrison does.

As party loyalty has declined, the popularity of the leader has become more important in determining electoral outcomes. The 1987–2016 Australian Election Study showed that rusted-on support-ers—those who vote Labor, Liberal or National in every election and in both houses—are now only 40 per cent of the electorate. In the late 1960s they were 70 per cent. Many of the uncommitted are not very interested in politics, but come election day they have to make a decision and some will base it on their judgement of the leader.

Liberal Party research since the 2019 election (reported in the *Sydney Morning Herald* on 28 July) revealed that the Coalition victory swung on the votes of suburban working mums in the thirty-five to fifty-four age group with loose political alignments. In Victoria there had been a massive twelve-point shift in their votes since the state election, which Labor won in a landslide.

Amanda Harris, a teacher and a mum with two children aged thirteen and ten, told the *Australian*'s Caroline Overington the day after the election that although she doesn't always vote Liberal, 'I looked at the Morrison family, and I thought: his family looks like us, a typical Australian family, wanting to get ahead…What's been really interesting this last few days is how many people there are, just like us. Waking up to look at the vote, I thought: oh, okay, we're not wrong.'

Just like us. People hope that a political leader who shares their experience will be more likely to govern to advance their interests. This is why in the late nineteenth century working-class men switched their votes from middle-class friends of the workers to their own kind, why farmers formed their own party in 1920, why feminists argue for more women in parliament, why there is a push for greater ethnic and racial diversity in parliamentary candidates. Our federal parliament is a long way from being a mirror of contemporary Australian society, but in positioning himself as a suburban family man, Morrison made himself recognisable to a huge swathe of loosely aligned voters. As well, Jenny, his wife, looked far more relatable than the glamorous Chloe Shorten. Liberal strategists surmised that she was a big factor in explaining his success, women seeing her as someone who would keep her husband in touch with the issues that matter to parents.

On election night, Morrison attributed victory to 'the Quiet Australians'. Howard had pitched his appeal to 'the men and women of mainstream Australia whose political voice has too often been ignored', battling to get ahead, or just to survive, as he described them in 1995 in a Liberal Party pamphlet, 'The Australia I Believe In'. Even further back are Robert Menzies' 'Forgotten People', whose quiet, family-centred lives were being overlooked by a Labor government already committed to post-war planning.

Menzies' 1942 radio broadcast did not have the political significance at the time that it has since acquired for the party he founded a few years later. Menzies never used the term 'the Forgotten People' again. In 1945 it was more important to set out the core beliefs of the new party in a philosophy and a party platform than to hone its rhetorical appeals. But since then, as the ideological identities of both major parties have blurred and voter alignment has loosened, the need to construct a distinctive rhetorical identity has become more urgent.

How similar are Morrison's Quiet Australians to Howard's Battlers and Menzies' Forgotten People? This question is about rhetoric as much as demography, about how Liberal leaders project their followers and the symbolic resources they draw on. Each is implicitly contrasted with noisy minorities who get all the attention. Quiet, ignored, forgotten: the message is the same. Also the same are their virtues as responsible people working hard to provide for their families, to 'get ahead', and to secure their well-deserved retirement. A neat fit is posited between their economic virtues and aspirations and the Liberals' promise of smaller government, lower taxes and careful economic management, which was on full display in the 2019 campaign. The re-elected Coalition government, Morrison told jubilant Liberals on election night, would give 'A fair go for those who have a go', for those who make a contribution and don't just seek to take.

When pressed, Liberals accept the need for government-provided services, but they have always been more committed to equality of opportunity than to equality of outcome. The praise for those who contribute and 'have a go' implies a bunch of lazy takers, whether they are named or not. Robert Menzies' called them 'leaners', in contrast to the 'lifters' who keep society going. It is a core Liberal Party belief that individuals should be encouraged to look after themselves and then rewarded for the effort.

It's not just the self-congratulatory appeal of seeing oneself as a contributor that gives this pattern its power, but the anxieties it evokes: of the never-ending demands that the needy, with the government as their agent, might make on the resources we've each marshalled to support ourselves and our families. Labor's tax and spend; Bill

Shorten's hand in your pocket, taking.

During the 2019 election campaign Morrison made no overt attacks on government-provided services. This would have opened him up to a Labor scare campaign, as well as reminding voters of Joe Hockey's 2014 budget, which took an axe to government spending on health and pensions. Nor did he indulge in demonising dole bludgers or asylum seekers. Instead he projected a world of scarce resources, with individuals and families competing with each other to get ahead, and a modest tax refund to reward their effort. He made them anxious and uncertain about what life would be like under a Labor government.

Virtues come in sets. There are the virtues of being independent and looking after yourself; and there are the virtues of compassion and looking after others. We each strike a balance between the two, shuttling back and forth as we try not to be too hard and unforgiving yet also to protect ourselves from fraudsters who will play on our sympathy and get under our guard. Peter Dutton is the Coalition's specialist in hard-heartedness, ever alert to the way asylum seekers might try to game the system: self-injuring to get medical evacuations, coming in the back door from New Zealand.

Morrison's Quiet Australians, Howard's Battlers and Menzies' Forgotten People share a common heritage in the Liberal Party's belief that individual effort is the basis of society rather than collective endeavour and institutions. But there are important differences. Howard and Menzies both worked their audience's accumulated grievances harder than Morrison. In part, this can be explained by the fact that both were in Opposition. Howard's Battlers in particular had a sharp sense of grievance built up after thirteen years of Labor government, a recession and three years of instruction from Prime Minister Keating about how they needed to change.

In 1942 Menzies positioned his Forgotten People between the idle rich and the organised working class, and though he did not overtly demonise the latter the speech did contain some pretty graphic negative images of the poor and uneducated in a society in which class was a major determinant of people's life chances. By Howard's time class-based rhetoric had waned. After four decades of immigration, a sexual revolution, second-wave feminism, environmentalism and Indigenous demands for justice and recognition, Australian politics was much more complex. Howard's solution was to push all these new political demands aside, and project an assimilationist nationalism as in the slogan of his 1996 victorious election campaign, 'For all of us'. He worked hard to fill out this projected national space. Speech after speech extolled the virtues of the Australian character and way of life. Praising Australians' practical mateship and open, unpretentious character, he constructed a flexible vernacular nationalism of broad appeal.

Compared with Howard's elaborated view of the nation, Morrison's nationalism seems more a matter of gesture than substance: 'How good is Australia? How good are Australians?' But exactly what is it that is so good about us? Compared with Howard's many speeches, Morrison hasn't really said.

On Indigenous Australians, though, Morrison's thinking does seem very different from Howard's. For a decade, from the mid-1980s until the defeat of the Keating government, some sort of reconciliation seemed possible between settler Australians and the descendants of those killed and dispossessed by the European invasion. Howard put paid to that. He refused to acknowledge the legality of prior ownership, the massacres and violence of the frontier, the truth of the forced removal of Indigenous children from their families. He dismantled Labor initiatives like the Aboriginal and Torres Strait

Islander Commission, and stopped the reconciliation process in its tracks. Two decades later it is slowly beginning again, and Morrison looks much more sympathetic than Howard was.

Morrison gave his maiden speech as the member for Cook on 14 February 2008, the day after Rudd's apology to the Stolen Generations, which finally acknowledged the terrible suffering inflicted on Indigenous children and their families by government policies of forced child removal. This suffering had been shockingly documented in *Bringing Them Home*, the report of an inquiry by the Human Rights and Equal Opportunity Commission, which called for an official apology for these past government practices. The problem was that the report had been commissioned by Labor but delivered in 1997, when Howard was prime minister.

For more than ten years, Howard had stubbornly refused to say sorry. Six Liberals left the chamber as Rudd rose, and Peter Dutton abstained from the vote. Next day Morrison made clear that he did not share the Howard era's stance on Indigenous issues. He began by acknowledging the Gweagal people of the Dharawal nation of southern Sydney. He recognised the devastation of the Indigenous population from two hundred years of shared ignorance and failed policies. He said he was pleased to say sorry yesterday, and that he hoped for true reconciliation. He did balance his recognition of the wrongs of Australia's past with the need to celebrate our achievements, but the defensive denial of the Howard era was gone. In 2019, in his speech at the Prime Minister's Literary Awards, Morrison spoke of the impact reading Kate Grenville's *The Secret River* had had on him, how it had opened his eyes and changed his thinking.

Morrison has committed to some sort of recognition of Indigenous peoples in the constitution, and he has appointed an Indigenous man, Ken Wyatt, as the minister for Indigenous affairs. But so far he has ruled out the Uluru Statement's call for a constitutionally enshrined First Nations Voice. Malcolm Turnbull's ill-considered and incorrect rejection of this as a third chamber of the parliament has stuck in the Coalition's collective thinking, so he needs to move carefully, if moving is his intention.

Compared with Howard, though, we know little about what Morrison really thinks about many matters. Take his policy speech made on Mother's Day, the Sunday before the 2019 election. Full of first names, it was more like a speech at a family celebration than an address to the nation about the intentions of a government he hoped to lead. Of course this was his intention, to project the nation as a large family, all working together to get ahead, contributing, saving, loving and supporting each other. It all sounds very simple. Except that it isn't. The nation is not a family, and the skills and experience one needs to run a suburban household, or a regional small business, are not sufficient to run the country. There are entrenched conflicts of interest to be managed, long chains of consequence from decisions, institutions to be reformed, a complex international environment, a faltering economy, a threatened planet.

Morrison's exuberant suburban public persona, with its baseball cap, high-fives and carefully crafted shots of Daggy Dad fixing a backyard chicken coop, gives us few clues to his thinking on key issues. Does he have a policy agenda, reforms he entered politics to work for, as Howard did with tax and industrial-relations reform? It seems not, and this has led some to look to his religious faith for clues to his political thinking. In a February 2019 essay in the *Monthly* James Boyce wondered if he believed in the Devil, and Erik Jensen called his *Quarterly Essay* on the 2019 election 'The Prosperity Gospel'. In the *Conversation* in May 2019 a historian of religion, Philip Almond, argued that Morrison's 'have a go' philosophy sits squarely within

Pentecostal prosperity theology, the view that belief in God leads to material wealth. But it also sits squarely within the traditions of the Liberal Party and its commitment to reward for individual effort. To be sure, the Liberal Party has deep roots in Protestant thinking, but we don't need Pentecostalism to explain the emphasis Morrison gives to aspiration and material reward.

In a 2015 interview with the *Women's Weekly*, Morrison said that he was not particularly denominational but wanted to go to a local community church. He was brought up Presbyterian, then became Uniting, and he and Jenny are now members of the Horizon Pentecostal church. Taking him at his word that he is non-denominational, which I take to mean non-doctrinal, perhaps he just wants to belong to a vibrant religious community.

The mainstream Protestant congregations—Uniting, Anglican, residual Presbyterian, Congregational and Baptist—are dying, along with their elderly members. If Morrison and Jenny wanted to reproduce the social role the local church played in their youth, they were not really an option. By contrast, the Horizon Church ministers to hundreds of families with well-attended Sunday services, and clubs and activities for all age ranges: midweek groups for young mums, Friday-night youth clubs, social meals, study groups, camps and conferences. It is bigger and flashier than the local church that was the centre of my family's suburban social world when I was growing up, and the music is different, but much looks familiar.

Secularists often see only the beliefs in religious observance, and miss the fellowship and social support churches can provide. Could it be that the heart of Morrison's Christian faith is not dogma but the desire to be part of a community and the chance for an enthusiastic singalong? Perhaps too he values its detachment from politics.

Morrison talks a lot about the 'Canberra bubble'. We all need places to go to re-centre ourselves, politicians more than most.

•

We have become so used to incoming governments promising to change things that we have forgotten it hasn't always been like this. Menzies never had much of a policy agenda. What he promised was that the Liberals would provide good government and would react to the crises that beset the nation with pragmatic common sense, guided by their general philosophical preference for leaving solutions in the hands of individuals and private enterprise. The contrast was with the adventurous radicalism of the Labor Party and its penchant for top-down government solutions. Instead of a detailed policy programme, Menzies offered himself, much as Morrison has done. The main aims were to keep Labor off the treasury benches and to provide competent, middle-of-the-road government.

Morrison failed dismally at his first crisis, when bushfires swept across south-eastern Australia in the summer of 2019–20, but he rose masterfully to the second, when the scale of the threat the COVID-19 pandemic posed both to the nation's health and economy became evident. He closed the borders, created a national cabinet to co-ordinate responses, and abandoned the Liberals' fiscal caution to pour billions of dollars into the economy. With Joe Biden in the White House committed to rapid action on climate change, with capital deserting fossil fuels and with business organisations urging government action, he is shifting the government away from its ideological denialism to a pragmatic acceptance of the inevitable. At his press conference in February 2021 to launch the parliamentary year, Morrison announced the goal of reaching zero net emissions by 2050 and preferably sooner. He did not commit to a target, but the intention was clear and we should welcome it. The climate activist Anna Rose (in her response to my *Quarterly Essay* 'The Coal Curse') has said that the planet doesn't have time to wait for a Labor government, so our best hope is a Coalition-led path to change, and that like John Howard's gun reforms, climate policies are more likely to stick if they are introduced by the Coalition.

The *Guardian* journalist Katharine Murphy has described Morrison as a shapeshifter, to capture the elusiveness of his policy agenda and core beliefs. But perhaps he doesn't hold tight core beliefs. Perhaps he is more concerned with competence than conviction. Government, he tells Murphy, is 'a practical exercise'. Answering a question at the National Press Club about his lack of bold reform proposals, he said: 'I am not one that likes to pursue things for the sake of vanity. I like to get things done and not waste time on things that don't get done because that doesn't help anyone.' So he stopped the boats because that was the job he was given to do; he protected us from the virus and its economic impact because protecting the national interest is the prime minister's job; he will steer his government towards committing to zero net emissions by 2050 because our allies will demand it.

The nickname Scotty from Marketing is meant to dismiss him as an opportunistic airhead, but it may inadvertently point to the secret of his success in his responsiveness to mainstream public opinion. Abbott was a conviction politician who tried to govern well to the right of the electorate and failed. Turnbull was much closer to the electorate, but because he was alienated from the party's right, as well as from the Nationals, he too failed. Morrison's miracle election victory in 2019, together with his competent handling of the coronavirus crisis, has given him authority over the right-wingers and the chance to steer the Coalition back to the centre of the electorate, away from adherence to the views of the Liberals' unrepresentative base and the stubborn Nationals.

In an interview before the 2019 election Leigh Sales asked Morrison who would have the upper hand in any post-election conflict between Liberal Party moderates and conservatives. He answered, 'I will,' and so far it seems he has. Apart from Craig Kelly, whose days were numbered, right-wing warriors like Dutton have been surprisingly quiet, and the Nationals don't really have anywhere to go.

Morrison's answer, though, points to the most troubling feature of his prime ministership: his and his government's lack of transparency. With chin thrust forward and mouth turned down, Morrison has mastered the art of not answering journalists' questions, often with barely concealed hostility. Then there are the scandals: the unsolved mystery of the doctored documents about Sydney mayor Clover Moore which appeared on Angus Taylor's website; the sports rorts, where government grants seemed not to be based on the merit of the submissions but on the Coalition's judgement of its electoral advantage; the Robodebt scheme which harried recipients of government benefits to repay unlawful debts, for which no one has taken responsibility; dubious overpriced buybacks of water in the Murray–Darling Basin from a Liberal Party donor; federally funded car parks in marginal Coalition seats, announced the day before the election was called; and on it goes. The proposed Commonwealth Integrity Commission is not independent of government and has no capacity to respond to exposures by journalists or whistleblowers; and funding to the National Audit Office has been cut in what looks very much like payback for embarrassing revelations.

Morrison's secrecy and general insouciance when scandals erupt give another meaning to his Quiet Australians. They are the people who don't ask awkward questions or make a fuss, who get on with their lives and trust him and his ministers to get on with their jobs.

They're certainly not active citizens whose engagement with public affairs keeps governments accountable and democracy alive. No. They're just noisy minorities.

PART III

Ordinary People's Politics

1 Writing Ordinary People's Politics

Monthly, September 2006.

'I can't stress enough how important it is for you to just be an ordinary person. You know, there aren't enough ordinary persons around. There are real high-flyers and jetsetters and all those sorts of things. There's a place for them. But I just think there are too many of them. There aren't enough just ordinary, okay guys.'

This high praise for ordinariness comes from a middle-aged, self-made businessman—Tjaart Reinkman, let's call him—born in Victoria around 1950 to immigrant Dutch parents. His commitment to ordinariness is many-layered. It began at school, where he wanted to fit in and hated his Dutch heritage: 'I wanted to be just like everybody else. You know, like Barry Lugg and David Higgins and Graeme Boyle—just ordinary names, being ordinary people. I didn't want to be different in any way.'

As Tjaart made his way into the wider world and joined the Young Farmers network, ordinariness took on the pleasures of sociability, and the belief that one should judge people by who they are and what they could do. He still doesn't really trust people who are 'bluebloods'. In his business, Tjaart's belief in the importance of ordinariness is expressed in the care that he takes to remember his employees' first names and their personal circumstances, and his shunning of conspicuous displays of wealth. It informs his concern at the way society has become more unequal over the past decade, and his compassion for people made redundant by the pace of social change—'the casualties of war', he calls them—whom he meets as a volunteer at a regular church-run breakfast.

The people Tjaart serves there are also likely to describe themselves as ordinary. Mark Peel said of the poor people he talked with for his wonderful book *Voices from the Lowest Rung* (2003) that 'If those to whom I spoke were best characterised as disadvantaged, they mostly called themselves "ordinary".'

·

For the past four years I have been writing a book with Anthony Moran called *Ordinary People's Politics*, and Tjaart Reinkman is one of the people whose life and political outlook it describes. It comes out of a large, two-part interview project. The first phase was in the late 1980s, when a group of researchers, including Foo Davies and Graham Little, interviewed people at length for a project called 'Images of Australia'. Then, earlier this decade, colleagues and I repeated that process, interviewing some of the original participants and some new ones.

Writing about ordinariness in today's political climate is a fraught enterprise. Since John Howard's election and the rise and fall of Pauline Hanson, being ordinary has become a contested political commodity. Howard's success is regularly attributed to his under-standing of ordinary people, as in Paul Kelly's claim in the *Australian* after the 2004 election that Howard 'doesn't have to imagine what ordinary Australians think—he has just to decide what he thinks because they are virtually the same'. Similarly, the failings of Howard's opponents are regularly explained by their being out of touch with ordinary Australians.

Howard haters are accused not of hating Howard's policies, but rather of hating all those Australians who voted for him. When David Williamson reflected in the *Bulletin* on the narrow materialism of his companions on a cruise ship, the *Australian* took up the cudgels against his sneering attack. Williamson's piece was less sociological observation than an expression of the Australian intelligentsia's continuing ambivalence about suburbia, giving the paper the chance, yet again, to attack the left art-establishment as arrogant and self-interested.

When I wrote in my *Quarterly Essay* 'Relaxed and Comfortable: The Liberal Party's Australia' (2005) about four ordinary people who voted for Howard, that ordinary chappie Christopher Pearson was seriously discomfited. He found them 'too close for comfort to clichés from the world of Fountain Gate, the land of *Kath & Kim*' and chastised me for not tackling Howard's more middle-class supporters. But these were real people I was writing about, their words I was reporting, their lives I was describing—and why to them voting Liberal seemed a reasonable thing to do. Who is uneasy with ordinary Australians here?

The enterprise of writing about ordinariness is just as fraught from the left. In appeals to ordinary people, a left-leaning ear hears the siren call of populism. After all, in her campaign of complaint about self-interested politicians, Pauline Hanson presented herself as just an ordinary person, and One Nation was a classic populist protest party, rejecting the compromises of representative politics for the chimera of the unified popular will. Jennifer Rutherford called her film on One Nation in Queensland *Ordinary Australians*, because that is what the people she was filming called themselves. So when I have told people that I am working on a book called *Ordinary People's Politics*, some have assumed that it is a book about Hanson's supporters, or at least Howard's.

But ordinary people lean both left and right. They are Howard haters, Howard supporters, Howard sceptics. Some follow politics closely; others are not really interested, though they take seriously their responsibility to vote. In a democracy, the views of ordinary people will always be of interest. They comprise the bulk of both the public and the electorate, and in both guises their opinions and judgements can affect the course of governments.

•

Since World War II, the detailed social knowledge and hunches which once guided politicians' and journalists' judgements about what the public thinks and feels have been replaced by increasingly sophisticated techniques of opinion polling. The professional pollster and market researcher have replaced the backbencher with his finger on the pulse as conduits of popular experience and feeling to the political elite. Opinion polls are now regular fare for political reporting in the media, for political parties fine-tuning their policies and self-presentation, and for governments developing new policies. Social research not only maps people's opinions; it also regularly checks their demographic and socioeconomic characteristics, providing policy makers with statistical maps of the country.

With these new tools, policy making has become ever more expert and technocratic. Despite the democratic impulse behind polling's attention to what people think, the techniques drain agency from people. Citizens as active members of the body politic become customers of government service-delivery or recipients of policy innovations. In the private talk of politicians and their factotums, they are often referred to simply as 'the mob'.

In our research we came at ordinary people's thinking about politics in a different way. What do Australians have to say when you engage them in conversation about politics, giving them plenty of time and a willing ear? How do they explain their views? What sorts of arguments and evidence do they use to support them? How do their political ideas sit with their social understandings and experiences?

Rather than scooping up opinions in huge vats to run through statistical strainers, my colleagues and I talked at length with a few individuals about their lives, and the place politics has and does not have in them. Quantitative methods, even as they stream and sort, also homogenise. Voices are turned into numbers, and the reasoning, the hesitations, the moral inflection, the emotional colour all disappear into rows of figures.

The trick and the fascination of this sort of writing is to capture both the individuality of people's ideas and experience, and also their representativeness or typicality. For it is the latter that makes the individual life a way into wider social knowledge. As much as anything, this is a literary challenge, and its achievement stands and falls with the writing and with the judgements made about which aspect of a life has been most significant: downward mobility, the expectations of gender, the experience of war, a lifelong occupational identity. And it is literary in the way that it aspires to a form of representation in which the depiction of an individual life draws the reader into an emotional identification with that life, and thus into a more general understanding of the place and times in which it was lived.

•

As Andrew Denton would say when he turned his attention from celebrities to ordinary people for 'Show and Tell' on *Enough Rope*, 'Everyone has a story to tell.' Life-history writing is burgeoning: biography, autobiography, memoir, interview, personal testimony of difficulties overcome. In the more naive of these, such as many of the personal-testimony narratives, the balance between biography and history shifts decidedly to the former, and the impersonal social forces which limit and shape experience slip from view. Even so, putting the individual at the centre of the story captures something of the reality of life in the early twenty-first century, when the erosion of traditional social and economic institutions is changing the conditions in which people make their lives.

The German sociologist Ulrich Beck has described the imperative to 'individualisation' in contemporary life, as social and economic changes compel people to experience their lives as individual, self-chosen projects, rather than as lived-out fates. This is not about the rise of individualism as a value, but about individualisation as the fate of many people in contemporary Western societies. As jobs for life disappear, as family forms multiply, as people learn to live among others with whom they barely even share a language, society no longer gives them a stable social identity with a life plan and taken-for-granted places of belonging. Because people move between countries, cities, jobs and families, fewer of them than in the past feel that the story of the nation or the class or the region is *their* story.

In place of what is shared and common, people want to hear and read about the individual and the particular. Time and again in our interviews, people responded to questions about collectivities and groupings with answers about individuals. A young Indigenous woman, Renee Simmons, who has struggled all her life between the prejudices and stereotypes of black Australia and white Australia, summed this up for many when she said, 'I don't look at groupings... culturally, socially, everything is just so diverse now. It's getting harder and harder to group. People are moving beyond structures.'

•

In Australia, the term 'ordinary' trails with it another set of associations which are not about politics at all, but rather about class and status. 'Very ordinary' or 'rather ordinary' can be class terms of disdain for people who lack manners, education and possibly intelligence. They invoke a status system based on degrees of refinement. Australia's egalitarianism of manners has never been universally practised. As John Hirst has argued, it was strongest among men working together and weakest among women, many of whom put a good deal of effort into maintaining the boundaries of class difference. So when people claim to be ordinary, they are saying something about what matters in their judgement of people and themselves, and cocking a snook at those who value refinement and social airs and graces.

Caroline Walker, a woman we interviewed who described herself as 'a very ordinary, average mother' and 'a pretty ordinary person', pointed out that 'there are lots of people with pots and pots of money who live very ordinary, simple lives.' The people she didn't like were people who regarded themselves as upper-class and lived in 'the social whirl'. 'I know some doctors who are very ordinary sorts of people, but others who are always partying and trying to outdo the next person, and flaunting their possessions. Still, in the same income bracket there are quite down-to-earth, ordinary sort of people.'

Many of the people we talked to were keen to refuse unworthy members of the upper class the deference and admiration they imagined them to be demanding. Interviews conducted in the 1980s included one with an elderly woman from one of Australia's wealthy establishment families, and even she was at pains to make it clear she was not a snob and that she despised the Toorak social set and 'that dreadful hairdresser', Lillian Frank.

Australians' preference for ordinariness expresses unease about putting people into social categories. A hardworking twenty-two-year-old who grew up in the country and was managing a takeaway restaurant put it like this: 'It's bad that we can class people as poor and middle and rich, because it's a way of saying that they're better people. But they're not better people at all. The richest man, Kerry Packer, is not necessarily a better person than the person who washes dishes at my restaurant who's in the poorer class, is he? All he's got is a lot more money.' And, as we saw in the extravagant public praise of Packer when he died, not even massive wealth need stand in the way of people accepting you as ordinary.

•

In Australia, the term 'middle class' often operates as a refusal of social categorisation based on economic role. In his paean to the middle class, Menzies claimed that the real life of the nation was 'in the homes of people who are nameless and unadvertised'. The decisive move in Menzies' system of social classification was to locate people's real life and the basis of their social identity not in the workplace, where Labor put it, but in the private world of home and family. As occupational identity has loosened, the plausibility of this has increased for many Australians.

Like Menzies, most of the respondents in our research believed that the real life of the nation was in the middle, where they put themselves. The dominance of the middle in Australian politics—the middle class, or middle Australia—has long been recognised, but just what it means is not entirely clear. It has often been interpreted as if it is the opposite of 'working class'—that this is the choice people are making. And in much research it is the choice that people are given. But the synonyms many of our interviewees used to describe their social position—average, normal, everyday, ordinary—suggest that for many people, the term 'middle class' has never been part of a two-class model at all. A married tradesmen in his mid-thirties working in the family business said that he was 'just average...I am very simple. I am not out there to big-note. I am just a very, very simple, average, middle-class—whatever you want to call it—person.'

Sometimes middle is just that: the midpoint in social schemas, loaded with judgements about respectability and moral worth. A forty-four-year-old housewife interviewed in 1967 for Don Aitkin's study of the social bases of the Australian party system, *Stability and Change in Australian Politics*, said, 'Friendly people are middle-class. Hotel types are lower-class. Upper-class are snobs.' Twenty years later, Lois Angus gave us a more elaborate version of essentially the same social map. She described her own position as 'middle of the road'. She felt out of place with people who were 'for want of a better word, snobby', but looked down on 'the yobbos getting drunk in the pubs'.

Lois constructed her schema on the basis of what she saw and what was of interest to her and the people with whom she felt comfortable. So do most people. Because people generally mix with people they regard as being like themselves, they perceive themselves as average and unexceptional. At the centre of their worlds looking out, people on the whole see others like themselves. The self-description 'middle-class' is linked to the idea of moderation and social harmony, as people project outwards from the general equality and consensus they find among their own circle of family and friends, to the society at large. 'Middle' thus becomes associated with positions that are sensible and level-headed, and a politics of compromise rather than one of conflict between entrenched positions.

John Howard's repeated appeal to the metaphor of the pendulum and the need for balance mobilises this meaning of 'middle' in Australian politics. This is not so much a matter of the substance of the argument, but of its form: the aim is to identify oneself with the moderate middle. Australia, we might speculate, has an Aristotelian political culture, where the best path is always the one between extremes.

•

In writing about ordinary people and ordinary life, it helps to be ordinary oneself. This, rather than the supposed political views of ordinary people, is the biggest barrier between many intellectuals, of both left and right, and ordinary people. Intellectuals' autobiographies are full of stories about how ill at ease they are with the people among whom they were born, the trials of solitude and how they never feel quite at home in the world. Sometimes, the tale is one where the intellectual or artist does eventually find people with whom to feel at home, socially or geographically far away from the place of their birth. Sometimes, the restlessness and alienation is endemic. Much twentieth-century intellectual history was driven by a critical and avant-gardist energy which pushed many intellectuals to explore the margins of social worlds and the dark side of human existence, and to expose the costs and repressions of particular societies and moral systems.

I have no objection to people doing any of this. The dark and marginal are part of human experience, just as the normal and ordinary are part of systems of social classification which construct opposites such as exotic, abnormal and deviant that can make life tough for people who don't fit in. It is essential to keep alive the understanding that human beings could live differently from the way we do now, and think about how that might be. As Marx showed us, the ordinary and everyday are produced and constrained by larger social and historical forces, and people live their lives in conditions not of their own choosing. We need to understand those conditions if we want to change things.

However, in writing about ordinary Australians, these intellectual approaches are of only so much use. Some of the people involved in our research were refugees from terrible wars; but others had lived uneventful lives, and the challenge in writing about them is to understand and map the contours of the everyday. I do not believe that the true or only meaning of the ordinary and the everyday is to be found in the people and experiences it excludes. It is also to be found in what it includes.

Writing about ordinary people, I am not so interested in the dark nights of their souls as in their view of the world on a sunny day, when they sit down to lunch with family and friends; or the view from the kitchen table midafternoon, when they are feeling a bit down. I am interested in the people who bring up the children, organise the barbecues, visit the old folks and generally keep the show on the road; in how they do it, their wisdom, their understanding of life's necessary compromises, and the perplexity of time and memory. To me, this seems as important as exploring the underworld, especially if you want to understand where politics sits in people's lives.

•

Because we talked with people for so long about their politics, we were able to get a sense of its place among their priorities. One of our older respondents, a man who has been politically active throughout his life, regarded politicians as ordinary people grappling with the complexities of globalisation. A couple of others also respected politicians and recognised the difficulty of the decisions they have to make: used to authority themselves, they identified with its demands. Others saw politicians as doing a necessary job, and apart from voting at elections were happy to leave them to it. Others, again, were turned off politics by its lies and deceit.

Yet, for all of them, family and friends were far more important. As Tjaart Reinkman said, 'Life isn't about having the most of anything. It's about relationships. It's about family. It's about love.' On this sort of scale, politics unsurprisingly starts rather low down.

2 Pham Dinh
Number One Son

From Ordinary People's Politics: Australians Talk about Life, Politics and the Future of Their Country, *with Anthony Moran, Pluto Press, Melbourne, 2006.*

Pham Dinh was born into leadership, the eldest son destined to be the head of his family's clan in a patrilineal society where property and political authority is passed through the eldest son: 'So when I was born there was a lot of expectations already. It's not like pressure, you enjoy it, psychologically it's good. You think, "I'm meant to be somebody."' Arriving in Australia as a twenty-one-year-old refugee in the early 1980s, Pham worked hard to become somebody in his new land, to match his inner sense of who he already was with what he could do and be here.

This is a familiar refugee story. It is strikingly different from the stories of migrants where the new land offers opportunities unavailable in the old, and where the travails and hard work of the first generation are justified by opportunities opened up for children. For many refugees the task is quite different: it is to regain what has been lost—or violently taken away—rather than to gain something new.

Pham's grandfather was a large landowner in North Vietnam. He was Catholic, a member of the westernised Vietnamese upper class. He was executed during the land reforms, and the love and respect the villagers felt for him had entered into family lore. Three times they were ordered to shoot, and three times all the bullets missed:

> People still talking about him with high respect. He became a myth, so you know when you grow up, you've got that on your mind. He's a great man. My father talking about his own ambitions, doing great things for the country, and I expect you to do things like that. It really helps you. I'm supposed to be doing something here like that. That's good.

After France's defeat at Dien Bien Phu in 1954 around a million North Vietnamese fled south, including many Catholics and members of the upper class who were able to re-establish themselves there in government positions. Pham's family was among them, and his father became a successful and well-respected district administrator. The family continued its close association with French Catholic culture and Pham was sent to an elite French Catholic school, where he excelled. The school provided him with a secure and ordered world where the dangers of the surrounding war could be ignored by concentrating on the immediate tasks at hand and cultivating his spiritual life. It also opened up for him the possibility of pursuing his education in France, a path taken by many members of the Vietnamese elite before him. He passed the exams for the French Baccalaureate and won a scholarship to study in Paris. Pham was in the last group of students to graduate from this school. Saigon fell before he could leave and, given his family's political history, he couldn't even get a university place in Vietnam. He worked in various jobs, and eventually escaped on a boat with eighty others.

Pham had little to say about the details of the escape and the journey. What he wanted to talk about was the interview with the Australian immigration official in the Indonesian refugee camp and how he made sure he was chosen. This is the episode which begins his Australian identity:

> We send delegations to the camp to interview people. I thought I would practise before the interview. I did my homework; I asked other people—'What questions she ask?' She a big woman. Everyone in the camp call her Madam Big because she's very big. We don't know her name. I had read an article, 'Australia and its People'. It's talking about people and life, even slang, so I had a rough idea. So at the interview I try to impress her, I say, 'Look, madam, I try to talk to you in English, my English not good, please speak slowly. Only use interpreter if I need him.' She impressed. She talk to me in English, easy English, I manage to understand. I call it the interview of my life, because it changed my life.

Madam Big asked Pham what he knew about Australia, and with the article as a source he had plenty to say:

> She asked people that before, so I was ready. 'Madam', I said, 'Australia is the land of opportunity.' She liked that. 'Oh, everybody equal, everybody have a chance if they work hard.' She liked that. And I used a big word I didn't even know how to pronounce properly—'The only country in the world know about egalitarianism.' 'What do you mean by that?' 'Oh, everybody equal, madam.' I knew she'd like it because she'd think I'm interested. 'So, do you know anything else?' So I started talking about 'the real Aussie ocker'. I tried to impress her with what I learn from the article—very good article. 'What do you mean?' 'Oh a typical Australian, madam, he's got a big belly, and zinc cream here and

there'—I point to my cheek—'And they love football—go to football with esky full of beer. Esky full of beer.' I remember that—I tried to impress her, because I know the jargon. She laughed. 'Oh, and they love gambling, madam. They can gamble on a fly on a wall.' And she laughed. Oh, I remember that. Then she asked me about my three-year plan. 'Oh, you let me go to Australia, I will do anything, madam, I will be a good boy. I go to night class and at day time I do anything, dirty job.' And she ask me about my ten-year plan. 'By that time definitely I would be able to speak English much better, get a good job.' And ten years later I did exactly that.

Quick-witted and well-prepared, Pham's use of phrases from the Australian Legend convinced the big woman with the power of fate to give him a refugee visa for Australia. She had recognised him for what he was and could be, but when he arrived in Australia no one else did. Living with other single men, he felt unwanted:

People talking about you all the time, the Vietnamese, the trouble-makers. It's not what I expected. I thought, 'Oh people will run up to you. Somebody will adopt you maybe because you're so smart, definitely there will be someone who will want you to stay with them, their family.' But the only people who visited me were the Mormon elders, very kind, but I'm a Catholic. Sometimes you feel, I didn't want them to come all the time. I was confused about Australian people, why not a non-Mormon come and take you to their home?

None did, but because he had been well known in Vietnam, 'a lot of people here already knew of my arrival' and contacted him, and they brought him to their homes. He learned English, began working in menial jobs like fruit picking and mail sorting, and looked around for opportunities to fulfil his ten-year plan. Pham's first step was to become a union advocate at the mailroom, where he worked alongside former army officers, lawyers and doctors. Many of them were too old to go back to school. He didn't like the way the workers were treated:

> Everyone was supposed to work like a machine—'Keep your head down, don't talk,' things like that. And they watch you all the time. I thought this was ridiculous, something wrong with Australia Post, and I got with the unions, I became a bit of a rep, stood up for people a bit, tried to make a few points with the supervisor. I tell people, 'Look, let me do it because Australia Post is not the rest of my life. Maybe the rest of your life, you need a job, you need to be settled, so let me do something.'

When he was interviewed in 2003, twenty-two years after the interview of his life, Pham was working as a community-welfare officer in an area with a large Asian population. He had gained some tertiary qualifications, and was an active and prominent member of the Vietnamese community:

> Because I had training, I got a lot of opportunity to represent the Vietnamese—youth issues, women's issues, elderly issues, you name it, I set up self-help groups, learned to deal with ethnic reporters. I enjoyed that. Even now I walk down the street I bump into people, now very successful people, used to be my street kids. I like that.

Pham was comfortable with the role of ethnic middleman, a broker between two worlds. It's a role his grandfather and father had inhabited before him, in the various Vietnamese colonial administrations; and it drew on his Confucian commitment to serving his community.

But Pham had not confined himself to Vietnamese community

politics. By about 1990, ten years after his arrival and in his early thirties, he was ready to move on—'away from community politics to the real politics. Mainstream politics.' This was a deliberate decision and he gave it a great deal of thought; and it is one he advised others to make:

> When I talk to young people I say, 'Look, the community is a training ground for you. Join a volunteer group, enjoy helping other people and learn. Learn to organise, learn to speak, to advocate for other people. To run ceremonies. Train yourself, and when you think you're ready get away from Vietnamese politics, join a political party, a union.'

He moved into another welfare job where he was working with people from other ethnic groups besides the Vietnamese—Turks, Greeks, Cambodians. He got involved with local government, stood for election as an independent and won. His plan was to do a stint in local government, then join a party:

> I played politics in a very positive way. Of course you can play in a negative way—but you had rules you had to play. You have to know what to ask, know the politics of the group, know the different factions, play the balance of power game. You learn when to shut up, and when to speak. I speak English still with an accent, so I have to rely on my homework a bit more. Seek advice from CEO, understand your role, when you know your role you can ask nicely. I enjoyed that. It's a learning curve; I learned very quickly.

Pham had come to Australian politics from the outside, without prior loyalties or commitments, with little if any knowledge of the political history of the local government area where he sought election. So he had to watch, observe, make moves and learn from how they went. Local government was a learning ground where he could enhance his skills and knowledge, but it also confronted him with the darker side of power and personal ambition, people playing politics in a negative way: 'I learn about real politics in local government. I don't know if you have watched the film *Rats in the Ranks*—very similar.'

Just as Pham had not wanted to stay at Australia Post, he did not want to stay in local government. There is an undercurrent of restlessness in Pham's political story, which is perhaps a consequence of his detachment. With few emotional anchor points to Australian political life, the game could sometimes seem simply a game:

> I always think you need to move on. People encourage me to stay but
> I'm not interested any more. State government maybe, or federal,
> I see it like a natural development, I want to go up. Sometimes I
> have the feeling, I've been there, done that.

So, looking for ways to move on, Pham joined the Liberal Party.

Why did Pham join the Liberal Party? The scope for political participation as an independent is limited: 'if you're really serious, you have to join a party. So I believe in political parties, but not so much in their philosophies.' Pham's view is again from the outside, looking for reasons to choose one of the major parties rather than the other. He lacked many of the bearings people born into the society have to orient their political choices, in particular a family history of party identification, but he was able to find some nevertheless to give him a rationale for choosing the Liberals over Labor:

> It was the Liberal Party which opened the doors for political
> refugees from Vietnam, and I remember that. And it's the Liberal
> government who sent our troops, our men to Vietnam. And again,

you know I come from a socialist country, and the Liberal Party anti-communist. Of course the Liberal Party is not that anti-communist, and Labor is not communist. But that is what it looks like to the Vietnamese community, particularly the older generation. It's displaced politics I call it, they've brought it from Vietnam. So because I so close to them, and they need support, I said okay, this is the party who can help the Vietnamese cause more.

And also I believe in, what you call it, individual commitment, hard work, reward, grows in my heart more Liberal values. Saying that, it's not that I don't like Labor. I like Labor, with their commit-ment to social issues. Of course, not to say that Liberals don't do that. They've got a lot of overlap, the two parties. I have a lot of friends in Labor, maybe I'd have more chance within the Labor Party.

Interviewer: Why do you think that?

Pham: I have friends, and because of the structure, the politics at the branch level, the preselection—I was very impressed with the so-called branch stacking. This doesn't mean that the Liberals don't do that. But very hard to get preselection for a seat I could win.

He had contemplated standing for preselection, but the area in which he lived and worked is Labor territory; as well, he had no realistic chance of Liberal preselection for a winnable outer-eastern seat, where you have to compete with 'high-calibre Liberal people who grew up in the suburb'. But he was not in a hurry, happy to bide his time, slowly building support in the Liberal Party by going to functions, networking, speaking up, showing what he could do and what he had to offer the party—so that when the opportunity arose, when it was his turn, he would be ready: 'But I don't see it as a matter of life and death.'

Even so, Pham did express some impatience with the party's failure to recognise what he had to offer. He saw much he could do to help the Victorian branch in its current rather parlous state, by building bridges for the party with the Asian community, participating in business and cultural exchanges with countries in the region, helping them overcome their image problem with the young as the party of the rich. The experience echoes his first months in Australia, when he naively expected his energy and intelligence to be immediately recognised and welcomed:

> I don't believe in tokenism. I say, 'You give me the job, I can be a great asset to you.' I am not begging for a job, but I am offering myself. I'm a committed Liberal, so I have to be an agent of social change in my own party. I have to speak up, challenge people around me. I think I can do the job. I'm ready. I speak English. I may not speak English with an Aussie accent but I've got my brain. And I could show the Asian community that the Liberal Party really exists. And that it is not just the party for the rich, the snobby eastern-suburbs people. Because when I go out and talk to young people, a lot of them think, 'Oh, the Liberal Party is the party of the rich, they don't care about youth, social-welfare-recipient people. No, they come and they screw you up and they don't care about social justice.'

In open societies, where it is not too hard to get onto the first step, politics can be a status escalator. It also provides an easy means for a person without connections to the mainstream to start to get involved with networks and associations outside their particular ethnic community. If we see Pham's task as the re-establishment in Australia of the sort of position of social and political authority he would have had in Vietnam, a position where he can be both useful and respected, then politics is an obvious choice. Business never interested him, nor the acquiring of material wealth. His satisfactions as he looked back over his time in Australia came from evidence of his acceptance by political elites, his increasing connectedness within the mainstream, his slow movement towards the centre. The more accepted he became in Australia, the more connected he felt to his Vietnamese past, to his family's social position, and to the sense of civic responsibility he was taught at school:

> Politics is the highest level of the participant in society, for good politics you need good people, you have to be ethical, look at politics as a vocation. When I was young in Vietnam I got a civic education. They trained me to be a responsible citizen, and promoted the dream about one day being able to do something good for society. Why not be a politician representing people?

Politics also helped him to think his way into the centre. That is, it was not just about gaining status but consciously building a sense of belonging. Here Pham is describing the early 1980s, just before he arrived in Australia:

> Because '82 we in Australia talk about whether we should accept more single men, because single men create a bit of a problem here at that time. Not criminal but troublemakers, and we do not want more single men, and I was a single young person at that time. It was very tough.
>
> Interviewer: When you say 'we did not want any more,' you're talking from Australia's point of view?
>
> Pham: 'We,' yes, that's very interesting that you pick that up, because sometimes when I talk like that, I think that's how I see myself, I see myself as an Australian from a Vietnamese background. When I say 'we' I really mean it. I'm talking about history, and 'We in Australia at that time, we didn't want them,' things like that, very interesting.

At a couple of other points in the interviews Pham used 'we' like this, identifying with the Australian perspective on migrants and refugees: 'We in Australia didn't want any more unskilled migrants, who would come here and become a burden.' It is indicative of the conscious effort he has put into becoming part of Australia. Multi-culturalism has made that easier, given a framework, and a clear message that it is possible for the migrant to be Australian: 'Being Australian means to work hard, be committed to Australia—this is your country, you've got the opportunity if you work hard.' The emphasis on work is interesting here; work is a matter of will and effort—outward, tangible evidence of the inner commitment being formed—it is how you show you want to belong. Even so, his sense of identity was fluid: 'When I go back to Vietnam, or travel round the world, I have a kind of global feeling. I don't feel I'm either Vietnamese or Australian when I travel.'

Despite Pham's identification with the Liberal Party's values of hard work and effort, his view of the role of government is a long way from the current belief that the state needs to be wound back and people made more self-reliant. He had a generally paternalistic belief in the responsibility of the state to look after people—and if need be to provide them with jobs:

> As human beings we need a job. To have smaller government, to have to save money, for me is a backward step. Because if you've got the money, you provide, everybody happy. Same with privatisation, I think it's a big pity, very important essential services should be provided by the government. Privatisation, for me it's a step backward. I'm a Liberal, but that's what I'm thinking.

The last questions Pham was asked were about Aboriginal Austral-ians, how he saw their position in Australia. Pham had a lot to say—this question was, he said, 'my hobby horse'—and he was very keen to sympathise with them. When he first arrived he tried to understand Australian politics through Vietnamese experience of nationalism and the war for independence:

> Vietnam, one thousand years under the Chinese, one hundred years under the French, they're still Vietnamese, they're still there. I think that's what Aborigines should be. We kick the French, we kick the Americans. They came but they have to get out. We Vietnamese, very proud it's still our country. And I look at these people, they should be boss. I remember one day after I had been in Australia about two or three months, an Aussie guy come up to me and give me two fingers and swore at me and told me to 'Go back to where you belong.' And I said, 'You're not an Aboriginal.' The guy didn't understand, I didn't understand even why I said that. I think in my head I thought, 'Only an Aboriginal can tell me this is my land, go back to where you belong.' Because I believe that this land is theirs and only they have the right to tell people to 'Get off my land. I don't want you here.'

But despite his desire to sympathise Pham had little understanding of the politics of native title or Indigenous demands for autonomy. He believed Australia was 'one country, one people', that Aborigines should not be treated like second-class citizens, and he could see no reason why they couldn't be given land rights. He had a bright idea about how to give symbolic recognition to Aboriginal ownership: 'Maybe I have a solution for the Australian republic. I want some sort of Aboriginal king in the role, like owner of the land. This land is theirs; you all borrow this land, that's my thinking.' Clearly Pham thought his ideas about an Aboriginal king were reasonable enough. He was thinking of writing an article about it. But they show the limits of his grasp of the politics of his new country, the shallowness of his understanding of the structures of economic and political power, and of Australia's history. They do demonstrate, though, his eagerness to engage.

Pham was forty-two when we interviewed him in 2003. Since he arrived in the early 1980s he had built a workable Australian identity for himself, but there was still a gap between his skills and talents and their realisation, which fuelled his restlessness, his urge always 'to move on'. Australia's growing integration with Asia opens up opportunities for people like him. This restlessness could at some point mean a move away from Australia. This was not something he was consciously planning, but it was a possibility he was willing to entertain, if the opportunity were to arise:

> It would be good to do something for the country you came from, because your roots are there, friends, relatives, ethnic origins. I don't know…maybe if I had children I would stay—but no such luck yet—which would turn out lucky then [laughs].

3 Everyday Multiculturalism

In 2007 I gave a number of presentations on ordinary people's understanding of multiculturalism, including to a conference at La Trobe University on the work of the historian John Hirst. The fullest account of this research and its interpretation is in 'Cosmopolitan Nationalism: Ordinary People Making Sense of Diversity', with Anthony Moran, Nations and Nationalism, *volume 17, number 1, January 2011. I also published a less-academic version, 'Australian Multiculturalism: Triumph of Common Sense',* Australian Literary Review, *May 2011. What follows is based on all of these.*

Al Grassby was the first person to describe Australia as multicultural, in 1973, when he was immigration minister in the first Whitlam Labor government. In a speech titled 'A Multicultural Society for the Future', Grassby said that the post-war migration programme had made Australia one of the most cosmopolitan societies on earth, but that Australians had barely begun to think about what this implied. Grassby lost his seat in the 1974 double-dissolution election but the term survived and was embraced by Liberal Prime Minister Malcolm Fraser. Multicultural policy as it developed during Fraser's time was largely about migrant-settlement policies and government service delivery, but a new national story was forming.

During the Hawke and Keating Labor governments, from 1983 to 1996, the term 'multicultural' came to be used to describe not just policy but the nation itself; and it acquired a companion word, 'multiracial', in response to the large, visible Vietnamese migration.

Australia was a multicultural, multiracial nation, with its national distinctiveness lying in its successful embrace of diversity. But just what did being a multicultural society imply? Was it one with a diversity of cultures or a diversity of culturally different people? And what did it mean for national unity?

During the 1980s a backlash developed against the term's implied divisiveness and its seeming to diminish Australia's British heritage to one fragment, albeit a relatively large one, in Australia's rich cultural diversity. When John Howard became prime minister in 1996, he refused to use it at all. It became the 'm' word as he strove to differentiate himself from Keating's supposed neglect of the mainstream in favour of minorities. But it was more than this. Howard had been expressing opposition to multiculturalism since his first period as leader of the Liberal Party, from 1985 to 1989, arguing then, as he was to argue when he became prime minister, that Australians needed to focus on what they shared rather than on what separated them. *Future Directions*, the Liberal Party manifesto published in 1988, criticised 'so-called multicultural programmes' which 'ensnare individuals in ethnic communities' and stop them participating in mainstream Australian life.

Howard was also publicly uneasy about the pace of Asian migration. In March 1984 the historian Geoffrey Blainey had warned in a speech to the Warrnambool Rotary Club that current levels of Asian immigration were too fast for public opinion and risked social disorder. This set off a furious debate in which Blainey received strong vocal support from the then president of the RSL, Bruce Ruxton, but was condemned by others for excusing racism, including by his colleagues at the University of Melbourne. In 1986, heeding Blainey's warning, Howard said that the government had the right to impose some form of restriction on the immigration intake in the interests of social cohesion, and he refused to back down in the face of the predictable furore.

When he became Liberal leader again in 1995, he softened his stance; and as prime minister, after the initial banning, the word 'multiculturalism' soon returned to his speeches and to government documents, though with the emphasis on inclusiveness rather than diversity. It was banished again in 2007 when the Department of Immigration and Multicultural Affairs (DIMA) became the Department of Immigration and Citizenship. This name change realised what has been evident since September 11, 2001, that policies encouraging ethnic and cultural diversity risked sending the wrong messages to new migrants about what is expected of them as Australian citizens.

What did ordinary Australians make of these debates? How did they think about multiculturalism, and what it meant to be Australian? The people we talked to for our study of Ordinary People's Politics were well aware of these issues. Forty-two of them were interviewed in the second half of the 1980s, when the debate about Asian immigration was in full swing, with the very visible increase in migration from Asia and the development of distinctively Vietnamese suburbs in Melbourne and Sydney. They were re-interviewed between 2002 and 2004, together with thirty-three new respondents, when anxiety about Muslim communities was high in the wake of the terrorist attacks on the Twin Towers.

All the respondents were interviewed multiple times in sessions of up to two hours and the interviews were semi-structured, with plenty of opportunity for people to give their own take on issues. The first session collected a life history and later ones canvassed views on the economy, politicians and government, settler–Indigenous relations, immigration and ethnic diversity, social change, the distinctive qualities of Australia and its most pressing problems.

Views on immigration and multiculturalism were expressed in answer both to particular questions about these issues and to general questions, such as 'How has Australia changed in the past twenty years?' or 'What are three things you would tell someone about Australia?' They also emerged in people's life stories, especially those of first- and second-generation respondents of non-Anglo background. We were interested in what people said of their own accord about multiculturalism and migration. Did they, for example, see it as one of Australia's pressing problems or name it as a distinctive feature of contemporary society? Most of all, we were interested in the way people talked about it, the sorts of arguments and evidence they used to support their views, the doubts they expressed and how they quieted them, and the timeframes in which they placed them. Some of the discussions of multiculturalism were quite brief and did not supply much data. Others were very long and considered.

All of our seventy-five respondents were living in Victoria when they were interviewed, mainly in Melbourne and two regional centres, with some in rural areas. This perhaps explains the mildness of their thinking about Australia's changing ethnic and racial mix. Victoria has a more liberal and progressive political culture than much of the rest of Australia, and Melbourne has not experienced the same conflict between ethnic groups as Sydney has. Only one interviewee, a young male sportsman, gave a clearly racist response. 'I'm a bit like Bruce Ruxton on the Vietnamese,' he said. 'We should be getting rid of them. I used to live in Springvale. It's spot-your-Aussie out there. Ruxton says what others think.' At the other end of the spectrum was a young community arts worker who was 'very against Bruce Ruxton' and didn't mind if she became part of a white minority. The rest gave more complex responses with varying degrees of balance between anxiety about and support for Australia's ethnic diversity.

Almost all used 'multicultural' and 'multiculturalism' as straight-forward terms of description for contemporary Australia: 'We are a multicultural race'; 'We are a multicultural society'; 'Multiculturalism is the new Australia'; 'Multicultural/multiracial, that's what we are. How could you not think that?'; 'Australia is multicultural, the different lifestyles, there's not only just one style like in other countries. That's what Australia's about, dealing with different cultures.' Race, nationality, background, culture and lifestyle were all used, often interchangeably.

Only two people explicitly expressed unease with the term 'multi-culturalism' itself, men interviewed in the late 1980s who were strong Liberal Party identifiers and hence sensitive to its contemporary politicisation by John Howard. For the rest it was non-problematic and carried little if any of the associations it had in elite public debates. While the term was clearly introduced and popularised through official discourse, policies and actions, it had acquired a life of its own as a widely shared commonsense description of the everyday social world of contemporary Australians. As an elderly Italian man said, 'Australia is a lot of migrants, a lot of cultures, what else you suggest?'

That is the word. What about the images people used to fill out and illustrate this description? Reflecting the diverse sources of Australia's immigrants, the most common was of a mix or variety of people. 'When I think of Australia I think of a lot of different cultures, different ethnic backgrounds, a lot of different faces. I don't know whether you'd find so many different cultures anywhere else.' One working-class man described Australia as having 'a good sprinkling of everything'; a young Indigenous artist described Melbourne and Paris as the most cosmopolitan cities in the world, in which 'people of all nationalities lived side by side'.

This mix was frequently illustrated with physical images: suburbs in which there was 'a mix of nationalities and food'; a street with Italian, Greek, Vietnamese and Turkish restaurants all in a row, or families of different ethnic types in the houses; a school classroom with different faces; the passing parade of tram conductors. This variety was even located in that quintessential space of old male working-class Australia: 'You go to a pub now, you walk into a pub and you see Turks, Irish, Poms, Chinese, all standing up in the bar drinking, talking to each other.' A forty-six-year old working-class man of Italian background commented in 2002 on the new ethnicities coming into the mix:

> I've noticed some huge changes, like a lot of Filipino people, now we're getting a lot of Pacific Islanders as well, which is really nice, more Vietnamese, a lot of other nationalities too, Indians and South Americans coming in as well. So in [the north-western suburb of] St Albans there are a huge mix of nationalities.

Said a twenty-three-year-old Chinese-Malay woman in 2003: 'The face of Australia is not just your typical Australian. It's everyone now. It's just a mix.'

A sixty-year-old Anglo farmer noted the succession of ethnic types in the agricultural sector, where different migrant groups had come with different bags of tricks: the nineteenth-century Scottish, with their sheep and cattle skills; the Chinese and Italians, with their talent for market gardening; the dairying skills of the Dutch and Kiwis; and the fishing skills of the Greeks and Croatians.

Twenty-one respondents illustrated the multicultural character of contemporary Australian society with catalogues of ethnic types when describing their friends and family. A fifty-four-year-old Italian woman who came to Australia in her early twenties had 'French friends, friends from Morocco, Spain, Chile, Argentina, Czechoslovakia, Yugoslavia, Chinese, Japanese. They're from everywhere.'

For some, cultural diversity was found within the family itself. A seventy-two-year-old working-class Anglo man in a regional town reflected in 2003, 'I sat down at Christmas dinner three or four years ago and there were twenty-two of us and there was about eleven different nationalities. So anybody comes to me and starts to whinge about multiculturalism I tell them, hang on, this is my family structure and we're all Australians.' A thirty-eight-year-old Anglo woman contrasted her parents' twenty-first birthday celebrations, which were 'all Anglo with a few Germans', with her own, which was attended by 'people from all over the world'.

Overwhelmingly multiculturalism was described at the level of the social. People did not immediately or particularly associate it with politics or government policies, but with the society they saw and experienced in their daily lives, on the street, at work, among friends and family. Contrary to the arguments which preoccupy much public political debate about multiculturalism, it was not predominately thought about as a mix of cultures or even groups but as a mix of people, individuals who ideally socialise together and talk to each other.

Nor were cultures imagined as abstract sets of practices or values which had an existence independent of the individuals. Cultural differences were carried by individuals, families at most, and only two respondents—a young Chinese woman and a twenty-year-old Muslim woman born in Australia whose parents had migrated from Lebanon in the early 1970s—raised the problem of language and cultural maintenance.

No one mentioned ethnic institutions or organisations, apart from religious ones. Only a few used the image of the melting pot, and none used the image of the family which was in Al Grassby's initial speech. On the whole, people's thinking about multiculturalism was based on first-hand experience and observation. They were describing changes observed over their life time, or comparing their or their children's experience with that of their parents.

•

Australians' attitudes to immigration, multiculturalism and national identity have frequently been collected in questionnaires based on the national identity module of the International Social Survey Programme, which includes standard statements such as 'It is better for society if groups maintain distinct traditions and customs' and 'Ethnic minorities should be given government assistance to preserve their customs and traditions', which Australians overwhelmingly reject. Many Australians don't agree with these and some researchers thus conclude that support for multiculturalism is weak. But when our respondents talked about multiculturalism they were not describing a society made up of different cultural groups but one composed of people and families with different cultural characteristics. What they opposed was group rights not cultural difference, and overwhelmingly they regarded Australia's mixed multicultural population as a good thing.

People mentioned a variety of benefits, including those migrants had brought to the economy with their skills and hard work, such as the migrant workers who built the Snowy Mountains Scheme. Some compared their own acceptance of difference with the intolerance of their parents. A couple of older respondents thought it was good for the health and vitality of the population ('it mixes up the breeding'). But by far the most common benefit mentioned was that an ethnically mixed population enabled one to know about, experience and learn from different cultures. People saw this as a benefit both for Australia as a whole and for themselves.

This was expressed with differing degrees of sophistication. One of the more complex responses was from a thirty-five-year-old Greek-Cypriot man, interviewed in 1989, who talked about the way multiculturalism enables people to see that their own culture is one of many; then 'they cannot pretend that people of another culture are a different species.' Coming from a country with deep ethnic and religious rifts, he had in mind the benefits to the migrants as well as to the Australian-born. A forty-three-year-old Palestinian man interviewed in 2004 welcomed the way here people forget about the disagreements back home.

Most responses were simpler. The accessibility of people from other cultures made Australia a more interesting place to live compared with more monocultural societies. A fifty-four-year-old Italian-born woman reflected:

> In Australia we have the whole world at our fingertips, we can be in contact with all the different parts of the world, with the cultures. In fact, when I went back to Italy that's one of the parts of Australia that I missed terribly. Of course, in Italy everything is Italian, there is the one culture which is fantastic, but that's it, it's limited. If you are interested in being in contact with others, you have to go out of Italy.

Many people mentioned the variety of food and the restaurants. The association of multiculturalism with food is so common in Australia that it can seem to be a trivialisation of the task of learning to live with cultural difference. But sharing food is a very basic human activity. Even if this is in restaurants or at market stalls, it embeds the benefits of immigration in people's everyday life like little else has been able to do. In the words of a forty-six-year-old son of Italian

parents living on a disability pension, different food can be a door
to different worlds:

> I think we're lucky here that we have all the world right in our lap.
> We can experience the feelings of the people by talking to them,
> seeing what they wear, and what they eat, and all that. Can go into
> a restaurant with music and almost feel as if you're over there.

He added, 'I don't go to restaurants much, can't afford it, but I love
talking to people.' Another working-class man, a twenty-eight-
year-old of Anglo background who had had a very rough life, said,
'I might never be able to get on a plane and go overseas, but I can
learn about places here—Turkey, India, China, Japan.'

Our respondents showed the same enthusiasm for and interest in
cultural diversity that media commentators often attribute to cosmopolitan elites, commenting on both the moral and the intellectual
benefits to be derived from exposure to different ways of living. To
be an Australian cosmopolitan one did not have to leave the nation
to discover the world, because the world had come to Australia.
Australia's ethnically diverse population had 'broadened outlooks',
'made us more tolerant', 'helped us see things differently'. Said one
young woman, 'You learn about all different races, cultures. I think,
wow, there's so many people live differently to us. It's great to be able
to communicate with them.' A barely literate working-class woman
who was annoyed that Vietnamese migrants got given so much by
the government nevertheless believed that multiculturalism is good
'because it's giving people a chance to see how other people live'. For
a fifty-two-year-old Australian-born female law clerk, Australia's
contemporary cultural plenitude was yet another attribute of the
lucky country.

You get difference in thought, difference in attitude, and I guess
they're like these jolting sorts of things that make you aware of
new ways…It's like a visible indication that there are alternatives,
alternative ways of thought, alternative ways of living…I've always
been very proud to be Australian. We really are the lucky people.
It's part of being a new country, with a mixed people, the particular
openness of the country—I think this must have an enormous
influence.

·

Despite all the enthusiasm and acceptance, about half of the people
we talked to also admitted to some anxieties about Australia's cultural
diversity. In the late 1980s some respondents expressed worries about
the Vietnamese, mostly associated with drugs and crime, and in the
early 2000s about Muslims, mostly associated with religious intolerance and attitudes to women. Most of the problems and anxieties
raised had to do with 'groupness': people sticking together in their
ethnic groups and not mixing; people not being able to speak English,
so you can't communicate with them; residential concentrations;
parents who don't orient their children to the wider society.

Some linked this to the insularity of the ethnic groups themselves.
A twenty-one-year-old second-generation Italian woman said that
it was unfair of Muslims to keep to themselves because then you
can't learn from them, a sentiment echoed by a thirty-year-old
Australian-born man married to a Chinese woman: 'You don't learn
by having people isolated in little groups.' A thirty-three-year-old
Anglo woman living in the outer suburbs of Melbourne believed
that interest in cultural diversity had to go both ways: 'I don't like
them not showing interest in our culture, or making fun of the
Australian skippies.'

There was some sympathy for the plight of newcomers who stick together at first for support, but this was clearly seen as a transitional phase. If the benefits of an ethnically mixed population were to be available to individuals, then people had to mix.

Analysing the interview transcripts, we were struck by how often the expression of an anxiety or a negative attitude was followed by a qualification or a counter-example, as if having expressed their anxiety the respondent was now at pains to calm and contain it. In the late 1980s, for example, some said that the claims made by Blainey, Ruxton or the media about the degree of public unrest about Asian migration were exaggerated. Others saw racism as the product of ignorance rather than entrenched dispositions, and a couple distinguished between racist language and racist action. 'You might hear racist talk but this did not mean people would not get on as individuals—Australians have compassion when they get to know people face to face,' claimed one man.

People also calmed their anxieties by appealing to history. Yes, there was some tension around the Vietnamese or the Muslims at present (depending on the time of the interview), but this would pass as it had with previous immigrant groups. A working-class Vietnam veteran who was very worried by current levels of racist tension reassured himself: 'The old man said the Greeks and Italians would never mix.' A middle-aged Italian man compared his experience as a migrant in the 1950s with that of the Vietnamese in the 1980s: 'If I go back thirty-five years, we were looked at like a beast in the zoo. At that time you have hostility, so you have a tendency to band together because the pack give you strength.' Now he had only a few Italian friends. 'But you've got to give time.'

The general narrative was of a new group which met with initial suspicion and hostility and perhaps banded together defensively, but of both the hostility and defensiveness dying down with the passing of time. One older man of British descent referred to sectarianism between Catholics and Protestants, both to challenge the idea of a past harmonious culture only now being disturbed, and to point to a historical process in which bitter and entrenched differences can dissolve.

Many of our respondents calmed their anxieties with universal arguments about human nature. There were two versions of this. The first was an explicit appeal to a shared human nature: 'Although there are different cultures, people are pretty much the same.' 'No matter what nationality, there are common bonds.' 'People are the same under the skin.' 'At the end of the day they're human beings, they eat, they die.' 'We're all here for one thing—to live and enjoy life.'

The second, more common version, was to point out that there are good and bad in all groups, races and cultures. The phrase was used by a number of people, as were variations such as 'You can't talk about a whole race, only a few unfortunate individuals'. 'In every country in the world there are some lovely and some horrible people.' 'I don't see slovenliness and disorderliness and crime as belonging to any particular group…Australians can stand up to anyone with regard to criminal activities.' 'If you look for good qualities in people you will find them wherever you look. If you want to find bad qualities you will find them.' 'Like any group of people you get all sorts.'

These arguments were used both to resist stereotyping of immigrant ethnic groups and to resist claims that Australia was racist: 'It goes both ways. All Australians are not the same,' said a fifty-four-year-old Italian woman. The implication of such comments is that moral qualities are properly ascribed to individuals and not to groups.

The image of society implicit in these comments is a liberal one, of a society composed of individuals and families mixing in the day-to-day social world, in which cultural differences are attributes of individuals and families, with institutions and structural constraints being of little interest.

In much conservative commentary a cosmopolitan outlook is seen as the opposite of a parochial attachment to the nation. This was not the case for our respondents. 'Australia' can refer to a continent, a country, a society, a nation or just a place, and in their talk about Australia people slipped around among these meanings. Overwhelmingly, however, they were positive. Our respondents were nationalists, but this did not preclude them from a cosmopolitan attachment to diversity. In fact, they used their knowledge of the nation's history to calm any anxieties they had. Imagining the nation moving through time, with its successive waves of immigrants, reassured them that, whatever the problems with the most recent newcomers, these too will pass. Attachment to the nation, far from being a barrier to accepting contemporary multicultural society, helped them to understand it.

4 Meetings, Bloody Meetings and the Decline of Trust in Our Parliaments

Edited version of Senate Occasional Lecture, Parliament House, Canberra, 27 July 2001.

Meetings, bloody meetings. I'm sure we have all been to too many of them. A ubiquitous feature of modern life, meetings are where we conduct much of the business of our working and community lives. Some families even have them. I want to tell you something of the history of the meeting as a very particular form of social interaction, in order to reflect on the way meetings have changed, and to suggest that this change is one of the reasons for contemporary disaffection with our parliaments.

There is a photo of me as a child of three in one of my mother's hats and holding a handbag. I was going to a meeting. Meetings were one of the places my parents went when they left the house. Many years later, when I was working on ideas of citizenship and their relationship to people's practical political knowledge, I came across a book called *Meetings, Manners and Civilization: The Development of Modern Meeting Behaviour* by a Dutchman, Wilbert van Vree.

The book surveyed the development of meetings as part of what the brilliant sociologist Norbert Elias called (in his book of the same name) 'the civilizing process', whereby Europeans learned to live more interdependently in the complex societies created by industrialisation.[1]

Meetings are occasions when people come together for shared discussion and for non-violent decision making. The medium is talk regulated by rules with which the participants are more or less familiar, and the intended outcome is some sort of decision. They are different from informal talk, from gossip, chitchat or conversation, and the procedures followed give legitimacy to the decisions made. Those who lose the argument accept their loss, and those who win know that they can now legitimately act on the outcome of the meeting. Further, they are now expected to act on the outcome. Most importantly, meetings are different from a physical fight or economic intimidation, in which outcomes are determined by the exercise of power.

The meeting developed as part of the broad historical process of the pacification of politics in Europe, in which rule-governed talk was substituted for force and violence as a way of settling disputes within increasingly large territorial units. As monarchs asserted their monopoly over coercive force and barons lost their armies, other, more peaceful means were needed for members of ruling elites to settle their differences and display their prowess. Debates and oratory replaced duels and tournaments, and parliaments, which began as advisory bodies to the monarch, gradually usurped the monarch's power to become the key site of national decision making. One could attack the words of one's opponent but not the opponent himself. This historical process, sometimes described by the rather ugly word 'parliamentarisation', took around three centuries in Britain, from the sixteenth to the nineteenth centuries, though it followed slightly different trajectories in other European countries.

Organised sport developed at the same time as another substitute for military combat, similarly organised around adversarial teams of men competing for an outcome, and similarly providing opportunities for individual men to shine. Sport and parliament followed their own lines of development, but their deep shared history has made sport a rich source of analogy for parliamentary events and behaviour.

In the eighteenth century, meetings percolated down from the ruling elites to the lower orders through voluntary associations, which were a response to the increasing complexity of social and political life. Strangers, new to town or city from their rural villages, needed ways to meet each other and co-operate. Voluntary associations were an answer. Adaptable to a wide range of purposes ranging from pigeon fancying to a political association, a workers' co-operative or a friendly society, clubs, societies, leagues and associations spread quickly, especially among urban men. All that was needed was a purpose, a set of rules, and a membership defined by a formalised act of joining. Independent of both the family and the state, these voluntary associations contributed to the rapid growth of civil society in the early nineteenth century.[2]

So ubiquitous did they become that in 1836 Charles Dickens could satirise them in *The Pickwick Papers*. Even children could form a club, as the March sisters did in Louisa May Alcott's *Little Women*, to rehearse the skills and forms of adult life. Daughters of politically engaged parents, they expected one day to be active in public life, for as politics became more about talk and rules and less about physical force, spaces were opened up for women beyond the home. Women wouldn't be able to vote or stand for parliament for decades yet, but they could form organisations and participate in political campaigns. By 1830, for example, almost every British town had a ladies' anti-slavery society.[3]

Meetings also transformed the politics of the working classes, as they too began to substitute meetings for violence: 'The poor, when suffering and dissatisfied, no longer make a riot, but hold a meeting—instead of attacking their neighbours, they arraign the Ministry,' noted an observer of the Manchester working class in 1819 on the eve of the Peterloo Massacre.[4] Of course riots, strikes and uprisings continued, as did the state's use of physical violence to repress them, but there were now more peaceful ways to press one's claims.

Australia was settled after the rise of the voluntary association in Britain. Nineteenth-century colonists brought their experience of voluntary associations with them and turned them to the purposes of community-building in the new land, where they had perhaps even more need for them than at home. With no traditional ruling classes to rely on, no local squire or gentry and few clergy, the colonists knew that if anything were to happen it was up to them. Like the settlers in the United States, they were building a new society. Alexis de Tocqueville had observed the range and effectiveness of associational life when he visited America in the 1830s, and he saw it as the basis of its successful democratic life: 'In democratic countries, knowledge of how to combine is the mother of all other forms of knowledge,' he wrote.[5]

In new areas of settlement, especially in the country, the provision of essential services such as hospitals or fire brigades depended on voluntary effort, or on convincing the government to provide them. By the end of the nineteenth century the typical Australian country town and suburb had a plethora of community organisations: sporting clubs for cricket, football, horse racing, tennis and lawn bowls, musical societies, literary and debating clubs, public halls, mechanics' institutes and subscriber libraries, agricultural societies to organise the annual show, and so on. There were also churches of various denominations supporting their own range of organisations, and women's auxiliaries raising funds for schools, hospitals, fire brigades and children's homes, as well as associations with an economic purpose such as trade unions, chambers of commerce, farmers' groups and business organisations. In the early 1940s a survey of 180 Victorian country towns ranging in population size from 250 to ten thousand found well over three thousand social organisations and seventeen hundred sporting organisations, as well as boards, councils and trusts, and the more formal organisations of political and economic life.[6]

So many meetings. Helena Marfell was the Victorian Country Party's first woman parliamentary candidate, unsuccessfully contesting the federal seat of Wannon in 1949. Her daughter remembers her as always between meetings.

> Mother would return home from an afternoon meeting, and, not even stopping to take off her hat, would get the tea, make a couple of sponge cakes, sandwiches or biscuits, eat and rush off again to an evening meeting...She ate most evening meals with her hat on.[7]

Before the 1960s and 1970s, when women started to challenge their exclusion from institutional power, the meetings of civil society were their main means of political participation, as well as welcome opportunities to socialise over a cup of tea.

All these meetings needed a chairman. As one meeting manual put it, 'there are few persons who do not belong to some local council, association, society or club over whose meetings he or she may not be called upon to preside.' To know how to run a meeting was 'a necessity of modern life'.[8]

It is an intriguing historical question how people like Helen Marfell and countless other Australian men and women learned to run meetings. All the more politically oriented clubs and societies provided some sort of training in political skills. The Australian Natives' Association, for example, held Mock Parliaments and Mock Banquets;[9] debating societies were popular, with their formal speeches for and against particular motions; and the political parties ran speaking and debating clubs where political activists could learn the skills needed for the hustings. After women were enfranchised, women's political organisations, such as the New South Wales-based Women's Political Education League, established classes in speaking and debating, and ran schools for citizenship.[10] As a teenager I was a member of a YWCA organisation called the Girl Citizens in which we were taught how to run meetings, introduce speakers and give votes of thanks.

Many people, though, called on to chair the local tennis club or hall committee, had recourse to meeting manuals, such as J. P. Monro's *Guide for the Chairman and Secretary*. Monro's *Guide* was part of a series of Everyday Useful Books available at newsagents which contained other titles by Monro: *Model Speeches and Toasts*, *Model Letters and Invitations*, a guide to Australian etiquette and a book on what to name your baby. Monro's *Guide*, first published in Australia in 1934, was still in print, in its fourteenth edition, in 1958.

Manuals such as Munro's, which began to appear during the nineteenth century, served a similar function to etiquette manuals, which spread the manners of the European courts to the middle classes. The very early manuals focussed as much on meeting manners as on procedural issues: one should not arrive late or depart early, fall asleep, fight, shout, spit or swear, but should rather endeavour at all times to listen attentively to the views of others and to maintain a calm and dispassionate demeanour when stating one's own.[11] Meetings were about rational talk, and to participate in them successfully one had to learn to talk and listen in rational and reciprocal ways: to take one's turn, to control one's outbursts of scorn or temper, to subordinate one's own interests and views to those of others, or at least to appear to do so. As innumerable meeting manuals told their readers, 'Common sense and common courtesy are the foundations of good meeting procedure.'[12]

As meeting manners became more widely known, and more people knew not to spit or throw things, not to interrupt and shout abuse, attention shifted from instructing the ordinary members and participants to advising the chairman, who was ultimately responsible for the effective and orderly conduct of the meeting. As the advice made clear, knowing how to run a good meeting is far more than knowing formal procedural rules. It is knowing how to balance competing interests and views; how to achieve an effective outcome; how to handle a potentially disruptive outburst of anger, or even violence; how, that is, to maintain public order, prevent it from descending into chaos and still get things done. Meeting manuals thus mix exposition of the rules with advice to the chair on controlling the passions and passing impulses in themselves as well as in the meeting's participants. The standard United States manual, *Robert's Rules of Order*, concluded its list of 'Parliamentary Don'ts for the Presiding Officer' with 'Don't lose your calmness, objectivity and impartiality.'[13]

A person's ability to run a good meeting was evidence of their general moral capacities. An obituary for Mrs Crocker who served as president of the conservative Australian Women's National League slid easily between her capacities in office and her general character.

> The outstanding qualities of Mrs Crocker were her wonderful sense of justice, firmness and wisdom. She never gave a ruling without considering the question from all points and consulting those with whom she was associated.[14]

Women were good at meetings because they relied on the same skills women used to manage their households and families: listening, talking, finding compromises and controlling emotions.

In the main the procedures for the meetings of civil society were modifications of the procedures parliament had developed to guide its decision making. Even though voluntary associations with meetings to run them developed across Europe, British manuals generally treat them as exclusively British achievements. The standard Canadian meeting manual, *Bourinot's Rules of Order*, first published in 1894, claims that 'On the basis of common sense and fair play, the British Parliament slowly, through the centuries, evolved a system of rules and conventions upon which are based the procedures and usages of all free parliaments.'[15] A manual published in London about the same time by a James Tayler, who was also the author of a practical guide to fly-fishing, links it to the right of the British 'to assemble at pleasure for the purpose of discussion', a right confirmed by the Magna Carta and the Bill of Rights.[16] Another claims that the word 'Parliament…embodies the spirit that has characterised the British people at home and abroad, through the generations'.[17]

People learning how to run a meeting could be in no doubt that this was valuable knowledge which linked them to the deep history of Britain. In the meetings of the tennis club one followed procedures developed in the mother of all parliaments, at Westminster. The smallest and the greatest meetings of the land were thus linked by their shared deliberative procedures. *Robert's Rules of Order* has a

frontispiece with the three simple words: CHURCH—CLUB—
GOVERNMENT. His Rules are sufficient for each, a shared woof
and weft in a single cloth.

Meeting procedures thus embedded knowledge of parliamentary
proceedings in the daily life of the community and the belief that
this was how civilised people resolved their conflicts and made
joint decisions. This was not abstract knowledge about a distant
institution, but was enacted in every meeting convened or attended.
As well, the etiquette of meetings—participating in reciprocal talk,
subordinating self-interest and impulse—accorded with widely held
ideas about the subordination of self and sectional interest to the
common good which was the hallmark of the good citizen. Learning
how to run a good meeting, people were learning about connections
between personal character and public order, between the ethics of
self-control and the effective pursuit of collective outcomes, between
the principles needed to run a good meeting and those necessary for
a good society.

We can see how widespread such knowledge is among ordinary
Australians in the troubles that beset Pauline Hanson's One Nation
Party soon after its inception. Although describing itself as a party,
One Nation was set up as a business without the formal participatory
structures and transparent financial management of a voluntary
association. Hanson and two of her close associates were not elected
office bearers but directors.[18] Members, however, thought they had
joined a party and the mismatch between their expectations and One
Nation's organisational structure was a recurring source of acrimony
and resignations. In 1998, after the party had won eleven seats at
the Queensland state election, one of its office workers described
it as a rabble;[19] and in early 1999 three of its sitting Queensland
members resigned over its autocratic structure.[20] Neither a rabble

nor an autocracy is a legitimate modern deliberative body, and the party's organisation has been its Achilles heel as people attracted to the party by its policies resigned over the way it was run.[21]

Since World War Two meeting practices have been changing. Many meetings still run along the formal procedural lines set out in manuals like *Robert's Rules of Order* and Marjorie Puregger's *The Australian Guide to Chairing Meetings*, but many others now make little use of parliamentary procedures, with the chair expected to do far more than keep order through firm and impartial adherence to procedure. Instead, as one manual puts it, the chair's aim is to 'find the will of the group while keeping group unity, as much as possible without identifying the minority, and while giving the greatest possible atmosphere for free and informal participation.'[22] In achieving such an end, parliamentary procedure is more of a hindrance than a help:

> Parliamentary procedure and motions should be avoided in reaching decisions in most conferences...Parliamentary procedure imposes a degree of formality on the conduct of the discussion which does not allow for the informality, spontaneity and permissiveness we strive for in the conference...members should feel free to speak up and make contributions at any time without recognition by the chair or first indicating their desire to speak.[23]

Formal turn-taking through the chair is replaced by the more informal techniques people use to take turns in everyday conversation, and discussion replaces debate. Even a recent edition of *Robert's Rules of Order* expresses reservations about the applicability of formal procedures for all groups. It advises that, although required in legally constituted meetings, 'in small groups the ponderous procedures involved stymie human interactions, and the flow of creativity. The rules stimulate a legalistic and mechanical way of thinking.'[24]

•

Two developments explain this shift to less formal meetings. The first is the commitment to grassroots participation by the social movements of the 1960s and 1970s, and their distrust of the authoritarian potential of formal leadership positions. Conventional meeting procedures smacked of the repressive values and practices they were seeking to overthrow. Many in the women's movement, for example, regarded them as a tool of the patriarchy, used to control women and silence their voices. Instead, it was argued that women should develop their own, non-hierarchical modes of organisation, which better reflected their more open-ended ways of thinking and acting.[25] Also at work here, though not always recognised, was the baby boomers' heightened individualism, which made them less willing than their parents to be bound by group decisions and majority votes.

The second development is the spread of the workplace meeting. At work, more and more people attend more and more meetings. This is most obvious at the top, where chief executives and departmental heads can spend up to half their time in meetings, but meetings are now a ubiquitous feature of white-collar work and rapidly spreading to blue collar, as horizontally co-ordinated work teams replace hierarchical command structures. Early meeting manuals were addressed to people in their community, non-work life. Monro, for example, said that people needed his *Guide* because of their increasing leisure time and participation in interest-based clubs and societies. Contemporary meeting manuals are more likely to be addressed to managers exercising authority in the workplace than to citizens holding elected office. Malcolm Reid's *The Australian Meetings Handbook* (1991) begins: 'This is a no-nonsense meeting book for the busy executive who finds that he or she is increasingly involved in convening, chairing or simply attending gatherings of all types.'[26]

Guides to workplace meetings draw on management theory and on social psychology, particularly group theory. Few make any mention at all of parliamentary precedents. The deliberative body is generally small, the team or the work group, and the aim is a consensual outcome to which people will feel committed and on which they will act. Also important is the continuing cohesion of the group. One guide lists a meeting's functions as establishing group identity, collective thinking, helping individuals to understand their role in the group, creating a commitment to the decisions made, and acting as a status arena.[27] Only the last has any connection with what happens in parliament.

The focus on small group dynamics has transformed the role of the chair from the impartial umpire of the rules to something more like a facilitator. One manual describes the chair as 'the social leader, keeping the group together', another as a meeting master: 'Meeting masters saw their meetings as if they were orchestral performances... Everyone was an expert, trying to do his or her best. The job of the chairperson was to facilitate, to help, to conduct the committee orchestra.'[28]

•

What has all this to do with parliament? We know from surveys that Australians' trust in their political institutions and in politicians themselves has declined in the past three decades, with a sharp drop after 2013, when the Abbott government was elected.[29] Writing in 1993, Hugh Mackay suggested that the decline could be explained by politicians' unruliness in parliament, especially during question time, together with the disappearance of clear and meaningful differences between the parties. With the parties apparently so close, he argues, parliament's adversarial forms seem pointless.

It is a source of widespread astonishment in the Australian community that, at the very time when parties seem quite capable of
stealing each other's policies or invading each other's territory, it
is not possible for politicians from all sides of the political fence
to work together in a more co-operative and harmonious spirit...
The common cry of parents in particular is that they would not
allow their children to behave in the way that politicians typically
behave in parliament.[30]

Other popular explanations for the problem are that today's politicians, compared with those in some rather vague past, are more
self-interested, more prone to feather their nests at public expense,
not as watchful as they might be about conflicts of interest, and so on.

I want to put forward a quite different reason: that the shift in
meeting behaviour away from formal proceedings based on parliamentary precedent to more informal and less adversarial practices
has weakened the threads that once tied ordinary people to their
parliaments. Neither in top-level negotiations between companies
nor in settling community disputes do most people any longer learn
to follow formal rules based on parliamentary procedure. Parliament
has cut loose from civic life and active citizenship no longer teaches
us to trust it. Quite the opposite, with the adversarial form at the
heart of the Westminster system viewed as a barrier rather than an
aid to co-operative action and good decision making. Long used to
the replacement of weapons with words in the settlement of political
conflicts, people in contemporary society are looking for more flexible
and co-operative ways to solve community and national problems.

This is why, since Don Chipp formed the Democrats in the late
1970s, so many of us have been voting to prevent the major parties
from controlling the Senate, despite complaints that this prevents

governments from governing. Ways to slow down decision making, enforce discussion and try to build consensus are far more in tune with contemporary meeting practices than the winner-takes-all of allowing majorities free rein.

These slower, more consensual practices are also far more in tune with the complex interplay of interests and values in contemporary society which our two and a half major parties struggle to represent coherently. The range of opinions in contemporary Australia has spilled well beyond the aggregative capacities of the two major party blocs, with their legacies of the simpler social and economic divisions of an earlier Australia. Just look at the tensions within Labor between its well-educated white-collar and professional supporters and the blue-collar trade unionists of its traditional base; in the Liberal Party over the irrelevance of its white-Anglophone traditions to our multicultural, multiracial society; in the National Party between farmers and miners. The adversarial, majoritarian basis of party conflict, and its neat fit with the conventions of the Westminster system, cannot represent the diversity of interests, values and opinions in contemporary Australia.

Neither is it conducive to good policy formation. In civil society, good policy development explores issues and conflicts, gathers information and canvasses options, before well-formed policy positions become hostage to the political fortunes of their partisan advocates. This almost never seems to happen in Canberra, where if one side puts forward a policy the other will often oppose it for no other reason than that it does not want to give the opponent a win.

What has been described as 'the parliamentarisation' of associational life, which lasted from the late eighteenth century to the middle of the twentieth, is now on the wane, and parliaments are left exposed to the criticism of a population which now does its daily politics in quite different ways. Where once parliaments led the way, establishing procedures and protocols which became the model for other assemblies, they are now being left behind, their rigid adversarial procedures deployed by our rigidly disciplined parties no longer according with the community's experience of the processes necessary for good decision making. No wonder we no longer trust them.

[1] Wilbert van Vree, *Meetings, Manners and Civilization: The Development of Modern Meeting Behaviour*, Leicester University Press, London, 1999. Norbert Elias, *The Civilizing Process: The History of Manners* and *State Formation and Civilization*, Blackwell, Oxford, 1969 and 1982; first published in German in 1939.

[2] R. J. Morris, 'Clubs, Societies and Associations' in F. M. L. Thompson (ed.), *The Cambridge Social History of Britain, 1750–1950*, vol. 3. Jürgen Habermas, *The Structural Transformation of the Public Sphere: An Enquiry into a Category of Bourgeois Society*, 1962.

[3] Linda Colley, *Britons: Forging the Nation, 1707–1837*, Yale University Press, 1992, p. 278.

4   E. P. Thompson, *The Making of the English Working Class*, Penguin, 1968, p. 456.

5   Alexis de Tocqueville, *Democracy in America* (1835), Harper & Row, New York, 1966, pp. 485–88.

6   A. J & J. J. McIntyre, *Country Towns of Victoria: A Social Survey*, Melbourne University Press, 1944.

7   Mirth Jamieson remembering her mother Helena Marfell; cited in Heather Gunn, '"For the Man on the Land": Rural Women and the Victorian National Party, 1917–1996', PhD thesis, La Trobe University, 1996, p. 139.

8   Morton F. Parish, *The Chairman's Pilot and Chart: A Practical Guide to Procedure and Law*, Sweet & Maxwell, London, 1936, 2nd edn, p. 1.

9   Marion Aveling (Quartly), 'A History of the Australian Natives' Association, 1871–1930', PhD thesis, Monash University, 1970. p. 266.

10   Marilyn Lake, *Getting Equal: The History of Australian Feminism*, Allen & Unwin, Sydney, 1999, p. 147.

11   Van Vree, *Meetings, Manners and Civilization*, p. 256 passim.

12   'M.P.', *The Young Men's Parliamentary Guide*, Macmillan Co. of Canada, Toronto, c. 1919, p. 6. Marjorie Puregger, *Mr Chairman*, Jacaranda, Brisbane, 1962, p. 10.

13   General Henry M. Robert, *Robert's Rules of Order*, first published 1876, Spire Books paperback edn, 1967, p. 167.

14   Tribute to Mrs H. S. Crocker by Mrs F. G. Hughes, *Woman*, 1 August 1930, p. 164.

15   Sir John George Bourinot, *Bourinot's Rules of Order*, revised by J. Gordon Dubroy, McClelland & Stewart Ltd, Toronto, 1963: from Introduction to the First Edition, p. x.

16   James Tayler, *A Guide to the Business of Public Meetings*, Effingham, Wilson & Co., London, 1893, pp. 5–6.

17   *The Young Men's Parliamentary Guide*, p. 5.

18   Glenn Milne, 'The Party Must Be Over', *Australian*, 6 July 1998.

19   Scott Emerson, 'Sacked Staffer Spills the Beans on One Nation "Rabble"', *Australian*, 2 September 1998.

20   'One Nation's Last Gasp', *Age*, 6 February 1999.

21   Amy Remeikis, 'Party Is Doomed: Common Themes in Gripes of Former One Nation Members', *Guardian Australia*, 16 June 2018.

22   H. P. Zelko, *The Business Conference: Leadership and Participation*, New York, 1963, p. 163. This book was first published in 1957 and is representative of the new genre of meeting manuals discussed by van Vree, p. 272–91.

23   Cited in van Vree, p. 286.

24   1978 edition, cited in van Vree, p. 291.

25   Verity Burgmann, *Power and Protest: Movements for Change in Australian Society*, Allen & Unwin, Sydney, 1992, pp. 92–93.

26   *The Australian Meetings Handbook: More Effective Meetings in Half the Time*, Business Library, Information Australia, p. 199.

27   Antony Jay, *How to Run a Meeting*, Harvard Business Press, 1976, pp. 7–8.

28   John E. Troopman, *Making Meetings Work: Achieving High Quality Decisions*, Sage, 1996, pp. xii, 3.

29   Mark Evans, Michelle Grattan & Brendan McCaffrie (eds), *From Turnbull to Morrison: The Trust Divide*, Melbourne University Press, 2019, p. 19.

30   Hugh Mackay, *Reinventing Australia: The Mind and Mood of Australia in the 90s*, Angus & Robertson, Sydney, 1993, p. 78.

PART IV

Issues

1 We Are Good at Elections

Adapted from From Secret Ballot to Democracy Sausage: How Australia Got Compulsory Voting, *Text Publishing, 2019.*

In the middle of the nineteenth century the south-eastern mainland states achieved manhood suffrage, and the Australian ballot transformed voting practices. These democratic achievements led the world. More followed. Australia was second only to New Zealand in granting women the vote, the first to give them the right to stand for parliament, and the first to establish a national non-partisan electoral machinery. It paid close attention to potential barriers of distance, literacy and mobility to voting, made registration compulsory and legislated for Saturday polling days.

All this was achieved well before 1924, when Australia adopted compulsory voting. In his comparative study of modern democracies, published in 1921, the British Liberal political historian James Bryce wrote that this 'newest of all the democracies...has travelled farthest and fastest along the road which leads to the unlimited rule of the multitude'. With compulsory voting Australia ensured that most of the multitude made it to the ballot box. Advocacy began in the late nineteenth century but it faced a number of hurdles: its sheer novelty and breach with British precedent, practical considerations about enforcement, and Labor's stubborn opposition to postal voting.

A few people worried about the infringement of liberty but not many, and none mounted a well-developed philosophical case. Federalism complicated matters, as did World War One, but the deep currents of Australian political life were carrying us forward to the day in July 1924 when we adopted compulsory voting. This was not, as has sometimes been claimed, an accidental decision carelessly made by inattentive parliamentarians, but the result of Australia's confidence in government and its commitment to majoritarian democracy.

Colonial governments ran elections in Australia as they ran so much else, opening up land for settlement, building infrastructure, providing law and order, educating the children. Australians might complain about venal and self-serving politicians but on the whole they trusted the government. In the middle of the nineteenth century, when manhood suffrage suddenly expanded the electorate exponentially, there was really no alternative but to employ salaried public servants to run elections and to manage the rolls. Political parties barely existed and local government was too underdeveloped to take on the tasks.

Clever, dedicated senior bureaucrats drove the rationalisation of electoral processes, to make them more efficient and comprehensive. South Australia's William Boothby pioneered the running of elections by salaried public servants and introduced continuous government-initiated enrolment. In 1911 the Commonwealth's second chief electoral officer, R. C. Oldham, persuaded Labor to introduce compulsory registration and argued that it should be accompanied by compulsory voting. This paved the way for the introduction of compulsory voting and ensured that, once introduced, it was efficiently and fairly administered. Australian's professional, non-partisan state and federal electoral administration gives great legitimacy to election results, with very few legal challenges.

Labor also legislated for voting on Saturdays. This was a boon for women, whose husbands could help them with the children while they voted; and it ushered in the distinctive culture of Australian election days. 'The spirit of Holiday hovers over our election boxes,' writes David Malouf in his 1998 Boyer Lectures. 'Voting for us is a family occasion, a duty fulfilled, as often as not, on the way to the beach, so that children early get a sense of it as an obligation, but a light one, a duty casually undertaken.'

Most polling places are in community, school and church halls, with schools particularly favoured. Here, where children learn the rudiments of their future adult civic responsibilities, they see them enacted in a familiar community setting. Volunteers quickly saw the fundraising possibilities of large numbers of people passing through their doors on election days, beginning with stalls selling cakes, jams and crafts. In the 1980s, with the advent of large portable gas barbecues, sausages in bread rolls joined the fare on sale at polling booths, especially at schools.

Since 2012 these have been called 'the democracy sausage', as social-media accounts were established to advise on the fare available at various polling booths. The term caught on and in 2016, a federal election year, it was selected as word of the year by the Australian National Dictionary Centre, a symbol of the egalitarian good nature of Australian elections and a jokey accompaniment to the serious act of choosing the government, celebrating what we all share no matter which side wins.

For some, election day's carnival atmosphere continues at an election-night party. In earlier days, before radio or television, election crowds would gather outside newspaper buildings and post offices where results were posted as they were telegraphed in. Later, people at home might listen to the wireless. Party workers got together at local halls, but election nights were not widely seen as opportunities for private socialising with friends, no matter whether one expected their side to win or lose.

This began to change with the arrival of television. People watched the results come in at the local pub or the house of a friend with a set. Thus was born the private election-night party, friends gathering early on Saturday night to eat and drink and wait for the numbers to come in. By the end of the 1960s, these were common enough for David Williamson to write a play about one, *Don's Party*, set on the night of the 1969 election.

I went to my first election-night party in 1975. It was a gloomy affair somewhere in Gippsland as we learned that Gough Whitlam had been thrashed. During the 1980s and 1990s my family would watch the federal-election results and the AFL grand final with the same families and with much the same range of emotions, from triumphant glee to fatalistic resignation. The adults would cheer and jeer and drink, while the kids would rattle around. It being Saturday night, they were allowed to stay up late.

In recent years the civic rituals of Saturday voting have been somewhat undermined by the greatly increased availability—and popularity—of pre-poll voting. Pre-polling makes life difficult for the political parties, who now have to hand out how-to-vote cards for weeks before polling day; and it alters the dynamics of the campaign, considerably dampening the impact of a dramatic revelation on poll eve. But its greatest impact may be on our Saturday festivals of democracy, when we line up with the motley crew of our fellow citizens to vote. Perhaps the democracy sausage will save the day.

Here is one blogger on her decision to forgo pre-polling at the 2013 federal election:

> I was going to complete my vote an early polling booth near work during the week until I stumbled upon the website which mapped out the election sausage sizzle locations and found that the primary school near where I am house sitting was one...As I walked down I felt such a sense of community. Here I was walking along ahead and behind other groups doing the same—families, housemates, singles—about to participate in our democratic right and have a say in the leadership of our great and lucky country.

•

The most common argument for compulsory voting was the majoritarian one: that the elected government should represent not just the majority of those who vote but the majority of those eligible to vote. This would increase the government's legitimacy and ensure it paid attention to the interests of all the people. Similar arguments were put in support of preferential voting, which was introduced federally in 1918. It prevents the election of candidates who win only a minority of the first-preference vote.

Majoritarian arguments for compulsory voting in Australia are a close companion of egalitarianism. If government is to deliver the greatest happiness to the greatest number, then the greatest number need to vote. Every one counts as one and property has no special claims. We know from voluntary systems that the poor and marginalised are the least likely to vote, but with compulsory voting no political party can afford to ignore a substantial group of voters. Policies pitched only at the comfortable just won't fly.

Without compulsory voting, the Liberal Party would have abolished Medicare long ago, relying on the fact that those who needed it most were least likely to vote to save it.

Compulsory voting and registration also fosters political engagement. Because young people reaching voting age and new citizens are compelled to vote, most pay at least minimal attention to parties, leaders and issues. There will always be some who donkey vote or spoil their ballots, but after a few elections many more will be better informed and more interested than had voting been a matter of choice. Some partisan feelings are likely to have developed and voting to have become a habit.

Progressives focus on the egalitarian benefits of compulsory voting, but there are also more conservative arguments. Here is the Melbourne *Herald* arguing for compulsion in 1876:

> In few instances do more than one-half of the electors go to the poll;
> and in some cases only a third. And these, as a rule, are the violent
> partisans of one side or the other. Those who might be expected
> to give an impartial vote for the best man simply remain away.

After the 1890s, as a well-organised labour movement began to mobilise the working class vote, some non-Labor politicians hoped that compulsory voting would get more of their supporters to the polls. Arguing for compulsory voting in 1906, Victoria's chief secretary, John Mackey, was most agitated about religious zealots, the Protestant temperance and anti-gambling groups who demanded that politicians pledge support in return for help mobilising the vote. Compulsory voting ensured that moderate citizens turned out to balance the zealots of both right and left, and create a sensible centre concerned with matters of general public interest.

A common argument against compulsory registration and voting is that it lets political parties off the hook. In 1915 Billy Hughes opposed compulsory voting because 'The driving force of the Labour movement has not been compulsion but inspiration. To force the people onto the roll is a most indifferent substitute for that enthusiasm which led many to walk sixty miles to vote.' More recently, the former South Australian Liberal senator Nick Minchin argued that voluntary voting would revitalise political parties, forcing them to rebuild their branches in both safe and marginal seats. In an article entitled 'The Denial of Rights', published in the *Parliamentarian* in 1996, he wrote, 'To date the political parties have conspired to use the law to do what in virtually every other democracy the parties themselves must do—namely maximise voter turnout.'

Minchin and Hughes both saw grassroots political organisation as the main means of getting out the vote: building branches, recruiting members, public meetings, personal canvassing. But as Mackey saw at the beginning of last century, moral outrage is also a great motivator, especially when backed by religious conviction. In the United States gun laws, abortion, same-sex marriage and climate change are all potent mobilising issues but they are also polarising, eroding social cohesion and making the country harder to govern as noisy groups on both sides raise the emotional stakes.

Commentators frequently suggest that Australia is heading down the same path, that Australia too is subject to polarising populist forces from both left and right and is becoming impossible to govern. Most weekends you can find such sentiments in the opinion pages of News Corp papers. I don't agree. Not only does religious belief have less political salience here than in the States, but compulsory voting tempers the impact of the passionate and committed voters of the base with the votes of the moderate and indifferent. It lowers the emotional temperature of our politics and keeps open the sensible centre. The angry and aggrieved will always be drawn to politics, but compulsory voting ensures that they're not the main occupants of the public square.

Since 2010, the number of rusted-on, lifelong party voters has plunged. Fewer people report very strong levels of partisanship, more are splitting their vote between the House of Representatives and the Senate and fewer are following the parties' how-to-vote cards. Accompanying this loosening of party loyalties has been a general decline in trust for our major institutions in politics, business and the media. Without compulsory voting many disillusioned voters would turn away from politics altogether and stop voting, but because they have to find someone to vote for, new contestants enter the fray to pick up their protest and offer an alternative. This is a very good thing.

Over the past three decades or so the Greens, Pauline Hanson's One Nation Party, Bob Katter's Australian Party and Clive Palmer's short-lived Palmer United Party, as well as prominent independents like Tony Windsor, Andrew Wilkie, Cathy McGowan, Helen Haines, Zali Steggall and Kerryn Phelps, have all benefited from voters' disaffection with the parties which dominated politics in the twentieth century. We mightn't like all of these new contestants, or agree with their positions, but it keeps the disillusioned voters in the tent engaged in the peaceful protest of changing their vote. It also encourages the major parties to modify their positions to try to win back some of their erstwhile supporters, as Labor is doing with the Greens and John Howard did when One Nation first appeared after Hanson's explosive maiden speech.

Dealing with newcomers is painful for the established politicians, as they see comfortable margins erode and career plans threatened. Unsurprisingly, there is plenty of ranting against irresponsible and divisive minorities, and hand-wringing over the difficulties of governing a fragmented nation. But there are real risks to the established parties of ignoring significant groups of disillusioned supporters. Compulsory voting keeps our political system flexible, forcing political players to adapt to the shifting sentiments and interests of the majority or lose office, and ensuring that no significant minority group ends up outside the political system altogether.

•

Australia's democratic achievements are not flawless. The disenfranchising of Indigenous Australians by the first Commonwealth Franchise Act was shameful and continued for far too long into the twentieth century. Non-white overseas-born residents were also disenfranchised, but at least their children born here could vote.

In one way we have gone backwards. The 1902 franchise bill that Richard O'Connor introduced gave the right to vote on 'one ground only…residence in the Commonwealth of six months or over by any person of adult age'. This liberal intention was compromised by racial exclusions, but it is more generous in terms of residence than our current law, which bases the right to vote on citizenship. Permanent residents who do not become citizens can't vote, even if they have lived here and paid taxes for years, so a significant minority of people subject to our laws have no say in them. New Zealand, by contrast, gives the right to vote to permanent residents after a year of continuous residence.

There are, too, other democratic deficits. For example, the light regulation and poor transparency of political donations and campaign finances, and the parties' processes for preselecting candidates. But the story of the mechanics of our voting—who can vote, where, when, and how our votes are counted—is a triumph of majoritarian democracy.

Compulsory voting is at the heart of this story. With preferential voting and our non-partisan electoral administration it forms a triumvirate protecting our majoritarian faith in democracy and our commitment to peaceful constitutional processes for resolving our conflicts and differences. From the invention of the Australian ballot to the humble democracy sausage, we have been innovators in electoral practice, concerned both with the integrity of the process and the communality of the day. There are many reasons to be disillusioned with Australian politics at present, as we suffer our sixth prime minister in eight years, but our electoral system is not one of them. We Australians are good at elections and we should celebrate it.

2 Fair Share
Country and City in Australia

Agitation Hill Lecture, Christ Church, Castlemaine, June 2011.

When I was growing up in the 1950s, like many of my friends I had country cousins. My father grew up on a dairy farm in the Goulburn Valley. He sought his future in the city but on holidays we went to the farm, visiting our grandparents, aunts and uncles, and we learned something of what the world looked like from the farm gate. In school we pasted bits of wool into our project books and watched jerky educational films on the wheat industry to teach us the importance of rural industries to Australia. That was over half a century ago. When I was teaching the politics of rural Australia to university students at the beginning of this century, only a few had any connections with the country. They knew about it from the media, but they had little understanding of its history and were far more likely to fly to Bali or Queensland for their holidays than to spend them in Melbourne's rural hinterland.

City and country in Australia share a history of interdependence and of watchful suspicion. The understanding of that interdependence was strong in the first two centuries of Australia's European settlement, when the attempt to build a vibrant and self-sustaining countryside was a major political preoccupation. The country made claims for support on the city, and by and large the city attempted to meet them as part of a compact in which Australians shared the costs of living in a big country by subsidising their country cousins.

Most often when Australians think about our egalitarian traditions, they think about the informality of manners and absence of relations of deference—such as sitting in the front of taxis and an aversion to tipping—and about high minimum wages and reasonable working conditions. They think, that is, about class relations. But there is another historically important strand of Australian egalitarianism that is focussed on regional or spatial equity. Australia was 'a nation for a continent' but outside the capital cities the population is spread thinly and it is costly for governments to provide country dwellers with the same level of services as those living in the closely settled cities.

Some of this commitment to regional equality was embedded in the constitution to persuade reluctant colonies like Queensland and Tasmania with small populations to join the federation. Each state, no matter what its population, would have the same number of senators; and none would have fewer than five members of the House of Representatives. So Tasmania, with its population of about 541,000, has more federal electorates than it otherwise would under the current quota of 173,647, and its senators, like Brian Harradine and Jacqui Lambie, have been able to exercise power disproportionate to their electoral base. The ACT, with a largely urban population of about 431,000, has only two senators.

The Commonwealth devised ways to redistribute its tax take

among the states, in what is called by the awkward technical term of 'horizontal fiscal equalisation'. Obviously it was more expensive for the governments of Queensland and Western Australia to provide services to their populations scattered over huge distances than for the governments in the more closely settled south-eastern states, yet before the minerals boom of the 1960s they had far less revenue per head. So the Commonwealth topped up the state's coffers. This was systematised in 1933, when the Commonwealth Grants Commission was established in response to the potential political fracturing of the federation in the early 1930s when Western Australia tried to secede.

There were also various devices to support agricultural producers, small farmers in particular. Sugar, fruit and dairy were protected by tariffs and import quotas, and statutory marketing boards were established from the 1920s onwards across the range of agricultural sectors: wool, wheat, dairy and so on. The idea was simple: a combination of producers would be able to get a better price, providing a countervailing power to the big purchasers and eliminating middlemen. These boards were more than voluntarist co-operatives; established by law, they regulated markets in agricultural produce. For example, only eggs which had been graded, tested and stamped by the various state Egg Boards could lawfully be sold, consigning backyard egg producers to barter or under-the-table exchanges. A friend of mine whose mother kept a well-populated backyard chook pen in the 1950s remembers the furtiveness accompanying the exchange of eggs for money in his otherwise respectable and law-abiding household.

The country also benefited from the fact that, until the neoliberal 1980s and 1990s, the state and federal governments were monopoly providers of many basic services and much infrastructure, making cross-subsidisation of city to country through taxation and pricing mechanisms a relatively simple matter. At federation the Postmaster General's Department (PMG) was given control of postal, telegraphic, telephonic 'and other like services,' with the obligation to provide these to remote areas. These new forms of communication promised to conquer distance for people living in Australia's remote and scattered communities, to knit them more closely into the nation, and to increase their access to basic services like health and education. The government was expected to provide the access, and not charge full cost.

The two living descendants of the PMG, Australia Post and Telstra, still carry a version of that obligation. Australia Post is required to carry a standard letter for a uniform price anywhere in Australia; and Telstra is bound to ensure that all people in Australia, no matter where they live, have reasonable access on an equitable basis to standard telephone services and payphones. In 2020 this was extended to access to broadband services under the Universal Service Guarantee. Broadband is the latest in a long line of promised technological fixes to the tyranny of Australia's distances.

Similarly, railways and irrigation schemes, established in part to support closer settlement on the land, made huge losses that disappeared into the consolidated accounts. State-owned enterprises also provided tens of thousands of jobs in the country. The old PMG employed postmasters and mistresses, postmen, mail sorters, linesmen, telephonists and technicians right across the country and was Australia's largest national employer, as was its successor, Telecom. The power companies and water utilities similarly provided thousands of skilled and semi-skilled manual jobs in the regions.

In this multitude of ways, since federation, the city has been subsidising the country, with country dwellers arguing that, although their numbers were small, their contribution to the nation was large so their subsidy and special treatment was well justified. The country supported this claim with three main arguments.

The first and overwhelmingly convincing claim that the country could make for special treatment was economic—the country rode on the sheep's back. This is the key to understanding the political power the country once had and why this has evaporated. Australia became one of the world's wealthiest countries in the nineteenth century because of sheep. Gold helped, but it was the export of fine wool that drove the economy. As well, much of the economic activity of the cities came from the links they provided between the rural hinterland and the world. Australian cities as they developed in the nineteenth century were port cities, transport hubs and service centres, through which farmers and pastoralists shipped their produce to the world economy.

The second claim was that Australia needed people settled across the land. A nation for a continent was the promise of federation, a political community for Australia's vast territory. But to make this happen, Australia needed more people. It was a truism for the men and women of the first half of last century, still believing the convenient fiction of terra nullius, that the vast empty spaces of Australia needed to be filled with people and that the people should be white. From the beginning of settlement governments in Australia have actively encouraged migrants. The urgency of 'filling up the empty spaces' was strongest after each of the two world wars, when people's sense of national vulnerability was understandably high. After World War Two, Australians were warned that they must 'populate or perish' and the massive post-war immigration programme was launched.

Until the 1950s, colonial and then state governments attempted not only to increase the population but to encourage it to spread across the country through closer settlement schemes. The lure of cheap land was used to entice migrants to cross the globe and, from the 1860s onwards, colonial and then state government land reforms attempted to break up the large pastoral runs. The family farm not the squatter's station was to be the ideal dwelling of rural Australia, for no matter how profitable the pastoral industry, under-populated sheep runs were not regarded as sufficient basis for a nation. Government-sponsored irrigation schemes were likewise used to increase inland settlement.

The third argument country people made to support their claims to special treatment was cultural: that they contributed disproportion-ately to the character of the nation, both to its national distinctiveness and to its moral character. The push for closer settlement had been driven not just by the need to fill the land with white people, but also by the yeoman ideal, the belief that it was better for people to live in the country than the city, that a nation filled with hardworking, independent farming families would be better and stronger than a nation of soft-bellied city dwellers.

For the growing Australian nationalism at the end of the nineteenth century, the real Australia was the country, where people had been shaped by their struggles with the unique problems of the land and so made what they were by Australia. Country folk were the bearers of the characteristics of resourcefulness, endurance and laconic, courteous good humour, which were widely seen as distinctive Australian attributes. Cities and city dwellers, by contrast, were much the same the world over, and so made no special contribution to a distinctively Australian character.

•

Since World War Two a range of economic, social and cultural changes have been draining the country of its nation-building significance and so weakening the city's willingness to subsidise it. World War Two was the watershed, when the focus of Australian nation-building shifted decisively from the country to the city, from agriculture to industrialisation. When war broke out, Australia couldn't even make the optical glass needed for telescopes, binoculars, periscopes and range-finders. Manufacturing capacity had to expand rapidly to produce the machines and equipment needed to fight a war: guns, tanks, ships, aircraft, trucks, scientific equipment, chemicals and so on. Australia's scientific capacity also grew rapidly, as did its skilled engineering workforce. This was the point when secondary and tertiary industries overtook agriculture in terms of share of GDP and of employment. Farmers' and country people's claim to be the economic backbone of the nation became ever less plausible.

After the 1960s minerals replaced wool as Australia's export staple. No longer on the sheep's back, Australian prosperity now rode on the top of railway trucks full of coal, and alumina and iron ore. Much of this mining development occurred in the north and west, far from the settled areas, so although it provided an effective substitute for agriculture in Australia's balance of trade, its capacity to support rural communities was marginal.

The second change has been in farming. Australia's agriculture is very efficient by world standards. Advances in technology have meant that fewer people produce the same amount of product. Thus, even as agriculture has modernised and adapted, it has undermined its capacity to fill Australia with people. Farm numbers have been declining since World War Two. Farm employment was 28 per cent of total employment in 1933, 15 per cent in 1954 and now in 2011 is around 4 per cent. There is thus a large gap between the economic performance of the rural sector measured in terms of output and its capacity to sustain rural towns and communities.

Although the drift of population from the city to the country stopped around 1970, as people moved to coastal New South Wales and Queensland, this did not halt the country's cultural and economic decline. Quite the contrary. The lifestyle communities of sea- and tree-changers remained city-focussed, with many living off the proceeds of their years of city work. The inland and the dry sheep and wheat belts are still losing population. Smaller towns have shrunk as the so-called sponge cities have grown, regional centres such as Shepparton or Dubbo soaking up the small service towns of horse-and-buggy days and becoming hubs for government and commercial services. A combination of increased mobility and government policy has marooned older residents, providing a rich reservoir for pathos in images of boarded-up shops and a few remnant locals with memories of grander days.

Then there's the environment. We now have a much better understanding of Australia's varied and unpredictable environment and the impact on it of two centuries of European farming practices. Two changes in particular have been profoundly unsettling for the country. The first is the rise of an environmental movement which values non-agricultural over agricultural land. Old-style agricultural country is no longer the taken-for-granted source of pride in the country's hard work and productivity that it was for earlier generations, but now also speaks of cleared forests and absent bird and mammal species.

The second change is the profound doubts that have arisen over the long-term sustainability of European farming practices in Australian conditions, with increasing evidence of serious degradation of the natural environment—in land salination, loss of soil cover and of biodiversity, and the deterioration of the inland waterways. The threatened collapse of the Murray–Darling river system has put agriculture and environmental sustainability into head-on conflict over access to water, as allocations for irrigation have been slashed. Agriculture, the city, country towns and a host of threatened ecological systems are all competing for the same scarce resource.

Country Australia's position in the Australian nation has been affected by a third major change since World War Two: the markedly increased ethnic and racial diversity which has resulted from the continuing immigration programme. Although post-war migration has increased the ethnic diversity of both country and city, this has been most marked in the cities where most of the new migrants have settled. There are of course notable exceptions, such as the Italians in Griffith and Mildura, but on the whole the country stayed white while the city brindled.

As Australia's cities were socially and culturally transformed by migration, city dwellers started to argue that Australia's distinctiveness lay not in its resourceful, friendly country folk but in its ethnically diverse and culturally sophisticated capitals. Australian cities, especially Sydney and Melbourne, felt they could escape their status as provincial cities, much the same as provincial cities the world over, to become bearers of one version of Australia's new national distinctiveness: the most successful multicultural nation in the world.

In the decades after World War Two these various economic, demographic and cultural changes were making the city more independent of the country and so undermining the basis for the country's claims to subsidy. However, it was not really until the 1980s and 1990s that politics caught up and started systematically to undo the subsidies to the country. Neoliberalism—or economic rationalism as it was then called—was suspicious of government subsidies of all sorts. The Hawke government, elected in 1983, embarked on a series of reforms designed to open up the protected parts of the economy to competition, floating the dollar, reducing tariffs and modestly encouraging research and development.

Australian agriculture too would be made more competitive by the reduction of protection. Tariffs and quotas on agricultural products were abolished or reduced, statutory marketing authorities dismantled and industry regulatory regimes simplified. A key argument used to support trade liberalisation and deregulation in agriculture was that there were too many farms. In large part this was the result of the closer settlement policies of earlier governments. The social and political goals of filling the land with people were now irrelevant to the overriding economic goal of creating an efficient agriculture which did not rely on government subsidy. 'Get big or get out,' farmers were told, and as financial markets were deregulated many borrowed heavily to 'get big'—only to come to grief when interest rates were hiked in the late 1980s and early 1990s. In the interests of the economy the countryside was being emptied of farmers as trade liberalisation exacerbated the difference between the profitability of larger enterprises and the rest. Government would mop up the social cost by helping the unprofitable 'adjust'.

Neoliberalism also inspired a radical rationalisation and restructuring of government service delivery. Just as national economies were to be transformed and revitalised by opening them up to competition and the entrepreneurial spirit, so too were the lumbering government bureaucracies. Developed to deliver relatively equal services to Australian citizens wherever they lived, these were redesigned according to market principles. This included the large state-owned enterprises, many of which were privatised during the 1980s and 1990s: gas and electricity companies, the Commonwealth Bank, public transport, airports and the two airlines. Other government enterprises, such as Australia Post, were corporatised. Many railways were closed.

Rationalisation inevitably followed, as the requirement to make a profit forced the closure of unprofitable branches and user-pays became the order of the day. Between 1991 and 1997, following corporatisation, Australia Post reduced the numbers of post offices by around a quarter, many in rural areas where they were popular local meeting places. But such social functions couldn't be costed.

Rationalisation in the delivery of services by the private sector followed similar patterns. The most visible was in banking, as main-street branches in their imposing historic buildings were downsized and eventually replaced by automatic tellers. Rural towns were dismayed. Since the founding of these towns, banks had brought in new families: bank managers to join the local golf club and chair fundraising drives, and tellers to play in the football team and marry the farmers' daughters. Now all they had was an ATM.

The waves of public and private rationalisations that broke over rural Australia during the 1980s and 1990s affected people living in the country in two main ways. First, and obviously, there was a decline in easy local access to many basic public services, such as health and education, which were centralised in regional centres, and to rail services. The quality of services in many large regional centres has improved, with more regional universities and much better regional hospitals, but at the expense of services available in smaller surrounding towns. Second was the loss of jobs. As government agencies and private businesses individually pursued efficiencies of cost, their decisions impacted on each other to produce social outcomes for which no one took responsibility—dying small towns, and confused and distressed Australians who felt abandoned and betrayed.

Earlier generations of Australians acknowledged that regional inequalities were structural, the consequences of living in a big country with a sparse population, but in the neoliberal 1980s and 1990s regions were encouraged to take responsibility for their own futures by becoming more self-reliant, more entrepreneurial, more creative. There was some assistance with this—for example, by providing leadership training—and there was much talk about the need to mobilise social capital, but the message was clear: don't look to government to bail you out; you're on your own. Like the farmers, regional communities were told they were responsible for their own future viability.

Once, the problems *of* the country were problems *for* the country as a whole. But then government stepped back to allow market forces and technological change to redistribute resources in the interests of economic efficiency, and made little specific commitment to country Australia beyond helping individuals and communities to 'adjust', although the welfare state did remain as a safety net for the worst affected. The problems of the country were seen as unfortunate for those affected but not likely to have much effect on the rest of Australia as the agents of neoliberalism cut the country loose from the city and left it to fend for itself.

3 Why Climate Change Defeats Our Short-Term Thinking

Monthly, *February 2014.*

In the middle of the nineteenth century, science forced a massive readjustment of the temporal imagination of the West. Geology and the theory of evolution expanded time from the Bible's few thousand years to millennia, of which humanity had been around for barely a sliver. At the same time German hermeneutic scholarship was turning the Bible from the word of God into a historical text and embarking on the comparative study of religion. It was all very disorienting. When Henry Bourne Higgins, the judge who gave Australia the famous Harvester judgment, read the classicist George Grote on the origins of myth in Ancient Greece at Melbourne University in the 1870s, it shook his world like an earthquake. What if the Wesleyan beliefs in which he had been raised had no firmer foundations than the Greeks' myths of Olympus? What indeed. Despite the large numbers of fundamentalists who have never accepted either evolution or the Bible as a cultural artefact, religion in the West gradually adapted, giving up its cosmological claims and accommodating other faiths.

We now face another massive assault on our temporal imaginations. The debate about global warming—its causes, its trajectory and its likely impacts—asks us to think in centuries, at least, and to project this thinking into the future, long after those living today will be dead. We are all used to shifting among overlapping temporal scales—the daily round, the weekly routine, the rhythms of the year and seasons, the phases of the life-cycle, and lived historical memory—but lay these across longer-term claims about the way the world's climate might be changing and possible future consequences, and it is as if our minds shut down. It is just too hard for most of us to think about, and seems almost impossible for our political processes to deal with.

We know that politicians are always trapped between the long term required for substantial policy reforms and short-term electoral pressures which, combined with vested economic interests, generally means that maintaining the status quo becomes the default option. In this case, the status quo is our carbon-based economy, and to dismantle it will impose serious short-term risks and costs, against the ever more serious long-term risks and costs of not doing so. For politicians, the short-term risks always loom larger than the long-term, as they do for most of us in our daily lives.

Even so, I am still puzzled about the motivation and the world view of those who refuse to take seriously the risks of a heating world. Yes, we can agree that the science is not 100-per-cent definitive—and may never be. Yes, we can agree that the forces governing the world's climate are complex and exact outcomes are hard to predict. But can't we also agree that if even some of the predictions prove to be correct, then these will have terrible consequences which it would be wise to avoid if possible? One can only conclude that many of the people who actively oppose attempts to mitigate the risk of global warming don't really believe it is a risk. Some, of course, don't care—those getting rich from the ownership and exploitation of coal deposits, for example, who want to dig it up and sell it as soon as possible, before the rest of the world stops buying coal. There is no arguing with them. The ones I am interested in are people like John Howard and Tony Abbott, who do care about the future of the world and whose actions could make a difference. If they really believed in the risks of human-induced global warming, they would act differently.

Kevin Rudd said that global warming is the greatest moral challenge of our time. True, there are grave moral issues raised by the fairness of the measures used to respond to the risks of global warming. There is also an intergenerational moral challenge, but this latter runs up against the limits of our temporal imaginations to about three generations ahead of us. What will the world look like for our great-great-grandchildren? It is impossible to imagine for most of us—except for scientists trained in long-term modelling.

Climate change is not primarily a moral challenge, one to do with how we treat each other, but a cognitive and emotional challenge. We can't live in constant anxiety about cataclysmic risk, yet we need to be able to formulate policies which respond to these risks. We live day to day and year to year, but the risks exist in a much longer timeframe. Denial is perhaps human beings' most common response to anxiety: *It can't happen to me*. And of course it probably won't to most of us alive today.

In November 2013, John Howard spoke to the Global Warming Policy Foundation, the London-based organisation of old men dedicated to climate change scepticism. To quote from its website, 'while open-minded on the contested science of global warming, [it] is deeply concerned about the costs and other implications of many of the policies currently being advocated.' The website makes it clear that the foundation sees the short-term economic risks posed by policies which mitigate emissions of carbon dioxide as far greater than the long-term environmental risks of not doing so. These they already know how to calculate and think about. The preoccupation with the data of the past fifteen years, in which world temperatures have not risen, shows how limited are their temporal horizons.

Howard's lecture is instructive for understanding the cognitive strategies of those attempting to hold back substantial policy responses to the risk of global warming, including Tony Abbott. Howard called his lecture 'One Religion Is Enough'

> in reaction to the sanctimonious tone employed by so many of these who advocate quite substantial and costly responses to what they see as irrefutable evidence that the world's climate faces catastrophe against people who do not share their view. To them the cause has become a substitute religion.

He then goes on to complain about the increasingly offensive language used against those who do not agree that drastic action is needed; to proclaim his temperamental preference for agnosticism; to present people concerned about global warming as opposed to economic development; and to describe with quiet satisfaction the politics of Tony Abbott's defeat of the Labor government's emissions-trading scheme.

Howard corrals the debate about the risks of global warming inside the old ideological left–right framework, where those concerned about global warming become extremists opposed to economic growth and technology, in contrast to pragmatic and humane economic common sense. This is how he makes sense of the debate, seeing it as primarily about political differences and so shifting the threat from the real natural world to the ideological battlefield, where he can recognise his enemies and use his familiar weapons. It is very much a case of shooting the messenger. To do this with any credibility at all he needs to marginalise the role of science in the debate, which he does like this:

> Scientists are experts in science. Judges are experts in interpreting the law...But parliaments—composed of elected politicians—are the experts at public policy making, and neither expressly or implicitly should they ever surrender that role to others...Global warming is a quintessential public policy issue.

This is an extraordinary move, given that we can only know about the climate through science. In a widely cited comment he made before giving the speech, he said, 'I instinctively feel that some of the claims are exaggerated,' leaving himself open to ridicule as substituting his gut instinct for science, though in the speech itself he only claimed to be 'agnostic'.

Of course we all hope that Howard's instinct is right—but his is not an evidence-based response. Of course the response to the risk of global warming is the domain of public policy, but the process itself is natural, and science is our only means of understanding it. Even if we think that what the science points to is a risk rather than a certainty, isn't it prudent to take the risk seriously? If even some of the predicted catastrophic consequences of climate change eventuate, then the emotional and ideological character of those who believed in it and those who did not will matter not one iota. Whether we are rude or courteous to each other, whether we are optimists or pessimists, sincere or not in our motivations, has no impact on long-term natural processes.

Some of those who warn of the risks of climate change may do so with the passion of the religious zealot, but they share none of the believers' faith in a divinely ordained universe. The supreme indifference of nature: this is the earthquake shaking the established politics of the West. There is no god who will rebalance the forces of nature for us to ensure his supreme creation does not go the way of other species into extinction. One suspects that neither Tony Abbott nor his mentor John Howard really believes this.

4 The Coal Curse

Adapted from Quarterly Essay *78, 'The Coal Curse: Resources, Climate and Australia's Future'.*

Shortly after Christmas 2019, when south-east Australia was burning and the impacts of climate change were uppermost in everyone's mind, I began writing my *Quarterly Essay* 'The Coal Curse'. By New Year's Day the fire fronts were roaring through much of south-eastern Australia. The day after, four thousand people were trapped on the beach at Mallacoota, waiting for the navy to bring in supplies and start an evacuation, car convoys were leaving Batemans Bay and the other holiday towns on the New South Wales South Coast, Corryong in northern Victoria was evacuating to Tallangatta, and fire authorities were warning of worse to come. In his press conference that day Prime Minister Scott Morrison batted away any suggestion that the catastrophic fires might push the Coalition to go harder on reducing emissions from fossil fuels, with arguments that were all too familiar.

Our emissions-reduction policies will both protect our environment
and seek to reduce the risk and hazard we are seeing today. At the
same time, it will seek to make sure the stability of people's jobs
and livelihoods all around the country. What we will do is ensure
that our policies remain sensible, that they don't move towards
either extreme and stay focussed on what Australians need for a
vibrant and viable economy, as well as a vibrant and sustainable
environment. Getting the balance right is what Australia, I think,
has always been able to achieve.

Everything about Morrison's initial response to the fires was wrong,
beginning with his ill-considered family holiday in Hawaii, flying
off when fires were already raging in New South Wales and the
smoke was so thick in Sydney that tourists couldn't see the bridge
from the Opera House. Morrison was determined to see the fires
as part of the expected pattern of Australian summers, and their
management as the responsibility of the states' emergency services.
After mounting popular outrage forced him to cut his holiday short,
he badly misread the reasons for people's anger. He thought his
absence made people anxious, as if he were a monarch whose very
presence reassured and gave comfort.

It was soon clear his presence was just as likely to arouse anger,
and that meet-and-greets with fire victims could not be relied on to
provide soothing photo opportunities. Visiting the fire-ravaged village
of Cobargo in the Bega Valley, he was heckled, two people refused to
shake his hand and it was filmed for the whole nation to see. What
people wanted was not a hug from Scotty, but leadership and decisive
action from their prime minister: to bring in the armed services, to
pay the volunteer firefighters, to provide national leadership and
co-ordination in an emergency that ignored state borders. And they

wanted him to talk about climate change, to admit that the ferocity and extent of these fires were what scientists had been predicting would happen as the climate warmed.

In December, with out-of-control fires burning in the Blue Mountains, Greg Mullins, the former New South Wales Fire and Rescue Commissioner, had described the fires as 'unprecedented' and called for the prime minister to convene an emergency summit on how the country should prepare for bushfires in a changed climate. The previous April, Mullins, along with twenty-eight other fire chiefs, had tried to warn the prime minister that fire behaviour was changing in Australia, and that a ramped-up and better-coordinated response and far more resources were needed. They made a number of practical suggestions, but, said Mullins, 'We weren't listened to.'

As prime minister, Morrison does not deny that the climate is changing, nor that the burning of fossil fuels is the primary cause. This, it must be said, is a major advance on Tony Abbott's position as prime minister, which was barely disguised denialism. But Morrison would not admit to the severity of the crisis, nor that his government was failing to respond to its seriousness.

In his carefully calibrated statement at the press conference on 2 January, he balanced two things: cutting emissions and protecting livelihoods 'all around the country.' Not everyone lived in these fire-prone areas, he was reminding us: some lived in mining regions, and they had interests too, which the government must look after. Economy versus environment, here it was again, and the misleading search for balance between two supposedly competing goods.

Over the New Year, as the fires burned, I was in no mood for balance. I was angry. Scientists had been warning of fires like these for decades. Ross Garnaut had warned of them in his 2008 report on climate change. The fire chiefs had warned of them not twelve months before, as the drought dried the land. The government had responded with Dorothea Mackellar's land of droughts and flooding rains to claim that fires were business-as-usual for the Australian bush and with a childlike theory of causation where the only cause of a fire is the spark that sets it off, whether it be the arsonist's match, the unattended campfire or a lightning bolt. Of course rising temperatures do not produce the spark, but they do create the conditions to make the fires more intense and destructive. Rainforest was burning that had never burned before, as it had in Tasmania in the summer of 2016.

Over the New Year my favourite place on earth was burned: the campgrounds at Thurra River and Mueller Inlet, near the Point Hicks Lighthouse in East Gippsland. I had camped there with family and friends for the past twenty years, and we were booked to camp there again in February. It was beautiful: magnificent old mahogany gums with snaking trunks and limbs, a short tannin-bronzed river and estuary, long white beaches and sheltered bays, enormous sand dunes which took you to the top of the world. For a few weeks a year it was all ours, as so many annual holiday spots on the south and east coast are to others.

I know that the loss of a loved camping ground is not in the same league as burnt houses, sheds and livestock, or a father, son and husband killed fighting the fires. We weren't there and we didn't face the horror of the walls of flame. Our comfortable city-based lives went on almost as usual. But awake at night I had losses to mourn: the habitat destruction, the reptiles, birds and the animals that have been killed, the stately lace monitors, the lyrebirds and red-bellied black snakes, the bright blue dragonflies. Maybe it will all bounce back; but maybe it won't. Maybe it will be burnt again before the plants and animals have recovered. It is not just the intensity of the fires that is new, but their increased frequency, and both will get worse as the planet heats.

Over the summer Australia's international reputation took a hammering. The world's media filled with apocalyptic images of kilometre-high flames, fleeing kangaroos and burnt koalas, a small boy in a boat on a wine-dark sea, devastated communities and cities smothered in smoke. Fresh in many minds was the shameful performance of Energy Minister Angus Taylor at the United Nations-convened climate conference in Madrid in December intended to ratchet up global efforts to reduce emissions.

Before countries could agree to higher targets the rules needed to be sorted out. In particular, should countries be allowed to carry over as credits towards meeting their Paris Agreement targets any overshoot in achieving the reductions they committed to at Kyoto? Australia argued they should. Australia had negotiated an easy target for itself at Kyoto by including changes to land-clearing laws. Now it wanted to use that easy target to reduce the effort needed to meet its Paris targets. Many other countries also had credits, but none planned to use them to meet their targets and most explicitly ruled this out as an accounting ploy which avoided the real task of cutting emissions.

With carry-over credits from Kyoto, Australia would easily reach its Paris target of a 26 per cent cut in emissions from 2005. Without them the reduction would only be 16 per cent, and we would have almost to double our efforts to meet the target. Carry-over credits were not allowed under the Paris Agreement and developing countries lobbied hard against them being allowed at Madrid. Taylor, though, was intransigent, so a decision on how to treat them was kicked down the road to the next conference, which was to be held in Glasgow in November 2020 until it was postponed to 2021 because of the pandemic. Morrison has since indicated Australia would not rely on these credits to meet its goal, though only after modelling made clear it wouldn't need to. Morrison would still not commit to a more ambitious target, let alone a timeframe to reach zero emissions.

Once, Australia prided itself on being a good international citizen, a middle-ranking power that could punch above its weight in debates on matters of global importance. Once, we cared what other countries thought of us. The high point of our reputation was 1988 to 1996, when Gareth Evans was Australia's foreign minister and made major contributions to the peace process in Cambodia, the control of chemical weapons and the formation of APEC. But since the Howard government refused to allow the captain of the Norwegian vessel the *Tampa* to land rescued asylum seekers in Australia, our cruel treatment of boat people has forfeited much of this reputation. Playing the spoiler in global climate negotiations is shredding what's left.

On his return from Madrid, Taylor wrote an op-ed for the *Australian* arguing that we 'should be proud of our climate change efforts'. He repeated the claim that we are 'responsible for only 1.3 per cent of global emissions, so we can't single-handedly have a meaningful impact without the co-operation of the largest emitters such as China and the US'. Because international targets are based on domestic emissions, Taylor did not mention emissions from the fossil fuels we export in the form of coal and liquefied natural gas (LNG). Add these in and we become responsible for 3.6 per cent of the world's emissions. China, the United States and India are the world's biggest emitters, but their populations are much larger. Per capita, our emissions are second in the world, only slightly less than Saudi Arabia's.

The rest of the world sees no reason for Australia to be proud of its climate-change efforts. After the Madrid conference, Australia was widely identified as one of a small number of countries wrecking the chance of effective global agreements to cut emissions. Said the UN secretary-general, António Guterres: 'The international community lost an important opportunity to show increased ambition on mitigation, adaptation and finance to tackle the climate crisis.'

Fires were already burning in New South Wales when Taylor was in Madrid. While the federal government was refusing to link them to climate change, to the rest of the world the links between climate, coal and the fires were obvious, as was the motive for the government's obfuscation. On 20 December, the Friday before Christmas, when Australia was the hottest place in the world, Ross Atkins of BBC News stood in front of a map showing fires all down the east coast and over much of the rest of the country. The impacts of global warming, which scientists had predicted, had arrived, he said, yet admitting this was politically controversial because fossil fuels, coal in particular, are a major export industry for Australia.

Writing in the *Atlantic* a week later, Robinson Meyer described Australia as 'caught in a climate spiral'.

> For the past few decades, the arid and affluent country of 25 million has padded out its economy—otherwise dominated by sandy beaches and a bustling service sector—by selling coal to the world. But now Australia is buckling under the conditions that its fossil fuels have helped bring about.

It is not just our reputation that is at stake. As global concern escalates about the devastating impacts of climate change, there are risks to our trade. In November 2019 the French foreign minister, Jean-Yves Le Drian, warned the Morrison government that a planned free-trade deal between Australia and the European Union must incorporate ambitious action on climate change.

The European Commission is calling for a goal of net-zero carbon emissions by 2050. At the World Economic Forum's annual meeting at Davos in 2021, its new president, Ursula von der Leyen, made clear that the EU was considering a carbon tax on imports from countries that do not support international climate goals, both to accelerate global action and to protect its own industries from a competitive disadvantage when dealing with recalcitrant global polluters. This is not yet EU policy, but it is not in Australia's long-term interests to be labelled a recalcitrant global polluter.

Australia has been cursed with a decade of poor national leadership on climate change, with our prime ministers lacking either the intellect or the courage to develop coherent policy responses to the threat. Much has been written on the sad litany of failed attempts: Rudd's squibbing of the greatest moral challenge; Gillard's bumbling over whether or not the emissions-reduction scheme was a tax; Abbott's ruthless exploitation of her blunder and the Coalition's weaponising of climate change; Turnbull's inability to face down the climate deniers in his party; the pernicious role of the Murdoch press in undermining Labor's modest efforts. The result is that we still don't have a workable energy policy.

Pushed by city Liberals who understand the urgency of the problem and fear for their seats as their electorates run out of patience, Morrison now talks of balance, which at least acknowledges that the climate is changing. But there is still a rump of deniers on the government's backbench, mainly Nationals, who resist any move to set higher targets for emissions cuts, no matter how small the increase, and want the government to invest in a coal-fired power station in Queensland, even though this makes little economic sense. Speaking in February 2020, Malcom Turnbull likened the climate-change deniers in the Liberal Party to terrorists, willing to blow the joint up rather than cede ground. He should know. As important are the climate-change minimisers: those who admit the world is warming, but say we have plenty of time to respond and worry about the economic disruption of acting too fast.

How has Australia ended up here? How has climate-change denial gained such a deadly grip on our political class?

I am a historian, so I look for explanations not just in the perfidies of the present, but in the decisions and events of the past. Social scientists talk about path dependence: the way established institutions and ways of doing things shape present actions and future possibilities. This is just a fancy way of saying that history matters, but it does shift our attention from the contingencies of events and personalities to structures and institutions, in this case to the history of Australia as a commodity-exporting nation and its political consequences. Economic history is unfashionable nowadays. Economists focus on the modelling and management of the present; historians are more interested in stories and experience, and in uncovering diversity and neglected voices. Economic history is dry and resistant to narrative. But how a country makes its living can explain a lot.

•

The story, as with so much in Australia's short European history, begins with wool, which was the mainstay of our exports until the middle 1950s. It was our good fortune that as artificial fibres began to decimate the market for wool, demand for our mineral resources was growing, especially iron ore from the Pilbara. Coal exports grew exponentially from the 1980s, to be joined in the twenty-first century by liquid natural gas. In 2018–19 Australia's top export earners were iron ore, coal and LNG, together comprising 41.8 per cent of total income.

Australia's success in exporting first wool and then minerals created an economy with a dual structure, in which the industries earning our export income produced far fewer jobs than the sectors producing goods and services for domestic consumption. For most of the twentieth century protected manufacturing for the home market was a big employer, but it was inefficient and uncompetitive by world standards. When it did start to compete in the 1980s, as Labor opened up the economy, it was too late and it is now in poor shape. The big employers are now health care and social assistance, retail, accommodation, hospitality, and education. Tourism and international students gave an export focus to the service sector, though this has been shattered by the coronavirus pandemic, in the short term at least.

The mining industry cannot be blamed directly for the weakness of Australian manufacturing, even though its success drove the dollar higher and undermined its competitiveness. The blame lies mainly with political elites of both sides of politics who waited too long to dismantle Australia's protective tariffs. Once the most recent resources boom roared into life most of our leaders gave manufacturing little thought. Climate change has turned the dependence of Australia's export income on minerals into a curse. As renewable energy sources are developed, we can continue to export iron ore, bauxite, gold and other non-fossil-fuel minerals without contributing to the rise in global temperatures. It is only coal and gas we will have to give up.

Parallel to this economic story is a political story about the successful capture of so many of our politicians by the fossil-fuel lobby, mostly on the Coalition side of politics, but Labor has not been immune. The lobby has benefited greatly from the polarised politics of the last three decades. It is a moot point when this polarisation started. Some date it to 1975, with the ill-will flowing from the

Dismissal, but I think the current period of discord began when Paul Keating was prime minister. Brilliant at invective, he sharpened up lines of division around race and Indigenous politics, and Howard transformed these into the culture wars.

When serious pressure began at the turn of the century for governments to reduce carbon emissions, many cultural warriors transformed smoothly into climate warriors. Although the issues were very different, the enemies were mostly the same, which for many politicians is what counts: environmental activists, the Labor Party, Indigenous Australians, the left generally. In the 1980s the mining industry successfully saw off the threat to its interests from the push for a veto over mining exploration and development to be included in land rights and native-title claims. The fossil-fuel lobby deliberately stoked the polarisation around Indigenous and environmental policy, fostered climate-change denialism among Australia's conservative political elites, and rewarded its political advocates with jobs. But it could not have created the climate wars so easily without the preceding culture wars.

The culture wars had little to do with economics. Howard could introduce an economic reform like the GST, and try to reform industrial relations, even as he denounced black-armband history. The climate wars are different. They are about what we export and how we produce the energy which drives our economy, and they have made it impossible for successive Coalition governments to sustain a coherent economic narrative to support reform. The past fifteen years of climate wars have, in the words of the economist Alan Kohler, 'ruined Australia's ability to conduct any kind of sensible discussion about economic policy and to achieve consensus on anything'.

The climate warriors' support for coal and gas has depended on a cascading series of arguments. The first is that the planet is not heating, so there is no need to cut fossil-fuel emissions; second, even if it is, this was not caused by humans; third, even if it is, Australia's emissions from both what we burn and what we export are so small that stopping them won't make any difference globally; fourth—the drug dealer's defence—if we don't sell the coal and gas, someone else will; fifth, the predicted environmental damage will not be that bad and doesn't warrant the economic costs. Greg Sheridan, writing in the *Australian* in mid-2014, even argued that if 'these crook environmental outcomes are going to come about anyway, would you rather confront them as rich people or as poor people?' The first, second and fifth arguments are refuted by science; the third and fourth, by both ethics and by political realism. We cannot expect other countries to allow us to escape contributing to the global effort to reduce emissions without some sort of payback.

Australia's fossil-fuel curse operates through the nexus of economic and political power, and both sides are now under pressure. The price of renewable energy has fallen faster than expected, and storage technology developed more quickly. Renewable energy is now a market disrupter with a logic of its own as the new technologies of solar, wind, electric vehicles and lithium-ion batteries disrupt global energy and transport markets. This, says Tim Buckley from the Institute for Energy Economics and Financial Analysis, is 'why we've seen ten coal-plant closures in the last ten years in Australia. New coal plant builds are not economically viable nor bankable.' Gas too is under threat from renewables. Building the expensive infrastructure needed to extract gas is a long-term investment and future returns are looking uncertain.

Capital is deserting fossil fuels, in part because renewables are threatening future returns, but also because of shareholder and customer campaigns for financial organisations like banks and superannuation funds to divest from fossil fuels. Adani has so far been unable to find a single bank willing to fund its Carmichael coal mine in Queensland's Galilee Basin, and three of Australia's big four banks have pledged to stop lending to thermal coal projects. In February 2020 BlackRock, the world's largest fund manager, announced that it was 'putting climate change at the centre of its investment strategy' and offloading its thermal coal shares. Whether or not it was doing this for environmental reasons or just for risk management, the effect is the same.

While our federal government continues to go slow on emissions reduction, Australia risks international action against carbon-intensive economies. Robert Gottliebsen, who writes a business column in the *Australian* and is by no means a green leftie, warned in February 2020 that in his judgement carbon-based tariffs are ahead: 'Business models in most industries are set to change, driven by three forces: government regulation, community demand and, perhaps most important of all, the allocation of capital away from carbon-based companies.' Even Australia's very own Vicar of Bray, the journalist Paul Kelly, who is never far from the orthodoxies of the powerful, observed in the same month that one of the Morrison government's problems with climate change is the risk of being boycotted by global capital and marginalised.

Australia's fossil-fuel industry is also under pressure from community activism. Since 2010 an alliance of local environmental, community and farming groups calling itself Lock the Gate has been opposing coal and coal-seam gas developments, mainly in New South Wales and Queensland but also in the other states and the Northern Territory. Its mission is 'to protect Australia's natural, cultural and agricultural resources from inappropriate mining and to educate and empower all Australians to demand sustainable solutions to food and energy production'. It calls on land owners to 'lock the gate' to prevent access to their land by gas companies and to refuse to negotiate the sale of their properties to coal companies.

'Lock the Gate' is a challenge to coal mining's social licence from the heart of Australia's farming country: Queensland's Darling Downs, New South Wales' Liverpool Plains, Victoria's Gippsland. These are David and Goliath contests, with small producers tackling the corporate giants, but as a new political formation, the coalition of farmers and environmentalists has been remarkably successful. Community protests have succeeded in having licences withdrawn or abandoned, and in forcing more stringent reviews. Except for Queensland, the states and territories have imposed restrictions on coal-seam gas exploration and development, although some, like the Northern Territory's moratorium on fracking, have proved to be temporary.

Also driving capital's desertion of fossil fuels is the attraction of renewables as an investment. At present in Australia this is being stalled by uncertainty over the Coalition's energy policy, but its potential is starting to be recognised more widely. In 2019 Ross Garnaut, who authored the 2008 Climate Change Review for the Rudd federal government, published *Superpower: Australia's Low-Carbon Opportunity*. In this book he argues that Australia can become a renewable-energy superpower. Our climate gives us a natural advantage in the production of renewable energy. With the cheapest energy in the world, minerals and food can be processed here rather than shipped off raw to China and then re-imported. Australia could expand its production of steel (using renewable energy to make hydrogen), aluminium, silicon and ammonia. These would be located close to the sources of the minerals in regional Australia, and could easily replace the relatively few jobs lost in mining fossil fuels.

It would also reduce transport costs. Australia would reinvigorate employment-rich manufacturing and gain new export industries.

It's a brilliant strategy, giving Australia a new source of export income to replace that lost from fossil fuels, reviving manufacturing and providing employment in the regions. What Garnaut shows is that action on climate change need not come at the cost to the economy, but instead can provide enormous economic opportunities. The competing goods of the economy and environment, a mainstay of arguments against environmental protection, need compete no longer.

PART V

Writing

1 The Bureaucratisation of Writing

Why So Few Academics Are Public Intellectuals

Meanjin, *volume 50, number 4, 1991.*

> A writer must stand on the rock of herself and her judgement or be swept away by the tide or sink in the quaking earth: there must be an inviolate place where the choices and decisions, however imperfect, are the writer's own, where the decisions must be as individual and solitary as birth or death.
>
> **—Janet Frame, *The Envoy from Mirror City***

> Professors Woods, Percy and Hocking are moderately talented and enterprising young men with whom philosophy is merely a means of getting on in the world...I do not respect them; I will not co-operate with them; and I am happy to be in a position now to wipe out the stigma of being even nominally one of their 'colleagues'.
>
> **—Professor E. B. Holt, resigning from Harvard University in 1918 (cited in Russell Jacoby, *The Last Intellectuals*)**

There are two necessary characteristics of a public intellectual: that the person's work is engaged with substantive social questions, and that the person actively attempts to communicate with a public. The general question that this essay addresses is why so few academics in the humanities and the social sciences are public intellectuals; why, for the most part, their work neither engages with substantive social issues nor reaches out to the public.[1]

Books, pamphlets, essays and articles are the most important means of communication between intellectuals and their public, even when, as today, they are supplemented by various forms of audiovisual communication. A public intellectual must write well, and this very few academics seem able to do. In *The Last Intellectuals* (1987) Russell Jacoby argues that, in America at least, academics are failing to provide the public with challenging, readable books on matters of broad public interest. The cause of this failure, as he sees it, is in the transformation of the intellectuals of the first half of this century, who made a living from their writing, into the salaried academics of today. Although Australia has never had many self-supporting public intellectuals, and probably has more people writing for an informed Australian public than ever before, Jacoby provides a devastating critique of the quality of most writing produced by academics in the humanities and the social sciences, one that I think is applicable to much of the writing done by Australian academics.[2]

That few Australian academics are good writers is a claim some readers may think needs supporting. May I suggest to any with such doubts that they spend some time reading through any Australian academic journal—*Australian Historical Studies*, say, or the *Australian and New Zealand Journal of Sociology*; or perhaps that they read a sample of recent books published by academics; or that they try to name twenty Australian academics who are important writers. They may even be able to name twenty, but when one remembers the thousands of people employed in tertiary institutions in the humanities and social sciences, part of whose job is to write, twenty is not very many.

The first answer to the question of why so few academics are public intellectuals is that very few academics can write in ways that engage an audience outside their discipline. In Australia there are other possible answers, particularly in the difficulties posed for the formation of an Australian public by the lingering effects of the colonial cringe, and in a pragmatic immigrant society's lack of interest in ideas; but such explanations are outside the scope of this essay.[3] My initial question has thus become: why are so few academics in the humanities and social sciences good writers? Or, conversely, why are so many of them such bad or indifferent writers?

The preconditions for good discursive prose are relatively simple: a fully imagined audience, a sense of urgency, something interesting and important to say. The biggest problem with most academic writing is achieving the first two. Many academics start out with important and interesting things to say, but very few feel compelled to say them in ways that engage an audience outside their discipline; and in the end this corrodes the importance of what they have to say.

The lack of urgency and the failure to imagine an audience are consequences of the role writing has come to play in the modern bureaucratic university. The organisational needs of a bureaucratic university interact with an empiricist understanding of truth to deflect the academic writer from imagining an audience and exploring the potential of language to shape reality and persuade others. Academics so rarely write convincing prose because the bureaucratic organisation of their working lives and the organisation of knowledge into disciplines make it very difficult for them to take writing seriously. To do so is to go against the grain of the job.

In describing the modern university as bureaucratic I am highlighting certain features of its organisation at the expense of others. The other major tradition that informs the position of university academics is that of collegiate co-operation. At present this is under attack from all sides—from staff associations' preoccupation with equity of job conditions and secure career paths; from governments' efforts to make academics more accountable to the society that pays them; from university administrators' ambitions to streamline universities' management systems. These various attacks are all, in different ways, attempts to bring the contemporary university into line with bureaucratic models of organisation.

The Bureaucratisation of Working Life

Max Weber described modernisation as a process of increasing rationalisation, and saw bureaucracy as one of the main agents of this rationalisation.[4] Through bureaucracies, various areas of social life could be made subject to rational and impersonal criteria. In their modern form bureaucracies developed to ensure the objective, impartial and equal treatment of individuals in their dealings with the state. They are opposed to the making of decisions on the basis of personal criteria—like considerations of friendship or kinship, or pecuniary reward. Ideally, the consideration of an individual's case is governed only by the application of rules and regulations worked out in advance of the case; ideally, every official will deal with the case in the same way.

The employment conditions of the bureaucratic official are designed to ensure that the bureaucratic organisation carries out its functions with impartiality and rationality. Impartiality and rationality must also govern the organisation's selection of its personnel—with procedures laid down for selection, appointment and promotion. Central features of bureaucratic office, such as security of tenure and ensured salary and pension, are there to protect officials from the temptation to use their authority to ensure their livelihood—by taking a percentage of the money collected, for instance, or by receiving bribes. They also ensure that the official will deal with all parties equally according to the regulations, and will feel secure in rejecting pressures for preferment from the rich and famous.

Such a form of employment is now widespread among white-collar workers, including tenured university academics. To qualify to become an academic requires long and rigorous training; people are appointed to academic positions by a senior authority and ideally they receive this position for life; promotion is orderly and governed by regulation. Like the tenure of a government official, academic tenure is designed to protect academics from personal pressures that might deflect them from the proper performance of their duties—in this case, the pursuit of truth and understanding and the dissemination of knowledge.

Being an official in a bureaucracy has profound effects on the writing of academics in the humanities and social sciences, for it pushes their writing away from its proper goal—the contribution to culture and society—towards the need of the bureaucratic university for objective and impartial criteria on which to select and promote its personnel.

The PhD, a long piece of writing of up to one hundred thousand words, is now the standard qualification for serious consideration for an academic appointment; and subsequent movement through the ranks depends on published writing far more than on the quality of one's teaching. In so far as universities are bureaucracies, procedures must be designed to judge this writing in ways that seem impartial. The number of pages published is the most obvious criterion, supplemented by the place in which the writing is published. For purposes of selection and promotion, the best places are refereed journals, international if possible. Books are treated uneasily. Perhaps the book is just popularising someone else's work? Perhaps it's too light, or derivative, or journalistic? The publisher may be used as a guide—and here a book published by a moribund Australian branch of a prestigious overseas university press is likely to fare better than a book published by a vigorous locally owned publisher. Articles in non-academic journals like *Meanjin* or the *Age Monthly Review* can be very difficult to deal with, though in the area of Australian literature they may be acceptable. These journals are not refereed, and acceptance depends on the decision of a single editor rather than the judgement of a number of peers in the field. Newspaper and radio reviews are not relevant at all—mere journalism. The rule of thumb seems to be that the more widely a piece of writing is read, the less use it is on an academic publications list. That a person is interested in reaching out to a public invites suspicion—here perhaps is the populariser rather than the dedicated scholar.[5] Recent surveys of promotions and tenure committees in the United States found that both brilliance and public contribution were viewed with suspicion as signs of a non-professional bent.[6] In my experience, rules are more often used to argue dullards up than to keep the obviously talented down, reflecting perhaps a difference between the two cultures.

It is important in a bureaucracy that the promotions system operate fairly. The expectation of the impartial administration of incentives is part of the basis of bureaucratic organisation and of individuals' performance within such organisations. The system of incentives and rewards thus needs to be public and to be administered in such a way that people can be confident that if they do what is expected they will be appropriately rewarded, however lacking in talent they may be. Because of its resistance to routinisation, talent is viewed with suspicion. The pressure is always towards the devising and refining of rules to decide individual cases and away from areas of ambiguity where individual judgement is needed.

The Bureaucratisation of Knowledge

The bureaucratic university's use of writing to select and appoint its personnel is greatly assisted by the bureaucratisation of knowledge in the modern university through its organisation into disciplines. There is here a congruence between the university's organisational needs and its way of perceiving its tasks.

Australian universities are divided into departments and schools: English, History, Political Science, French, Sociology and so on. There is some variation, but, whatever the names, the view of knowledge implied by the formal organisation is that it divides reasonably easily into disciplines. Disciplines are organised across universities through their various professional associations, and the professional academic's career ideally takes place within these disciplines. One is trained as a historian, sociologist or literary critic, keeps up with the literature in one's field, attends and give papers at appropriate disciplinary conferences, and writes for the refereed journals run by these disciplinary organisations. At various points—when one is competing for scholarships, applying for grants, offering papers to conferences, submitting papers to journals—one's peers in the discipline judge one's work in terms of its contribution to the discipline; and one's position within an employing institution will partly depend on one's standing within the discipline's professional organisation.[7]

The discipline is conceptualised in terms of shared subject matter, shared methods and techniques, shared conventions of writing and shared canonical texts. The picture is of scholars working together to build knowledge in their area, of work parcelled out, and of limits to what one needs to know in order to be effective. Disciplines offer some reassurance that, in the face of the overwhelming possibilities of human knowledge, a small field can be distinguished as being all that one really needs to know.

But knowledge, in the humanities at least, does not operate according to the model of organisation embodied in disciplinary associations and university departments. The humanities are constituted through their joint endeavour—the interpretation of human culture. Their primary activities, reading and writing, are common; and despite passing fashions of technical jargon, they share a common language. Developments in one affect the others. Theoretical arguments about human nature, culture, society, language or interpretation will affect work across the humanities. For example, the waves of theoretical argument emanating from France since the 1960s and associated with people like Lévi-Strauss, Foucault and Derrida have transformed thinking across the humanities, particularly among younger scholars, who often have far more in common with each other than they do with their older colleagues within the same discipline. Feminism is another example of a shift in thinking to which disciplinary boundaries are irrelevant. I would argue that the same is true of knowledge in most areas of the social sciences, but this is a more controversial claim that would be resisted by those still under the sway of positivist models of knowledge.

The power of bureaucratisation can be seen, though, in the organisational responses to these theoretical challenges to disciplinary boundaries. Even when the theoretical challenges are such as to raise profound doubts about the very idea of disciplines, the scholars influenced by them become absorbed in fighting for their acceptability within the academy—arguing for new disciplines, forming new disciplinary associations. Whatever radical impetus the new ideas might have had is easily lost in the business of constructing the organisations necessary to give legitimacy to new academic career paths—conferences, journals, networks of referees.

In the 1960s the New Left challenged the entrenched academic disciplines with the theoretical weapons of Marxism. Now most disciplines in America have their dissenting journals—*Dialectical Anthropology, New Political Science, Radical History Review*. But, as Russell Jacoby points out, an influx of Marxists into the academy has not transformed American universities and has had little impact on American culture. The threat of unemployment has kept one-time radicals busy ensuring their futures; academic politics has replaced the broad public politics of their youth.[8] Similar fates threaten other intellectual challenges, where the impetus for change, though beginning outside the academy, becomes absorbed by the academy's organisational imperatives. Feminism, Australian studies and cultural studies are more recent examples of intellectual challenges from outside the academy that are in danger of becoming the basis of new careers and so losing their engagement with broad social and political goals. Bronwen Levy has remarked on the recent trend for the term 'gender studies' to replace 'women's studies', substituting a neutral term for one that has obvious connections to a political movement.[9]

Truth and Objectivity

The bureaucratisation of writing and of knowledge within the academy is underpinned by the hegemony of empiricist and positivist models of truth as the goal of academic inquiry. This, rather than the need to have a means of selecting personnel, is what legitimises disciplines' authority over the work of their members. Particular disciplines are seen as particular ways of approaching the truth, particular ways of ensuring objectivity. Commitment to truth and objectivity has a deep affinity with bureaucracy's ideal of the impartial application of rules and regulations. Both seek the ideal of a space in which any observer/officer will see/do the same things.

Both believe that if the method/rules can be got right, truth/justice will be guaranteed. Both are hostile to subjectivity's resistance to routinisation. The ideal of objectivity is embodied in the notion of research that the humanities and social sciences have taken over from science. This, it must be stressed, may have very little to do with the way contemporary scientists actually operate; it is about the way a particular understanding of science is wielded against more subjective, language-based ways of knowing in struggles within the academy over the legitimacy of different forms of knowledge.

Scientists do their research, and then write it up. The writing is seen as ancillary, after the fact, and in no way constitutive of the research itself. The adoption of this way of talking about research masks the centrality of language and writing to the humanities and social sciences. The fiction is of reality apprehended prior to language and of the act of writing as a simple one of reporting on or describing that apprehension. The true work is thus seen as collecting the facts, the arguments, the findings, and the writing is simply the report, written in the plain, impersonal style characteristic of reports, as if the author were absent. The role of language in shaping and probing reality is denied and all questions about style are avoided.

The humanities do not seek truth but understanding, and while the concern with objectivity is an important value, it can easily become an end in itself, replacing the true end of work in the humanities, which is its contribution to living human culture, to a society's sense of a cultural context and to the understanding of its possibilities for freedom. Without that ultimate end, and without the engagement with a public it implies, the work becomes meaningless. I would argue that the same is true of the social sciences, but again this is to invoke a very complex and bitterly fought battle over the nature of social knowledge.

In a recent essay on Australian history writing, Stuart Macintyre points to the connection between commitment to objectivity and the loss of any sense of a public among Australian historians.[10] Whereas the earliest writers of history in Australia were men of affairs, writing the history of the recent past to argue for the policies that should direct the present, present historians are academics concerned with thorough research and documentation, exactness in references, and sound, unbiased interpretation. The writing of Australian history is now professionalised, and while there have been many gains, there have also been costs. Ideally, professional historians are detached from particular social groups and interests that might affect the objectivity and impartiality of their interpretations. But in detaching themselves from contemporary social goals and interests, they have detached themselves from the public.

The picture Macintyre draws of contemporary writing in Australian history, particularly by younger historians, is gloomy indeed. He describes the way university historians have lost the ability to instruct or entertain a reading public, the way the huge increase in the volume of research has stifled historians' confidence in bold hypotheses, the development of narrow specialisations and closed forms of communication, and the lack of conviction among many historians that they have anything to say. Macintyre points to Geoffrey Blainey and Manning Clark as exceptions among contemporary Australian historians. Both are conscious stylists, addressing themselves directly to the reader without the encumbrance of weighty scholarly apparatus; and both are convinced they have something to say. But, he says, their colleagues view their popularity with suspicion. 'Similarly, the flight from academia of Humphrey McQueen, among the most gifted of the next generation, is symptomatic of professional constraints.'

The processes Macintyre describes in history can be seen in other disciplines. Few of the young academics working in philosophy, political science, literary criticism or sociology write for a public, even though they are all working in intellectual traditions that once had close and vital connections with public life.

This is not to say that it is impossible for academics to write well. Many of our most important books are written by people who at some time during their lives have occupied academic positions. One thinks of Bernard Smith, Hugh Stretton, Germaine Greer, Peter Singer and Henry Reynolds. Some academics are able to develop and retain their sense of commitment to a general culture against the pressures of bureaucratisation; some academics are able to retain bases of identification and experience outside their academic careers. Important for the ability to do this is a deep commitment to extra-academic goals and values—to political or religious beliefs, for example, that give meaning to the writer's vocation beyond the service of a career and that give a basis from which to develop something to say.

To return, then, to the two absences in academic writing that I am trying to explain—the absence of a fully imagined audience and the absence of any sense of urgency. These two absences can be understood if we look at the institutional and discursive practices in which the writing of academics is embedded. The bureaucratic university combines with the organisation of knowledge into disciplines to disconnect writers both from a public and from their own subjectivity, the two traditional sources of energy for good writing and good books.

Academic writers in the humanities and social sciences so often fail to imagine a public audience because they are never trained to think of one. University academics do not write to persuade but to impress and gain approval within a hierarchy. They are trained to write for approval. From their student essays to their PhD theses, they are writing work to be submitted for examination. Even when they have received their PhDs, they must submit work to refereed journals in order to accumulate the publications necessary for appointment and then to accumulate the publications necessary for promotion, and so on. At every point their writing is subject to external criteria—approved topics, accepted methods of research and styles of writing, the norms and conventions of the discipline.

Never in this process need academics think about an audience outside the hierarchy of authority within the discipline; never need they think about the relationship of their work to a public: as I have indicated, to think about this relationship may very well jeopardise their career. The use of technical language or jargon, which is so characteristic of academic prose, has its origins here—in the need to indicate to higher authorities that one has mastered the current literature. Once, such technical language was motivated by the positivist dream of a language that would describe rather than constitute reality. That dream has long since faded, but the technical language persists and proliferates.

The institutionalisation of disciplines within the bureaucratic university and the continuing power of positivist models of knowledge also disconnect academic writers from their own life and subjectivity as a source for their writing. This is not to argue for the primacy of autobiographical writing, but for a deep connection between one's intellectual preoccupations and one's human experience. Academic writing unfolds within the concerns of the institution, the discipline and the career, rather than the lived life. To follow one's intellectual life where it leads is almost impossible within the academy; it can blur one's disciplinary identification to the point that one may no longer be recognisable by the institution. And the awareness of mortality, which can be so important to a writer, has no place within a bureaucracy. Bureaucracies map the futures of their personnel in terms that serve the organisation's needs to have trained and willing officers available at all times—its needs to recruit, to provide incentives and to maximise its investment in its human resources. As the organisation must assume its own immortality to be able to operate effectively, so the mortality of its members fades. Death does not continually illuminate the bureaucrat's working life, but has its proper place, outside the institution, in retirement.

Academic writing is writing that never leaves school, that never grows beyond the judging, persecuting eye of the parent to enter into a dialogue with the society and culture of its time, as an adult among other adults, with all the acceptance of mutual imperfection which this implies. Always seeking the approval of a higher authority, the academic writer endlessly defers responsibility. I write in this way because I have to pass the exam, to get my PhD, to get a job, to get tenure, to get promotion. I write like this because it is what *they* want. I don't write in the way best suited to what I have to say, or to win people to a cause, to change the world, to humiliate my opponents, to help people understand their lives, to please my readers, or even to please myself. Never is the academic writer in that inviolate place described by Janet Frame where the choices and decisions, however imperfect, must be the writer's own, as individual and solitary as life and death.

1   This makes the class of public intellectuals much smaller than the class of intellectuals, according to the very broad definition of intellectuals in James Walter and Brian Head's *Intellectual Movements and Australian Society*, Oxford University Press, Melbourne, 1988. They define intellectuals in societies like Australia as 'all those who engage in the production, transmission and adaptation of ideas about society and culture'.

2   Russell Jacoby, *The Last Intellectuals: American Culture in the Age of Academe*, Basic Books, New York, 1987.

3   See particularly Walter and Head for some discussion of these questions.

4   H. H. Gerth & C. Wright Mills (eds), *From Max Weber: Essays in Sociology*, Routledge & Kegan Paul, London, 1948, chapter 8.

5   These remarks are based on my observations while a member of the University of Melbourne's Promotions Committee in 1984, 1985 and 1986, and my membership of numerous selection committees.

6   Jacoby, p. 144.

7   For a much more thorough account of the operations of academic disciplines see Harry Redner, *The Ends of Science: An Essay in Academic Authority*, Westview Press, Boulder, 1987, pp. 116 ff.

8   Jacoby, chapter 5.

9   Bronwen Levy, 'Writers and Critics: Recasting an Opposition', *Arena*, 5, 1988, pp. 75–76.

10 Stuart Macintyre, 'The Writing of Australian History', in *Australians: A Guide to Sources*, Fairfax, Syme & Weldon, Sydney, 1987, pp. 1–29.

2 On Writing Robert Menzies' Forgotten People

Robert Menzies' Forgotten People was published in 1992, almost a decade after the Meanjin essay of the same title. This is the introduction to the 2007 edition, published by Melbourne University Press.

The origins of this book are the 1980s when Menzies had been dead less than ten years and I was young. Hated, loved, revered, scorned, he was a cultural touchstone for Australians to organise their memories, communicate their political allegiances and mark their generational differences. A political celebrity, for some he had borrowed glamour from his much-loved royal family, and for others had done deeds of such political mendacity that Australia was able to feel itself part of the twentieth century's moral and political struggles.

When the book was published in 1992 and I was doing the media rounds as a very new author, interviewers from Bert Newton to Phillip Adams were far more interested in telling stories about their encounters with the great man than in anything I had to say. He was always just Menzies, the name heavy with the jowls of masculine power but also familiar and homely. Menzies might have been the embodiment of political power, but he was ours, and in having spoken with him, seen him at a rally or school speech night, known his driver or an ex-neighbour, one could feel part of Australia's history.

The manuscript I delivered to Hilary McPhee in 1991 had an introductory chapter, describing the book's theoretical context and methods, which did not survive her editorial judgement about popular readability. In my work as editor of *Meanjin* I had become adept at ridding academic articles of their theoretical superstructures, and I followed her advice, though with some regret. I would have liked to have shown readers how I developed my interpretations and arguments, so that they could better judge what I had done with the evidence. I left clues to my theoretical sources in the choice of words, in expository half sentences and in endnotes, but if anyone noticed the clues at the time, no one will now. Books are part of conversations, and many of the conversations this book was having are long over.

The book began with an article I published in *Meanjin* in 1984. In 1980 I was teaching a course on Australian political parties at the University of Melbourne and wanted to give the students something to read on Menzies that was neither hagiography nor polemic. Whatever one thought about him, he was Australia's longest serving prime minister and young politics students needed to know about him. Finding nothing, I turned to the archive, where I found a pamphlet, 'The Forgotten People', on shiny paper with black, deeply indented type you could run your finger across. It was a speech Menzies had written for radio in May 1942, when he was on the backbench of a demoralised Opposition. In 1941 he had resigned as prime minister and shortly after the government had fallen. John Curtin became prime minister and led the country for the remainder of the war. I was bowled over by the speech and started having ideas about it, lots of them. In fact, I have been having ideas about that speech ever since, and have returned to it again and again as a lever to prise apart the interconnections between political ideas and social experience in twentieth-century Australia. Here was Menzies in his prime, pitting the language of the home against the impersonal world of work and organised labour. Here was Menzies talking about class even as he denied its relevance, citing Robbie Burns, and speaking in the prose and rhetorical forms of countless Sunday sermons. Here, it seemed, was Menzies in his own words.

But of course they weren't just his own words. They were also the words he shared with the people to whom he spoke, words and ideas from contested political traditions, parts of arguments about what was important in life and what politics could and should do about it. I have come to see Menzies' speech to 'The Forgotten People' as a crystallisation of a tradition of Australian thinking which rejects the relevance of class to the way people understand themselves and others in favour of a commonsense moral individualism where a person's worth is in their character rather than their job or their bank account. The roots of this tradition are in nineteenth-century colonial liberalism's faith in the opportunities the new land of Australia offered to ordinary men and women to make something of themselves, free from the Old World's strictures of status and deference. Its arguments could still be heard at the end of the twentieth century, when ordinary men and women talked about class.

When I first read the speech, class was the big question for scholars of politics and history. The strength and early success of the Australian labour movement, its bitter schisms and its spectacular failures, were a magnet for scholars who interpreted Australian history in terms of an underlying class conflict in which the ruling class, or at least ruling class interests, always came out trumps. There were more and less sophisticated versions of this, but the majority of Australians who voted for non-Labor federal governments far more often than for

Labor were always a problem. Also a problem was that the Liberal Party repeatedly denied that it was a class-based party. It was easy to dismiss this as hypocrisy, but to do so was to fail to engage with the party's self-understandings and political traditions, and so to be locked into a lopsided understanding of Australia's political history, which left the motivations of some of its key actors obscure.

The doyen of Australian class analysis was Raewyn Connell. Her and Terry Irving's *Class Structure in Australian History* was published in 1980. Ambitious and enormously influential, the book put forward a chronological framework for the analysis of social power in Australia which took antagonistic class relations as fundamental. The protagonists of this conflict were the working class and the ruling class. The book's avowed aim was to help people to a clear understanding of the pattern of class relations that shaped their lives so that they would be better able to change them. 'The Forgotten People' was included in a section on 'The Political Crisis of the Ruling Class', and the authors pointed to the skilful identification the speech made between the social customs and prejudices of the people addressed and the strategic interests of capitalism.[1] A painting by Noel Counihan called 'Election Eve' adorned the book's cover. Menzies leers from the gloomy canvas across a podium draped with a Union Jack, rubbing his hands together at having conned yet another victory out of a duped and anxious electorate.

Class was indeed able to explain a great deal about Australian politics, in particular the links of the major parties to different economic interests and producer groups, their characteristic stances towards industrial relations, patterns of financial support, and the power of class identification in mobilising Labor's working-class vote. It was less able to explain the basis of the Liberal Party's electoral support, why time and again the majority of Australians voted it into government. In my lectures I would quote the judgement of the Labor historian Fin Crisp that the Liberal and Country Party are 'first and foremost the owners and controllers of private productive and commercial capital, urban and rural'.[2] It was the orthodox class-based reading of the time, but it didn't quite ring true to me. I would scoot over it, fingers crossed that no student would ask me to explain. 'Owners and controllers of private productive and commercial capital, urban and rural' seemed too grand and powerful a description for the Liberal Party supporters I knew: the fathers of people I was at school with in Nunawading, clerks and accountants of modest means and their home-making wives; the good women my mother worked with at the YWCA, who lived out the importance of service; the men who turned up to working bees at the church and the school; my paternal grandparents on a dairy farm who had little time for Labor; my returned-servicemen uncles and my respectable, genteelly poor maternal grandmother; and so on. These were the salaried officers and white-collar workers, the small-business people and the farmers Menzies had addressed in 'The Forgotten People'. Did they know they were serving the strategic interests of capital? And even if they were, might not they also be serving some interests of their own?

The big problem for the standard class-based analysis of Australian politics and history was the middle class, which provided the core of the Liberal Party's electoral support. Australian historiography on the middle class was thin in the 1980s.[3] When the middle class did appear in historical narratives it was not generally the major villain, for after all most of the middle class were ordinary people of modest means; but they entered from stage right as the dupes of powerful interests which played on their fears to frustrate Labor's progressive political goals. The mobilisations around honest finance in the Depression, against Chifley's plans to nationalise the banks, in the moral panic about the excesses of the Whitlam government, were all interpreted in this way. Part of the problem historians had with the middle class was the failure to resolve whether it was an analytical term in a schema of social classification or a term of self-description. I was interested in it as a term of self-description, what people meant when they described themselves as middle class, and what it said to them about the basis of their political identification. I still am.

In 1980, though, the support of the middle class for the Liberals was something to be explained rather than understood, as was the support of the substantial number of working-class people who voted Liberal. Class analysis provided answers, with concepts like ideology, false consciousness and hegemony to explain how the ruling ideas of any time served the interests of the ruling class, and how alternative, oppositional understandings were marginalised and suppressed. Such arguments were powerfully attractive to intellectuals and political activists, who were able to believe they knew better than the subjects they were studying; but they were of limited use to historians intent on understanding how people thought and felt.

If Marxism and class analysis created the problem of how to interpret middle-class politics, developments in Marxism also provided the solution. The translation into English of the writings of the young Marx in the 1960s had led to a resurgence of interest in Marxism, and in particular in the nature and role of ideology.[4] No longer was this to be understand, as it had been in classical Marxism, as a simple reflection of the economic base of society. Rather, ideology was granted a relative autonomy and reconceptualised through the ideas of culture and language as a complex system of meaning. The standby excuse of false consciousness for the failure of the workers' revolution was rejected. Ideology was not illusion, as in Marx's infamous dismissal of religion as the opiate of the people. Rather, people's ideas, beliefs and commonsense understandings were seen as attempts to make sense of real experience. For me, this was summed up by Louis Althusser's dictum 'Ideology is the partial representation of real experience.' This provided me with a way of thinking about both the distortions and partiality in all systems of representation, and their grounding in people's everyday lived experience. It gave me a way to think about how the Australian middle class understood themselves.

Successive theoretical waves broke across the humanities and social sciences from the middle of the 1960s to create an extraordinarily productive and exciting couple of decades: structuralism, semiotics, structural Marxism, discourse theory, Lacanian psychoanalysis, cultural studies, deconstruction, postcolonialism, ending in the melee of theories that get bundled together as postmodernism. New writers, ideas, concepts and movements came at a bewildering rate and it was easy for young scholars to lose their footing. Some undoubtedly did, but the collective result was a much-expanded and greatly enriched repertoire of ideas and concepts for understanding human experience.

The axiom on which all these theories were based was the relative autonomy of language, and by extension of other systems of representation. Language was conceptualised not as a transparent medium for the description of the world nor the expression of thought, but as a dense, complex reality constructing the world and the self in ways which neither could resist. Rival theories put forward different ideas about how to explain this autonomy of language, and how to understand its effects. Different interpretive techniques were developed. Different balances were struck between the play and fictiveness of language, the resistance of reality and the imperatives of power and control. How to respond to so many new ideas and theories? Promiscuous eclecticism and rigorous discipleship were the two poles. I tended to the former, though decided early on that my interest was in the usefulness of theories for the tasks of interpreting the world, rather than in the arguments among the theories.[5]

My first go at this was my PhD on the Austrian fin-de-siècle poet Hugo von Hofmannsthal. I did this thesis in a Politics Department in the second half of the 1970s under the indulgent eye of Alan Davies, and I shudder now at my headstrong commitment to following my nose and his carelessness with my job prospects. Like *Robert Menzies' Forgotten People*, the thesis began with a short text, stumbled on accidentally when I was reading Alan Janik and Stephen Toulmin's *Wittgenstein's Vienna*.[6] The text was 'The Letter of Lord Chandos' (*'Ein Brief'*), a fictive letter from a young poet to his patron in which he describes the breakdown and slow rebuilding of his relationship with a language which had once flowed from him so easily into lyric poetry that he felt that he and language were one. The text had been studied before, as an expression of the crisis of meaning in fin-de-siècle Vienna, and it was clearly autobiographical. As a precocious sixteen-year-old poet, the young Hofmannsthal had been the darling of the Viennese coffee houses, only to find his gift and his words desert him in his early twenties. The Chandos Letter was his first published piece after this breakdown, and marked his move from the intense subjectivity of lyric poetry into more public and contained forms of writing. He never wrote lyric poetry again, and soon after began the collaboration with Richard Strauss through which his poetry has lived on. The thesis used psychoanalysis to interpret the crisis and its resolution, mainly the work of Melanie Klein and British Object Relations theory, but also the ideas of Jacques Lacan. It proceeded through detailed, close readings of selected texts by Hofmannsthal, returning again and again to the central *Brief* as the pivotal text in a story of profound psychological and literary transformation.

I now see that my PhD on Hofmannsthal was a rehearsal for my work on Menzies. Both take a central text and use it as a pivot, both develop their arguments from detailed close readings, and both ponder the interplay between private meanings and the publicly available forms for their expression. I didn't realise this until after the book on Menzies was published, and it was, I must say, a great relief. The five years of my twenties spent poring over German and reading a huge amount of difficult theory redeemed what might otherwise have been a huge waste of time.

My PhD on Hofmannsthal was also a rehearsal in the use of psychoanalytic theory to interpret the interplay between language and lived experience. It being about literary rather than political language, the balance between personal and public meanings was different, but all language has an inner and an outer face to which biographical interpretation must attend. The task I set myself in writing *Robert Menzies' Forgotten People* was to develop interpretations adequate to both faces of the language. Work on ideology, discourse and rhetoric guided my readings of the public face and psychoanalysis the private. But how to understand the way they interacted? I was not interested here in the labour of theoretical reconciliation but in the challenge of interpretive practice. I came to understand the task as locating the points of interconnection between the dominant public forms of Australian Liberal ideology in which Menzies was so skilled and deep themes in his own psychology and biography.

Menzies and Howard

In 1994 the Liberal Party celebrated the fiftieth anniversary of its formation, which coincided neatly with the centenary of Menzies' birth: 1894, 1944, 1994. There was a five-part ABC documentary; a couple of conferences; an exhibition at the National Library of Australia, which holds the papers of both Menzies and the federal Liberal Party; and much media commentary.[7] The celebrations were edgy, because the Liberals had just suffered their fifth successive electoral defeat, in which Paul Keating wiped the floor with the hapless John Hewson. Perhaps the past would hold clues to help the party regain its electoral ascendancy.

Prominently displayed at the National Library's commemorative exhibition was a bronze bust of Menzies by Victor Greenhalgh, captioned 'Founding Spirit'. This bust, visitors were told, normally stands in the meeting room of the Federal Council of the Liberal Party and occasionally travels to meetings of the council held outside Canberra. We heard time and again in the media that 'Menzies had founded the Liberal Party'. Gerard Henderson even called his book on the Liberal Party *Menzies' Child*.[8] To be sure Menzies had a big hand in it, but as the historian Ian Hancock has argued, it defies common sense to think that one man could found a party.[9] Menzies may have been the new party's most prominent spokesman, but its successful formation out of a score or so of other organisations depended on a huge amount of organisational work by many people. Common sense, however, is no match for people's need for heroes, and the identities of these organisations and people have all but disappeared from Liberal Party memory. Only Menzies remains. The myth of the party's origins had thus become the myth of leadership, the myth of the great man who can gather into himself the competing tendencies of the historical moment to rise above all other contenders for power, quietening their ambition with his incontestable superiority.

In 1993 Allan Martin published the first volume of his biography of Menzies, which took the story up to 1943; and in 1999, the second, which dealt with the revival of the Australian Liberals and the long period of the Menzies' governments.[10] These were landmark publications, embraced with admiration and gratitude not only by the Liberal Party but by journalists, historians and the general readers for whom Martin wrote. Martin wrote in full awareness of a fact of which I was careless: that many of his readers had no memory of Menzies as an active politician and only the sketchiest of knowledge of Australia's political history. So he wrote carefully researched and contextualised history, on which one could rely absolutely for a factually based account of Menzies' life and political career. I wrote as if I were having arguments with people who already knew the facts and would be impressed by my arabesques. I admire enormously Martin's achievements, and I could never have done it. Even so, I think he fudges some of the most difficult questions about Menzies: his struggle with ambition in the first twenty years of his political career and its often transparent rationalisations, and his shifting, ambivalent positionings on civil liberties during the Cold War. And to say, as Martin does in the introduction to the first volume, that he will not formally deal with Aboriginal, women's or environmental history, because they were not 'on the agenda' in Menzies' time, seems to me to be wilfully naive. Aborigines, women and the land were all in the world in which Menzies grew up and worked, and the processes which kept them from 'the agenda' surely warrant the historian's attention.

Pondering the limitations of Martin's biography of Henry Parkes, and his turning away from the 'murk of the personal' when earlier in his intellectual life he had been more daring, Inga Clendinnen argues that, in the end, with his self-effacing moral temperament, he could do no other.[11] In the case of the Menzies biography I think there was another reason. The project was initiated by Menzies' family and they made various family papers available. Menzies' daughter, Heather Henderson, and her husband, Peter, read the manuscript. Martin makes clear that the family made no attempt to influence his interpretations, and I am sure this is so. However, imagining them reading his words could not but have inhibited Martin's interpretation, and strengthened his decision to limit himself to the observable public life. The children of politicians have a difficult lot sharing their parents with the public, and if they want to protect their memories and idealisations, this I respect. It is a reason, though, for historians to be wary of getting too close to their subjects' families. I doubt that Martin gained much not already available on the public record from his closeness to the family, and he told us virtually nothing about Menzies' family life.

Of the three competing ways of remembering Menzies circulating when I was writing my book during the 1980s, the villainous Menzies has faded with the passing of the old communists; and the coming of Whitlam swept away my generation's sense that Menzies was holding Australia back. The Liberal Party's Grand Old Man is the one that has survived. This is not surprising. Liberals have good reasons to continue to remember their longest serving leader, and have institutionalised occasions for remembering, most notably the annual Sir Robert Menzies Lecture. Given by prominent Liberals, this always includes homage to Menzies and the achievements of his government. He is also remembered by dissenting Liberals such as Malcolm Fraser and Petro Georgiou, who appealed to him as the standard bearer of Liberal values in arguments with the Howard government.

Howard in particular enjoys remembering Menzies, and his belief that he has been maligned by left-wing historians is one of his motives for starting the so-called history wars. Journalists inevitably peg his electoral successes against those of Menzies, and speculate about whether he, like Menzies, will choose the time of his departure, and the fate of the government he will leave behind. The uses of Menzies to subsequent Liberals are rich and contradictory, as are the uses of the life and words of any political leader who has moved from the realm of history into myth.

Since John Howard returned the Liberals to federal electoral ascendancy, there has been a new reason for Australians to remember Menzies. Does he help us to understand Howard? What, if anything, do the Liberal Party's two most successful prime ministers have in common, apart from the obvious fact of their political success? These are historical questions, and until Howard's success has run its course are hard to answer. There are obvious parallels in their governing during periods of economic growth, and in the problems experienced by the Labor Party in finding a leader able to match their political skill and powers of communication. These are superficial resemblances of circumstances, however, and do not get us very deep into the inner workings of their relationship with public power. The big moral question for any historical judgement of John Howard is his handling of asylum seekers and the war on terror. Did he manipulate fear, racism and xenophobia to win the 2001 election? Did he overreact to the threat of Islamic terrorism by introducing draconian legislation that breached fundamental principles of civil liberty? Similar questions have always surrounded Robert Menzies' uses of anti-communism during the early years of the Cold War, in particular his unsuccessful attempt to ban the Communist Party of Australia and his role in the defection of the Soviet diplomat Vladimir Petrov on the eve of the 1954 election.

Here I think there are interesting parallels to be explored between the way Menzies and Howard handled the global threats of their times. Trying to understand how Menzies reconciled his strong and genuine commitment to civil liberties with his belief that Australia and the free world faced a real threat from communism, I read the political historian Richard Hofstadter's marvellous essay 'The Paranoid Style in American Politics'.[12] Hofstadter argued that the anti-communism of the 1950s was a version of a paranoid belief system which, at different times in American history, has posited a threat to the American way of life of such magnitude and evil that the most extraordinary and urgent responses are required by the state. Hofstadter wrote his essay in the 1960s, to explain the excesses of McCarthyism, but the paranoid style he describes fits many aspects of the beliefs fuelling the war on terror, in particular the belief in a vast, sinister conspiracy to undermine a whole way of life, and the construction of the enemy as an agent of pure evil. He links this to the history of Manichean thought in the United States, and its belief in a cosmic struggle between good and evil which affects both the way the enemy is perceived and the understandings of the self. George W. Bush's response to global terrorism since September 11 was the latest appearance of this belief system. This is not to say that the enemy is not real, but to draw attention to the deep cultural discourses which Bush mobilised in the way he responded to it. Small people like David Hicks and Jack Thomas who found themselves on the wrong side in this black-and-white world quickly became scapegoats.

Historical judgements about the reality of perceived threats and the appropriateness of responses to them are extraordinarily difficult to make, particularly if these threats do not come to much in the end. Were they successfully thwarted by firm and timely action, or were they largely imagined in the first place? If the latter, were these imaginings honest mistakes or opportunistic political manipulations? Answering such questions is tricky, not just because it depends on assessments of what might have happened, but also because it deals with deep psychological differences among humans in how they experience and respond to aggression. When is an aggressive response to threat realistic, and when is it a distorted, paranoid overreaction which magnifies what it was meant to hold at bay?

Australia has a much more secular and pragmatic political culture than the United States, yet as allies in global wars our leaders are drawn into its constructions of political reality. How do they fare? The contributions of political opportunism and conviction in Menzies' anti-communism have been matters of fierce historical debate among scholars, many of whom were themselves minor players in the politics of Australia's Cold War. To my mind the most convincing account is by David Lowe, who brings a younger scholar's fresh eye to the arguments and evidence, arguing that Menzies' anti-communism was based on real fears of Soviet military aggression, but that he was nevertheless fully alert to its political benefits.[13] The question which interested me about Menzies' anti-communism was: what symbolic strategies did he use to strengthen the paranoia in his make-up to enable him to do what he believed was necessary? Some of my argument seems quite speculative to me now, but I stand by its underlying assumption that Menzies had to do a good deal of psychological work on himself to overcome his commitment to civil liberties for the fight against communism, and that the ways in which he activated his paranoia are revealing of deep emotional structures.

In the end Menzies was saved by the Labor leader, Herb Vere Evatt, who threw himself into the fight against the anti-communist legislation with the passion of a madman. More prone to paranoia than Menzies, Evatt saw in the legislation threats to Australians' civil liberties which the government at the time argued were scare-mongering exaggerations. One of the most contentious aspects of the bill was the reversal of the onus of proof. People accused of being members of a proscribed organisation had to prove they were not members, rather than the state having to prove that they were. This, it was argued, was necessary to protect the security agency's sources of information, and because of the elusiveness of communists and their organisations. Reflecting on the failure of the referendum to ban the Communist Party many years after the heat of the events, Menzies wrote the following curiously ambiguous reflection:

> The whole matter offered interesting evidence that the electors, when they have the chance, are not only reluctant to vote for new powers for the Commonwealth, but are also, by deep instinct, unwilling to modify in any way the old principle that 'a man is innocent until he is *proved* guilty'.[14]

In Menzies' political thinking, the deep instincts of the electors are generally to be respected as bearers of historical wisdom and moderate good sense. Do we hear him breathe a sigh of relief that they saved him from breaching one of Britain's most ancient civil liberties?

The politics of anti-terrorism since September 11 and the Bali bombings share some features with the anti-communist legislation proposed by the Menzies government. The term 'terrorist' is as vague and general as was the term 'communist' and functions similarly as a bearer of pure evil lifted clear of historical motivation to become a generalised threat to all that is good. In the Howard government's anti-terrorist legislation, as in the anti-communist legislation, people are found guilty on the basis of beliefs and intentions rather than actions. This of course makes perfect sense when the purpose of the legislation is to thwart destructive actions, but intentions are far more difficult to prove than actions, so the chances of gross abuses of individuals' civil liberties are greatly increased. The net of suspicion is cast wide, and a significant minority of Australians feel afraid of arbitrary government power, and of social ostracism and persecution. Just how this will all play out is not at all clear. But any future biographer of Howard will need to think long and hard about why he played the politics of terror as he did.

A Personal Coda

I argue in this book that to be successful an ambitious politician must find a group to serve who will carry him to prominence and public power. A similar argument can be made for ambitious historians and biographers: they need a subject of sufficient public interest to win them readers. Menzies did this for me. As I was a young scholar and writer, it was my subject matter that initially drew readers to my book. I got more publicity for this book than for anything I have written since, and won more prizes. And it gave me the public profile to participate more generally in Australian political debate. It also gave me the subject matter for my next book. Having finished *Robert Menzies' Forgotten People*, I wanted to know more about the history of the political traditions Menzies had so successfully deployed in his speech to the Forgotten People and what had happened to them. I thus embarked on another ten-year project, to write the twentieth-century history of the political traditions of the Australian Liberals and their shifting relationship with middle-class experience. This became *Australian Liberals and the Moral Middle Class: From Alfred Deakin to John Howard*. It is dedicated to my grandparents, none of whom voted Labor, and their grandchildren, most of whom do, because in writing it I found I was writing the history of the people from whom I came. This is something I could never have imagined in 1980 when I went to the archives to find something by Robert Menzies. His forgotten people were my own.

---

[1] R. W. Connell & T. H. Irving, *Class Structure in Australian History: Documents, Narratives and Argument*, Longman Cheshire, Melbourne, 1980, p. 349.

[2] L. F. Crisp, *Australian National Government*, Longman Cheshire, Melbourne, 1965, p. 227.

[3] A four-volume paperback history produced for the Bicentennial virtually ignored its existence. Edited by Jenny Lee and Verity Burgmann, it was called *A People's History of Australia Since 1788* (McPhee Gribble, Melbourne, 1988). Influenced both by labour history and by social history's commitment to history from below, it included a great many interesting and valuable articles. The middle class, though, was virtually absent. It was clearly not part of what the authors meant by 'A People's History'.

[4] *Writings of the Young Marx on Philosophy and Society*, trans. Loyd D. Easton & Kurt H. Guddat, Doubleday, New York, 1967.

[5] The concepts of which I made most use in interpreting Menzies' language were discourse, rhetoric and ideology, and the writers I found most helpful were Michel Foucault, for his conceptualisation of discourse as structured patterns of meaning; Claude Lévi-Strauss, for his attention to the way binary oppositions structure symbolic systems; and Kenneth Burke, for his argument that language is strategic symbolic action, persuasion directed both to the self and other which can be more or less successful.

[6] Alan Janick & Stephen Toulmin, *Wittgenstein's Vienna*, Simon & Schuster, New York, 1973.

[7] *The Liberals: Fifty Years of the Federal Party* (five episodes), ABC, Sydney, 1994. The papers for the NLA conference were subsequently published in *Voices*, 5, 2, 1995.

[8] Gerard Henderson, *Menzies' Child: The Liberal Party of Australia 1944–94*, Allen & Unwin, Sydney, 1994.

[9] Ian Hancock, 'Menzies and the Liberal Party, 1944–66', *Voices*, 5, 2, 1995. See also Hancock, *National and Permanent?: The Federal Organisation of the Liberal Party of Australia 1944–65*, Melbourne University Press, 2000, ch. 1.

[10] *Robert Menzies: A Life*, Volume 1, 1894–1943; Volume 2, 1944–1978, Melbourne University Press, 1993 & 1999.

[11] 'In Search of the "Actual Man Underneath": A. W. Martin and the Art of Biography'. Inaugural Alan Martin Lecture, Pandanus Books, ANU, Canberra, 2004.

[12] Richard Hofstadter, *The Paranoid Style in American Politics and Other Essays*, Alfred Knopf, New York, 1965.

[13] David Lowe, *Menzies and the Great World Struggle: Australia's Cold War 1948–1954*, UNSW Press, Sydney, 1999. See especially chapter 4.

[14] Robert Menzies, *Central Power in the Australian Commonwealth: An Examination of the Growth of Commonwealth Power in the Australian Federation*, Cassell, London, 1967, p. 20.

3 The Bin Fire of the Humanities

Monthly, *March 2021*.

I couldn't wait to start university. Over the summer of 1967 I read and re-read the Arts Faculty handbook for the University of Melbourne, trying to decide my subjects. I did the suggested preliminary reading for Modern Government A, began reading the novels for English I, and even covered my books, just as I had at the start of every school year. I had worked hard in my matric year at Nunawading High and done well in the exams, so I was planning to do a four-year honours degree rather than a three-year pass. In those days, you enrolled in honours from first year for an extended curriculum in addition to the extra year and writing a short thesis. I planned to do honours in English, but I couldn't decide between politics and philosophy for my combined degree. As each only required an extra two-hour seminar, I chose to do them both and decide which to go on with at the end of the year. As the evening lectures in philosophy had a different lecturer from those in the day, I went to both of them too.

This gave me twenty-four contact hours in my first year, including seven hours for German language. The university year was divided into three terms and subjects ran for the full year. During the two three-week breaks between terms, I wrote essays and caught up on reading. This added six weeks to the time available to learn, compared with today. I am telling you this not simply to out myself as a swot, but to document how much time universities then made available to students to learn.

I had been dux of humanities at Nunawading High, but I was in a much bigger pond now and thought that the students from the big private schools would have the jump on me. They were certainly more confident in tutorials and seemed to have more extensive general knowledge. So I worked extra hard to bridge the gap, and read pretty well everything on the reading guides. At the end of the year, I had shared the top mark in both politics and philosophy, but received a disappointing H2A in English. I got an H1 in English language but bombed in literature for reasons I couldn't understand. Looking at my other results, my tutor said, 'You must be bright, but...' Perhaps I was too earnest; perhaps I lacked the cultural capital to know what was wanted in those Leavisite days of confident moral judgement. So I dropped English and embarked on a combined honours degree in politics and philosophy. I also relaxed a little. I didn't have to work quite so hard. But I still worked steadily. All that reading, note taking, indexing and summarising of lecture notes: it was like going to gym for the brain, and developed capacities for clear thinking and argumentation I have relied on ever since. Philosophy, now seen as the most impractical and contentless of subjects, was the most useful. In tutorials and seminars, we didn't so much discuss philosophy as *do* philosophy. It was here that I learnt how to structure an argument and control its consequences.

First-year lectures were huge, but tutorials were small—ten to twelve students—and most staff were permanent. There were dull and lazy lecturers, but there were also stars, men and a few women whose knowledge and dedication were exemplary. Teaching is as much about modelling ways of thinking and instilling a passion for understanding as it is about conveying content, and inspiring teachers impress something of themselves onto their students. It's hard to see how this can be achieved with online learning.

Some of these intensively taught honours students went on to postgraduate degrees here and overseas, and became leading intellectuals, writers and academics: Raimond Gaita, Peter Singer, Stuart Macintyre, Graeme Davison, Sheila Fitzpatrick, Robert Manne, Arnold Zable, Patrick McCaughey and Helen Garner were all honours arts students at Melbourne University in the 1960s. Similar stories can be told for other sandstone universities: Marilyn Lake and Dennis Altman from the University of Tasmania; Raewyn Connell, Ann Curthoys and Kate Grenville from the University of Sydney.

Elitist, I hear you say. Yes, it was. In 1967, when I enrolled, there were around 95,000 university students; by 2003 there were more almost 830,000; and today there are more than a million domestic students. Many more people can now benefit from a university education, but Australia no longer provides the intensive undergraduate education it once did. And it hardly seems to have been noticed, as we live off the capital of earlier times.

As more students began to go to university, honours arts degrees were wound back to just the extra year, perhaps with a special seminar in third year, and entry depended on one's marks rather than on preference and financial means. There was some loss here, but an overall gain in equity and access. Subject choices increased markedly during the 1980s and 1990s, as did the overall quality of the teaching staff. If there was a golden age in Australian universities it was from the mid-1970s, after Whitlam abolished university fees, until sometime in the 1990s, when the Dawkins reforms were transforming the sector. As students started to contribute to the cost of their teaching through HECS payments, the quality began slowly to decline.

When I started teaching in politics at La Trobe University in 1989 there were four first-year courses and a wide range of second- and third-year subjects. Robert Manne, Joe Camilleri, Robin Jeffrey, Dennis Altman, me—we all taught first-year courses for years, as well as upper-level courses, and we all took tutorials. In the 1990s, the teaching year was semesterised, replacing the old terms. Students went on holidays in the midyear break and six weeks of learning time vanished. We had to pare back our content and could no longer run large themes across the year or expect students to read during the breaks. Some universities also lopped a week or two off the standard thirteen weeks of teaching.

There were other changes too. As more students were also employed, the pressure was on for flexibility in course delivery. Lectures were recorded, tutorials discretionary, exams abolished. To pass you didn't really need to do the whole course at all, just to write a couple of essays and assignments on selected topics. I liked to include an exam so that students were obliged to review the whole subject, but there were plenty of exam-free subjects available. The comparison with sport is revealing. Everyone accepts that sport requires commitment and rigorous training, that muscles need to be worked and endurance built. So does intellectual work. I think of all those hours I spent before we had photocopiers, summarising articles and indexing my copious lecture notes, as building my brain's pathways.

It is fifty or more years since that eager young girl in Nunawading covered her books in anticipation of a new world. Were she starting university today, she would not find the same opportunities to learn. Today, humanities and social-science departments in Australia's universities are imploding, shedding staff and subjects, teaching online or in large classes with a highly casualised workforce, and expecting less and less of their students. While the public frets about what students will pay for their degrees, the people doing the teaching are as likely to worry about the decline in the quantity and quality of what students are getting for their money, and the poor standard of too many of the graduates.

As universities were forced to compete with each other for funds and students based on ever-shifting metrics, university managers put teaching faculties through restructure after restructure to reduce their costs, diverting teaching revenue to fund research, executive salaries and marketing. Teaching became less valued as progress in an academic career shifted to the measured achievement of specified research outputs. Bizarrely for the humanities, articles read by a few came to count more than books read by many. People competed for grants to 'buy out' their teaching, or to win one of the prestigious Australian Research Council (ARC) fellowships, which did not permit its holders to teach. This always struck me as a misguided policy, denying undergraduates the opportunity to be taught by academics at the height of their powers. Just how far teaching has slid down university management's priorities was evident in the peak body Universities Australia's response to the loss of seventeen thousand jobs in the sector since COVID-19, with more on the way. The emphasis was on the impact on the country's research capacity, with not a word about the effect on undergraduate teaching.

As permanent staff slid out of teaching, they were replaced in the classroom by casuals, who have become the underpaid workhorses of undergraduate teaching. Most casuals are dedicated and professional, but they cannot provide the same levels of contact as permanent staff. They are only paid for a minimum consultation time, if at all, and are certainly not available for extended conversations with keen or anxious students, let alone for casual socialising or to organise extracurricular activities. The cost of the casualisation of university teaching, though, is largely borne by the teachers themselves. Permanent staff, many of whom started their teaching career in much-better-paid circumstances, know that casuals are exploited and underpaid; but, restricted by tight budgets, they are rarely able to do anything except apologise a little guiltily.

Once, casuals were mainly postgraduate students taking some tutorials in a course run and carefully supervised by a permanent member of staff. Now they are employed to design and teach whole subjects. The permanent staff member credited as the 'co-ordinator' is often a fiction, palming off their teaching so they can get on with their research. With no job security, casuals are vulnerable to exploitation and most do a good deal of work for which they are not paid, in administration, answering student emails, talking to students after class and the preparation of material. The hourly rate is high, but the hours allotted to many tasks are unrealistic. For example, a casual is generally paid three hours to prepare and deliver a one-hour lecture. Perhaps that's reasonable, if a lecture is based on a textbook, or an already existing course, but it took me around fourteen concentrated hours, or two working days, to prepare a new politics lecture—and I was efficient. In some disciplines it would take longer; for example, English literature, when one also has to read the novel.

I have often wondered how the three-hour figure was arrived at. Was it based on an empirical study of a sample of academics preparing a lecture? Was it dreamt up by someone in a human-resources department who had never written a lecture? I got the answer reading the submission of the Australian Higher Education Industry Association (AHEIA) to the Senate Economics Committee's inquiry into unlawful underpayment of employees. Defending the sector's current practices, the AHEIA sourced the casual-employment payment regime to determinations made by the Academic Salaries Tribunal in 1976 and 1980, which were subsequently included in federal awards. But employment practices in 1980 were very different from today. This was more like an honorarium than payment for work done. Then, a casual lecture was generally a one-off, given by a visiting industry specialist in a course run by a permanent staff member. I would invite a local MP to give a lecture on parliament to my first-year Australian politics class, say, or someone working for a non-government organisation or industry association when we were discussing pressure groups. Casuals were never employed to design and run whole courses, and it would not have occurred to the tribunal that someone preparing and delivering twenty-six lecture hours might be paid for just seventy-eight hours of work, when at the time this would have represented around two-thirds of a permanent staff member's work for a semester and they would have had ample time to prepare before teaching started.

Interestingly, the same reasoning is not applied to the salaries of vice-chancellors, which the 1984 Academic Salaries Tribunal recommended be set at 42 per cent above that of a full professor ($72,000 and $51,000 respectively). Following those guidelines, with full professors' salaries now averaging around $180,000, today's vice-chancellors would have salaries around $256,000, not the million or more they now receive. In late January, the education committee of the New South Wales Legislative Council released a report titled 'Future Development of the NSW Tertiary Education Sector', which, among other things, considered the high salaries of vice-chancellors in the context of extensive losses of academic jobs. It commented:

> The vast disparity between the salaries paid to senior university administrators and the casual and insecure payments made to so many of the staff who actually conduct the teaching and research in universities is a matter of real concern to the committee. If the role of universities is to create new knowledge and disseminate that knowledge to students then the people who do this critical work need to be valued and respected. The current system that sees University Vice Chancellors paid 25 or thirty times more than many of the people undertaking the core work of universities must be reviewed and the failure to do this by the governing bodies of universities is evidence of a failure of leadership. This is a matter that should be reviewed by the Auditor-General.

The attraction of casuals to the universities is obvious. As the AHEIA submission to the Senate so blithely puts it, the extent of casualisation in the higher education sector has structural reasons relating to 'the high costs associated with continuing employment'. From this perspective, it is wage avoidance, rather than wage theft, and perfectly legal.

With no leave entitlements, no research support, and often with no provision of either office space or equipment, casuals are cheap compared with permanent staff. But even then, some universities have not been able to resist squeezing them further. In a little-noticed case at the end of 2020, the National Tertiary Education Union took the University of Melbourne to the Fair Work Commission for wage theft with respect to underpayment for marking in the Faculty of Arts. Wage theft! Just like 7-Eleven franchises or Domino's Pizza! Just before Christmas, the venerable institution sent a letter of apology and a cheque to at least fifteen hundred casuals. The bill was millions of dollars.

•

The Institute of Public Affairs has just published another of its reports complaining about the takeover of humanities and social-science teaching by identity politics, with themes of class, race and gender pushing aside traditional disciplinary content. Putting aside how you would teach twentieth-century history or literature without reference to class, race and gender, the IPA is missing the main story. It is not identity politics but the shrinking of humanities and social-science faculties and curriculums across the country that is the biggest threat to their valued disciplinary traditions, as universities seek to save money on teaching by restructuring faculties, departments and courses.

I ended my academic career in 2012 in such a restructure, during which a lively, productive school of social sciences that was more than paying its way was dismembered for reasons that are still obscure to me, and for no discernible gain in enrolments or research output. In fact, both went backwards, which made me wonder if that, indeed, was the intention; or perhaps it was just incompetence. But that way bitterness lies, and whatever the circumstances of my experience, and the perfidies of the perpetrators, similar things were happening across the country.

COVID-19 has now turned an incremental decline into an existential crisis. At my old university, La Trobe, already-diminished teaching programmes have been instructed to reduce costs yet again, which means losing more staff, offering fewer subjects, increasing class sizes and doing more teaching online: Zoom instead of rooms, because that accommodates more students and you don't have to pay for cleaning. And La Trobe is not alone.

When a university decides to phase out a subject area or a degree—such as when La Trobe announced at the end of last year that it would cease teaching modern Greek and Hindi, or Monash University that it would close its Centre for Theatre and Performance—it draws media attention, and provides an opportunity for the public to respond. Sometimes a subject area is even saved. For example, the Greek community is supporting La Trobe to retain modern Greek. But when a university restructures degrees and shrinks subject choices, the public barely notices. When the next cohort of students enrol, they don't know what they're missing.

Across the country, humanities departments are becoming barely credible: minimal language teaching; faculties without philosophy; English departments without a subject on Shakespeare, let alone Australian literature; visual-art departments studying no art history prior to 1900; politics departments with nothing on America and barely anything on Australia; and so on. You wouldn't know any of this from online university resources, so it's hard to build a complete picture. Perhaps the Australian Academy of the Humanities could do an audit. On most university websites it is near impossible to find the actual subjects offered, and a keen student has no chance of discovering who will be teaching them, as it will likely be a casual who probably doesn't yet have a contract. Instead, there are boasts about research achievements, promises about career prospects and testimony as to why enrolling at this institution will change your life.

Today's Australian universities promise their students a world-class education, but what they offer is not world class. Though Australian universities do remarkably well in world rankings, these can be seriously misleading. For example, in the QS World University Rankings, English language and literature studies at the University of Melbourne are ranked eighteenth in the world, between Canada's University of British Columbia and Cornell in the United States. Drill down and you find that English and theatre studies at Melbourne lists fifteen faculty members (excluding those in ARC-funded research-only positions), most of them professors who will be doing little or no teaching. By contrast, English at UBC has forty-nine faculty listed on its web page, and Cornell has fifty-one. English at the University of York, in the United Kingdom, which is ranked twenty-second, has forty-five faculty members, and in all these overseas universities theatre studies are in another department to English, with its own staff. Given that staff–student ratios are one of the six performance indicators used to determine the QS rankings, it is hard to know how the Melbourne department did so well. Perhaps it listed all the casual staff. Other universities would not regard fifteen full-time faculty, no matter how highly regarded their collective research, as sufficient to teach the discipline—so why do we? If I had a child now contemplating a liberal-arts degree, and I had the money, I would send them to Canada or the United States, crossing my fingers that they wouldn't fall in love and not want to come home.

The situation may be better in subject areas outside the humanities and social sciences, with which I am less familiar. Those requiring external accreditation, such as psychology, law or social work, are protected from university cost-cutters. But in humanities and many social sciences it is a serious crisis with far-reaching implications for the country at large—for the education available to our young people, and for our shared cultural life. Why do the perennial discussions about problems in secondary education and declining standards not also consider what is happening in universities, not just in the education faculties but in the arts and science faculties that provide many teachers with their disciplinary knowledge. If the teachers are less well-trained than in the past, is it surprising there is less rigour in our secondary schools? In January it was reported that only 38 per cent of Year 10 students who took the most recent national civics and citizenship assessment demonstrated proficient knowledge of Australia's system of government and the workings and values of democracy. Might this not have something to do with fewer Australian politics subjects being available for prospective teachers to study than a decade ago?

As universities have taken over from dedicated institutions the teaching of art practices such as painting and sculpture, acting and directing, music performance and creative writing, the historical and theoretical subjects that provide their context have declined: art history, musicology, literary studies, theatre and drama studies. Much of this decline is disguised in repackaged 'creative arts' courses, but decline it is. Since COVID-19, La Trobe, Newcastle and Monash universities have announced the closure of their theatre and drama programmes. Monash will no longer offer musicology and ethno-musicology streams. Emphasis is on careers in the creative industries, such as performance and curation, in line with a pragmatic focus on graduate job outcomes. The implication is that unless you are aiming to be an arts practitioner, such disciplines are of little value to you.

Does this matter, beyond its production of an oversupply of people who believe they are trained for an artistic career? I think it does, and not just because we will lose expertise and again become dependent, as we were before the 1960s, on knowledge and ideas produced in the northern hemisphere. Coupled with the general decline in our study of humanities and social sciences, Australia's broad cultural literacy will diminish. Fewer people will want to watch a performance of *Hamlet*, or a new play, or know how to appreciate them if they do.

Fewer people will be able to appreciate the wonderful collections in our galleries or read a challenging novel. Fewer people will know anything at all about the cultures of Asia, or Africa, or South and Central America, or the Pacific. Fewer people will know how to unpick flawed logic or construct a compelling argument. Add to this our current federal government's parsimonious support of the arts, and the annual efficiency dividend whittling away our cultural institutions, and Australia is well on its way to becoming the most philistine country in the West.

At the heart of Australian universities today are two morally compromised relationships. The first is with their casual underpaid staff. The second is with their students, and beyond them with their families and future employees, who are made false promises of a world-class education but delivered much less. There are many causes of the erosion of teaching and learning at Australian universities over the past decades, and for the mendacity that has crept across the sector. Some are due to government policies and some to actions of the sector itself: the reforms by Labor Education Minister John Dawkins at the end of the 1980s, changes to university governance, shameless vice-chancellors, the Liberal Party's hostility to intellectuals, to name but a few. They are for a different essay. This one is about effects, not causes. Our degraded tertiary sector needs to be seen for what it is, so we can start to repair it—for the sake of eager young people hungry to learn.

PART VI

Psychoanalysis

1 The Tasks of Political Biography

First published in a collection I edited, Political Lives, *Allen & Unwin, Sydney, 1997. Reprinted in Robert Reynolds and Joy Damousi (eds),* History on the Couch: Essays in History and Psychoanalysis, *Melbourne University Press, 2003.*

To admit to using psychoanalytic ideas in biographical work is immediately to find oneself on the defensive, facing a salvo of arguments ranging from 'Freud is bunk' to 'You cannot psychoanalyse the dead.' As one argument is rebutted, a new one is produced, and then another, until the first one reappears in a slightly altered form: the language is so ugly; psychoanalysis is reductionist, determinist, anti-humanist, patriarchal; literature is a better guide to the inner life; and, in these post-universalist days, Freud is of only historic interest. This essay is a defence of the usefulness of psychoanalysis for political biography.

The task of political biography is to tell the story of a political life in such a way as to make that life intelligible. In describing this task, I am deliberately avoiding the word 'psychobiography', not only because there have been some very bad books published under this description, but also because I want to avoid its implication of the primacy of psychoanalytic ideas and concepts among the biographer's tools. Instead I want to advance a more modest claim, that psychoanalytic concepts and methods should be present in the biographer's toolkit. This does necessarily involve tackling some of the arguments against the applications of psychoanalysis to historical material, although I will not cover them all and recommend to interested readers Peter Gay's lucid little book *Freud for Historians* (1985), which deals in a systematic way with the most common arguments against the applications of psychoanalysis to history.

Leon Edel argues that contemporary biographies which do not use the knowledge of psychoanalysis are incomplete, belonging to a time when lives were entirely exterior and neglected the reflective and inner sides of human beings.[1] Few contemporary biographers are content to see themselves as chroniclers of the exterior life. They want also to convey something of what their subject thought and felt about the key events and conflicts and the passing moments of their life; to bring out something of their personality—the characteristic patterning of gestures and responses which are uniquely theirs, the characteristic strategies which contribute to their successes and failures; and to convey something of the way they changed during the course of their life. The contemporary biographer moves continually between the outer and the inner, between the events and the culture of the times and the idiosyncratic and personally felt responses of the life.

Edel is writing from the experience of literary biography, where the biographer's subject, by definition, is a person who spends their life cultivating and transforming their inner life into words that others, including the biographer, can read. But what if you are writing about someone who themselves neglected their inner and reflective side, who lived in the external world of action and event, and who left little if any of the sorts of writing which seem to give some access to the inner life—no records of dreams, no diary entries about emotions, no intimate letters?

One solution is to look to the details of the private life. As Eric Erikson says, in psychoanalysis deeper often seems to mean sexual and repressed.[2] Psychoanalysis can seem to be mainly useful to the biographer for its attention to what is hidden, secret, taking place behind closed doors, in the innermost recesses of the private life. Psychoanalysis can thus seem a method particularly designed for digging up dirty secrets. It is this conception of psychoanalysis that evokes so much hostility, as it seems to denigrate and trivialise worthy public lives. This criticism aside, the problem with such a conception of psychoanalysis is that it confines it to the investigation of the private life, and the private lives of some individuals may not be particularly illuminating. Kenneth Morgan, in a 1988 article on political biography, writes:

> The relentless emphasis on Lloyd George's sexual adventures—real or alleged—for example can lead to extreme misinterpretation of the career of one who was above all, night and day, a supremely committed politician, obsessed with the issues of the time. Nothing, not even sex, could interfere with that.[3]

The reliance of much psychoanalytic thinking on metaphors of depth maps easily onto a distinction between the public and the private life, in which the private life seems to hold the clues to the meaning of the public life. Such a mapping, though, is misleading for the biographers of many politicians who are faced not only with a paucity of material, but with a private life that is scarcely lived. If psychoanalysis is to be useful to the political biographer, it must be useful in understanding the public life; and it must begin not with what is hidden and secret but with what is right in front of its nose—the publicness of the public life. It is, if you like, the publicness of the life that marks it as political. It is thus not so much a matter of searching for the real person behind the public person, but of realising that the public person is the real person and so learning to read the public political life for what it reveals about the distinctiveness of the person whose life it is.

It has been argued that men who seek and win public political power share certain characteristics. Harold Lasswell, one of the first to apply Freud's ideas to the systematic study of political lives, argued that men who devote their lives to the pursuit of high public office seek power and deference in order to overcome estimates of the self which they regard as inappropriately low. Such men typically come from backgrounds which put them at some distance from the centres of power and significance in their society: colonials, small-town boys, members of minorities, those from the wrong side of the tracks or the blanket. Lasswell's theory aims to illuminate the lives not of those born to power, but of those who strive for it.[4]

Central to the psychology of such men, argues Lasswell, is the psychological mechanism of projection, by which inner conflicts are displaced onto objects in the outside world and dealt with there, generally rationalised in terms of the public interest. These men are externalisers, dealing with their inner conflicts and struggles not by changing themselves but by changing, or attempting to change, the world. Fighting for the nation against colonial oppressors, serving the king, advancing the interests of a class or party, such men are also advancing their own interests, attempting to forge a pact between their own claims to power and deference and the interests of those they would represent. In popularly based politics ambition must be hitched to group goals, for it is only by successfully advancing such goals that the political type has any chance of reaching high office.

The close link between political ambition and self-interest is widely recognised in a settler democracy like Australia, where cynicism about politicians' motives has always been high. In the absence of a traditional governing class, Australian politics seems full of what Michael Kirby, arguing for a constitutional monarchy which would keep at least one job beyond their grasp, has called 'the pushing, shoving types'.[5] But while Lasswell's argument about the necessary link between projection and political ambition might lend support to this sort of real-world cynicism, it is also an argument about the deep sources of political energy; about what it is that makes some men and women go on fighting when others have compromised, or called it a day and gone on to do other things with their lives; about what it is that makes some men and women unable to leave politics alone. One thinks of Maggie Thatcher and Bob Hawke. Here it is important to go beyond the easy cynicism which recognises the ambitious politician's pact between self- and general interest, and to see that great good may flow from such pacts, that the interest of the class or the nation may indeed be advanced by an ambitious man or woman seeking power and deference. Indeed, Erik Erikson in *Young Man Luther* (1958) argues that in raising their deep personal conflicts to a general level, such people may be catalysts for major social change.

Lasswell's work makes two major contributions to political biography: it points to the centrality of psychoanalytic theories about the self (theories of narcissism) for understanding political leaders; and, in the mechanism of projection, it gives the biographer a powerful tool for linking the inner life of their subject with the public life of the times. Both of these contributions challenge two of the most popular misconceptions about the limitations of psychoanalysis for biography: the first, that it is all about sex; and the second, that is only interested in the individual and so is blind to history.

Is Psychoanalysis All about Sex?

In the view that psychoanalysis is all about sex, psychoanalysis becomes synonymous with the early work of Freud on the drives and his discovery of childhood sexuality. It thus seems to be about digging up dirty secrets, or reducing adult achievements to the playing-out of childhood wishes. These misconceptions very easily slide into another one, that psychoanalysis is about pathology, and hence to apply it to so called 'normal people' is inappropriate.[6] Not only are these wrongheaded understandings of the complexity and contribution of Freud's work, but they completely ignore the development of psychoanalytic theory since Freud. It is not sufficient when dismissing psychoanalytically informed biography simply to make a few insulting remarks about Freud; one must also take account of the developments of psychoanalytic theory since Freud. Of particular relevance to the essays in this collection is the work of Melanie Klein and the British Object Relations school, in particular Wilfred Bion and Donald Winnicott, as well as of the Americans Karen Horney and Heinz Kohut.

Despite their many differences, these psychoanalytic thinkers share a focus on understanding the way the human self emerges from the child's very early relations with its parents, and develops through childhood and youth and into adult life. The experiences of childhood sexuality are thus placed in the context of the way in which the parents respond to the child's emerging self. From this perspective the core of the Oedipal crisis is not the sexual wish and its denial but a lesson about the limits and possibilities of the self. For the biographer, childhood experiences of humiliation may be far more important for understanding the adult subject than childhood sexual fantasies, and far more accessible.

The argument here is not that sex is never of any relevance to the political biographer, but that psychoanalysis is about much more than the origins and vicissitudes of adult sexuality. In relation to some political lives, the biographer may, indeed, need to think a good deal about the subject's sexuality, particularly in political contexts where the subject's sexuality becomes part of the way in which they express their political power.

To a very great extent, liberal societies, with their separation between the private individual and the authority of the public office, keep a check on the more florid aspects of human sexuality affecting the actual exercise of state power. Sadists, for example, do not get their hands on state power. But even in liberal democracies, the projection of a certain sexual style may be part of a politician's bid for public power; one thinks here of Jeff Kennett's flamboyant virility, which was displayed as a sign of tough-minded worldliness and general lack of sentimentality.

Ambition and Ideals

In his early foray into the field Lasswell stressed the ambitious politician's craving for deference, thereby putting too much weight on grievance as a source of energy for political lives. Grievance is undoubtedly a powerful source in many cases, but a more flexible theory of the self is needed by biographers dealing with a wide range of political lives. Some political biographers have found Karen Horney's work useful, in particular her *Neurosis and Human Growth: The Struggle Toward Self-Realization* (1950), in which she develops the idea of an idealised self as a response to the insecurities and anxieties engendered by unempathic parenting.[7]

Horney's discussion of the various forms of the construction and defence of an idealised self—the different paths taken by those who search compulsively for glory—is very suggestive for political biographers. Her formulation of the idealised self in terms of neurosis does, however, imply that the vicissitudes of self-realisation she describes are pathological.

The work of Heinz Kohut sharply breaks with this implication. Rather than seeing narcissism as a stage through which individuals pass in their development towards psychological maturity, Kohut argues that the construction and defence of the self's cohesion is a lifelong task. Psychoanalysts thus need to rethink their generally negative evaluation of narcissism, which is as implicated in the joys and creativity of human life as in its selfishness and destructiveness. His work pertains to all people but is especially helpful for political biographers, who are often dealing with people extraordinarily endowed with self-regard.

Kohut looks in detail at the processes by which the idealised self is constructed, and he distinguishes two stages in this process. The first is the grandiose self of very early childhood, the child who feels herself the centre of the universe and delights in her own existence. The second is the idealised self of the slightly older child, who is starting to be aware of the relative powerlessness of children but retains the sense of her own power and uniqueness through identification with an admired parent. *I am perfect becomes you are perfect but I am part of you, so I am still perfect*.[8] The grandiose self, Kohut argues, is the seat of ambition, the drive to reach the social position where one's true self will be recognised. The idealised self is the seat of the self's desire to live up to and serve ideals. One is driven by ambition but strives for one's ideals.[9] Throughout life there is an interplay between these two aspects of the self: one is driven by ambition to reach one's 'rightful' place, to receive one's due rewards and recognition, but one strives for one's ideals, to put one's life and talents at the service of something beyond the self but with which the self is deeply identified.

Both ambition and ideals are of central interest to political biographers, and Kohut's work is very helpful in providing a dynamic model for thinking about the way these interact in a political life. Kohut leads one to ponder how and why one's subject invests a part of themselves in political causes, ideas or institutions, and he is a check against the too-easy cynicism of those who only see the self-serving ambition and fail to see the struggle to harness that ambition for some more general purpose.

In my thinking about Menzies, Kohut's formulation of the self as both driven by ambition and led by ideals was extremely helpful. Menzies was a man of powerful ambition, who carried into adult life a pleasure in his own capacities and achievements which many of his contemporaries found extremely galling. But Menzies the man of ambition was not the whole story, despite what many of his critics would like to believe. For Menzies was determined to turn his ambition to good use, and strove to serve and protect loved ideals, such as the British empire, the law and parliamentary democracy. These ideals controlled and gave meaning to his ambition, although at times the tables turned and the ideals became transparent rationalisations for the ambition. Although it took me longer to see Menzies' commitment to his ideals than to see his driving ambition, when I did it gave me a more complex way of understanding his political life; and it gave me a basis for understanding the tenacity with which he hung onto his early ideals even when, as with the British empire, their star had faded.

The Historical Context

The second misconception implicitly challenged by Lasswell is that psychoanalysis is of little use to the central biographical task of making subjects intelligible in their historical context. This misconception derives from the view of psychoanalysis as primarily concerned with analysing individuals in terms of the working-out of ahistorical drives. From the beginning, however, psychoanalysis has been concerned with the traffic between the inner and the outer world, with how real experiences of the outer world are transformed by fantasy and the unconscious, and with how the objects of the outer world come to carry meanings derived from the inner world, through processes of introjection and projection respectively. This is most developed in the work of Melanie Klein and the British Object Relations school.

Through introjection and projection one takes into or expels from the self thoughts, emotions and ideas. In introjection one makes part of the outer world one's own; in projection one disowns part of one's self and expels it into the outer world. These are the processes through which the institutions, people and events of the subject's life come to carry their emotions and fantasies, and so provide the biographer with ways of thinking about how the inner life of the subject is knitted together with the outer life of the times. Conventional life-and-times biography, by contrast, has few ways of showing the dynamic connections between the life and the times, except for notions such as influence which are far too weak to explain the passionate commitments and hatreds of political lives. There is thus much reliance on good descriptive writing to evoke the historical context, as well as frequent resort to truisms like 'In his love of England Menzies was a man of his times', which say nothing at all about the reasons for the particular intensity, even for his times, of Menzies' love of England.

Of course, in some aspects of a subject's life they may simply be of their times. As Freud said, sometimes a cigar is just a cigar. There is no established way of determining when one's subject is revealing their inner self rather than simply behaving according to the accepted social habits of the day. Here psychoanalytic biographical interpretation (as with psychoanalytic clinical interpretation) depends on the art of listening—of listening as carefully as possible to the traces of the life, and of knowing the historical context as deeply as possible, so that one can hear the individual nuances one's subject is giving to the shared social and historical experiences of the times. It is also a matter of listening as carefully as possible to one's own responses—both for clues as to the subject's emotions, and for warnings as to the possible interference of one's own psychological and emotional patterns. In biography, psychoanalysis is more about practising an art than applying a scientific theory, and it can be done more or less well.

In tracing the inner life in the outer actions and events of a person's life, or the impact of outer experiences on the inner life, biographers are writing, in good part, about their subjects' emotions—their hates, loves and fears, their joys and griefs, their angers and triumphs, and so on. Psychoanalysis provides the biographer with a grammar of the emotions to guide this interpretive task. Psychoanalysis is the body of modern thought which has reflected in the most systematic and sustained way on human emotional life. The term 'grammar of the emotions' conveys the way psychoanalysis is interested in emotional sequences and consequences, and in emotional exclusions and incompatibilities: for example, in such relationships as that between envy and idealisation, anger and despair, fear of dependence and the propensity to blame. Psychoanalysis thus provides the biographer with theories which help guide their attempts to understand the conflicts and emotional dramas of their subject's life. Without it, the biographer has only the various understandings of the emotions embedded in common sense, in religious understandings, and in literature. Common sense, religion and literature are all important sources for the understanding biographers bring to their subject's emotional lives, but they are not systematic, and so do not provide a systematic guide with which to control one's reflections and intuitive hunches. Neither, I would argue, are they always as successful at penetrating the hidden logic of emotions, at revealing patterns not otherwise discernible.

In tracing the emotional patterns of a person's life the biographer is not necessarily revealing anything that is secret or hidden, but is rather tracing patterns across a life which are there for all to see if they can read the connections. This brings me to the very vexed questions of time and causation in psychoanalytically informed biography, and the relationship between the patterns of the adult life and the subject's childhood. One of the common points of resistance to psychoanalytic interpretations in biography is that it reduces the adult life to the playing-out of childhood experience.

Freud stressed the formative role of childhood in human life, not just as a stage through which we pass on our journey through life, but as a period which reverberates throughout life, as the child's relations within the family are transformed into the relationships and attachments of adult life. It is in the family that the child first confronts the constraints and the pleasures that make him a 'civilised' member of society. Children's relations with their parents are thus fundamentally and inevitably conflicted and ambivalent, as the parents impose controls and meanings on their children's aggression, sexuality and narcissism.

The conflicts and ambivalences, the fears and anxieties, as well as the joys and intense pleasure of childhood, retain their psychic reality into adult life. Many biographers seem to regard the childhood as something for chapter one, with as much period detail as possible to disguise the often thin primary material. But the fuller and more real one can make the childhood, the richer will be the adult life. To keep the childhood confined to chapter one obscures the continuing presence of childhood in the memory of the adult. The grown-up remembers they were once a child, even if some biographer may be tempted to forget. Graham Little stresses the need for the self of childhood and the self of adulthood to work out a story on which they can both agree.[10] Childhood has its uses for the adult—an excuse for later failures, a repository of wisdom or of innocence, a measure of the distance travelled (*look how far I've come...*), and so on.

Childhood also has its uses for biographers, who are generally writing about people older than themselves and who thus always run the risk of seeing them in the larger-than-life terms in which they once saw their own parents. To be reminded that one's subjects were once children helps to remind the biographer of the continuing vulnerabilities of the adult, and to provide a check on their temptation to turn their subjects into either villains or heroes.

These uses aside, however, the vexed question remains of the relationship between the experiences of childhood and adult life. Freud's work fundamentally altered our view of the relationship between childhood and adult life, but it did so within an essentially causal and determinist framework of thinking. As Juliet Mitchell puts it, Freud's 'historical imagination examines the present (the adult illness) and from it reconstructs a hypothetical past determinant'.[11] In Freud the past produces the present. It is just this point to which many people object: it can seem to reduce the achievements and the failures of the adult life to an epiphenomena of some past events, often traumatic; it can seem to reduce the grown man or woman again to a little child; it can seem, almost, to wipe out adult life. These are oversimplifications of Freud, but nevertheless they are responding to the primacy which Freud gives to the past.

Many later psychoanalysts, however, and in particular Melanie Klein and the British Object Relations school which developed from her work, operate with a quite different understanding of time, one in which past and present are one, in which psychological positions, first experienced in infancy, continue to exist as permanent possibilities in the adult psyche. From this perspective, psychoanalytic interpretations of adult life are not uncovering some past determinant of that life, but a present psychological reality in which past and present may share the same patterns, without the implication that the past caused the present. Juliet Mitchell again:

> Klein is not a scientific theorist in the nineteenth-century tradition. The great theorists of the nineteenth century—Darwin, Marx and Freud—explain the present by the past. The dominant sociological phenomenologies of the twentieth century in which Klein participated study lateral, horizontal, not vertical relationships.[12]

Psychoanalytic interpretation can thus be understood not as a matter of digging up causes but of revealing patterns—both within a particular slice of time and across time.

The English biographer Richard Holmes says of biography:

> All biographers work essentially in a narrative mode—they tell the story of a life. Yet the truth they reveal is essentially figurative, the symbolic or representative elements within a life, and to that extent [a] timeless, transcending story…Partly this seems to me a question of biographers using two *kinds* of time. One is historical time, which produces chronology, 'the plot', the daily events of a life,

set against their unfolding historical background. The other may be called interior time, the inner life of the subject, which makes patterns of impulse and imagery, repetitions and recollections, constellations of self-myth and self-understanding, links between childhood and adult experience, which obey the quite different, unhistorical, or 'dream laws' of memory and imagination.[13]

Add to this the Kleinian and the later Object Relations theorists' attention to the traffic between inner and outer reality, and you have what I see as the key contribution psychoanalysis can make to biography: attentiveness to the patterns of interaction between the inner and outer life which, although they are often right before one's nose, only reveal themselves when the biographer lifts their attention from the moving edge of time, the sequence of people and events of the subject's outer life, to an essentially spatial contemplation of the whole—the life spread out like a landscape, the biographer's eye roving back and forth for patterns and disruptions, evasions and telling absences, projects started but abandoned, self-defeating repetitions, recurring strategies for success and obstacles surprisingly overcome.

There is one last point I want to make: some objections to the use of psychoanalysis by biographers are aesthetic rather than intellectual. Much psychoanalytic terminology is ugly; it introduces technical-sounding words into what is primarily a literary form and so disrupts the pleasures of reading. Leon Edel, who is committed to the biographer using psychoanalysis to develop his understanding of his subject, counsels that, nevertheless, the biographer should eschew psychoanalytic terminology:

Having arrived at an understanding of his subject he must now recreate him in words, and as a palpable, living being, in language proper to himself and to those who will read of him...The main duty of the literary biographer, it seems to me, is to gain his insights, understand the motivations of his subject, and then cast aside this special language, bury completely the tools that have served him in attaining his ends. He must write as if psychoanalysis never existed.[14]

This is a perfectly defensible position, but it is motivated primarily by a romantic aesthetic. To embed one's interpretation in a good read seduces people into accepting as certainties what are, after all, only provisional, artful interpretations. Psychoanalytic interpretations are just that—interpretations. A biographer may well want to let the reader in on the making of them, to lay on the table the steps through which that interpretation was developed so that the reader can make up their own mind. This disrupts the identification of the reader with the subject of the biography, but that is the point. It must be admitted, however, that this is a risky strategy, for the more visible the psychoanalytic basis of the interpretation, the more are the various preconceptions about psychoanalysis aroused, preconceptions which can easily come between potential readers and the book.

Conclusion

Psychoanalysis begins from suspicion. It holds that things are not always as they seem, that people do not always say or even know what they mean, that human beings are not transparent to themselves or each other. In this core of suspicion psychoanalysis seems ideally suited to political biographers in the liberal tradition, in which one always has a weather eye cocked for potential abuses of power. That it is not more popular is perhaps because it does not stay with suspicion and its comfortable bedfellow, cynicism, but moves on to compassion. For psychoanalysis also began in the quest to heal. Of course biographers are not in the business of healing, but those who use psychoanalysis are implicated in its quest to understand human lives in all their moral and emotional complexity. To look long and hard at a life, to remember that this person was once a vulnerable and dependent child, to realise that the person's achievements may only be possible because of their self-deceptions, to remember, above all, that this person is not a god or a saint or even a hero, but only a man or woman, is to refuse both denigration and idealisation. For those who want a world of villains and heroes psychoanalysis will never be convincing, but for those who want to understand political leaders and their quest for power it has much to offer.

[1] Leon Edel, *Writing Lives: Principia Biographica*, W. W. Norton, New York, 1984, p. 145.

[2] Erik Erikson, 'On Psycho-Historical Evidence', in *Life History and the Historical Moment*, W. W. Norton, New York, 1975, p. 158.

[3] Kenneth O. Morgan, 'Writing Political Biography', in Eric Hamburger & John Charley (eds), *The Troubled Face of Biography*, Macmillan, London, 1988, p. 33.

[4] Harold Lasswell, *Psychopathology and Politics*, University of Chicago Press, 1977 (1930), pp. 76–77; for discussion of Lasswell's theory of the political type, see A. F. Davies, *Skills, Outlooks and Passions*, Cambridge University Press, Cambridge, pp. 5–7, 24–50.

[5] Michael Kirby, 'A Reformer's View of Constitutional Monarchy', speech to launch South Australian Branch of Australians for a Constitutional Monarchy, 16 November 1993, p. 2.

[6] See discussion of this in James Walter, *The Leader: A Political Biography of Gough Whitlam*, University of Queensland Press, St Lucia, 1980, chapter 1.

[7] Karen Horney, *Neurosis and Human Growth: The Struggle Toward Self-Realization*, W. W. Norton, New York, 1950; Robert C. Tucker, 'A Stalin Biographer's Memoir', in Samuel Baron & Carl Pletsch (eds), *Introspection in Biography: The Biographer's Quest for Self-Awareness*, pp. 249–72.

[8] Heinz Kohut, *The Analysis of the Self*, International Universities Press, New York, 1971, pp. 25–27.

[9] Heinz Kohut, 'The Bipolar Self' in his *The Restoration of the Self*, International Universities Press, New York, 1977.

[10] Graham Little, 'The Uses of Childhood', *Eureka Street*, September 1994, pp. 28–32.

[11] Juliet Mitchell (ed.), *The Selected Melanie Klein* (Penguin, London, 1986), p. 27.

[12] Mitchell, p. 29.

[13] Richard Holmes, 'Biographer's Footsteps', *International Review of Psychoanalysis*, 19, 1, 1992, p. 2.

[14] Leon Edel, 'The Biographer and Psychoanalysis', *International Journal of Psychoanalysis*, 42, 1961, pp. 4462–63.

2 Graham Little's Theory of Political Leadership

The first version of this piece was 'A Psychosocial Approach to Politics', Arena, *number 72, 1985; a later version was published in the* International Journal of Applied Psychoanalysis, *volume 6, number 2, June 2009.*

In my thinking and writing about Australia's political leaders, I have been immeasurably influenced by the insights of my late friend and colleague Graham Little and his theory of political leadership.* It is a theory of extraordinary power and sophistication, with roots deep in psychoanalytic theory. Connecting the insights and knowledge of psychoanalysis with the public world of politics and finding ways to communicate these to a wide audience were the central quests of Little's intellectual life. From the 1980s until his death in 2000, Little was a regular contributor to the Australian media with profiles on political leaders such as Malcolm Fraser, Bob Hawke, Paul Keating, Jeff Kennett, Maggie Thatcher and Ronald Reagan.

Little came to psychoanalysis from sociology in the tradition of David Riesman's *The Lonely Crowd* (1950), in which intensely focussed case studies are used to explore the relationship between individual experience and broader social themes. He worked briefly in the 1960s with Robert Lane, Fred Greenstein and Daniel Levinson at Yale, and learned from Levinson in particular the close reading of life-history interviews using psychoanalytic categories. His early work in the late 1960s was on the student experience, when politics was an inescapable part of student life and campuses were exciting places to be—full of idealism, argument and optimistic confidence in the possibilities of creative social change. It was indeed a Time of Hope, as Donald Horne called his book on the same period, and it gave Little an abiding faith in the capacities of politics to inspire hope in people, to capture their dreams. Joining Melbourne University's Department of Politics in 1971 as Whitlam's campaign for government was gathering momentum, Little found his interest drawn to the way leaders represent particular emotional possibilities for the public, to the emotional and psychological meanings they carry for both their supporters and for those who reject them. The heady days of the Whitlam government, followed by its descent into disorder and recrimination, convinced him of the value of his approach.

Little organised his profiles of students into three political styles and later linked these to three originating family climates, making some use of psychoanalytic ideas, particularly about the enduring importance of childhood experience. His concept of style was fairly loose, used to notice similarities and isolate themes, and the types were descriptive, without a generative mechanism. In 1985 he published *Political Ensembles: A Psychosocial Approach to Politics and Leadership.* It was the product of ten years of hard work: countless interviews; extensive reading in psychoanalysis, particularly of the case-study-based British Object Relations school; and hours on the couch with his own memories, fears and dreams. It set out the solid basis of knowledge and insight which enabled Little later to engage so apparently effortlessly with the shifting moods of the public world and to produce powerful interpretations of contemporary leaders in his journalistic writing. The typology towards which Little had been groping in the earlier work on students and their families had been transformed into a theory of astonishing range and power. As Theodor Adorno claimed for the typologies in *The Authoritarian Personality* (1950), the types were no longer simply descriptive, but integrated traits according to their inherent logic, the way they related to certain basic psychological conflicts and dilemmas and their resolution. The dilemma at the root of Little's typology could hardly be more basic. It is the self–other dilemma, the dilemma of our human need both for other people and for a sense of ourselves as individuals.

Little posits three broad possible solutions to the balancing act in which we are all engaged, between the needs and demands of the self and the other. The evidential and theoretical base for this is Wilfred Bion's classic work *Experiences in Groups* (1961), in which he describes three emotionally based group formations which demand three different types of leaders. Little slightly reworked these, broadening the implications of Bion's observations of the therapeutic group out into relations between leaders and followers in society at large, together with the characteristic emotions evoked by different types of leaders and their inevitable failures.

Bion describes three group formations which demand three different types of leaders. He calls them the Dependency group, the Flight–Fight group and the Pairing group. Little matches these with three types of political leaders—Group, Strong and Inspiring.

The Dependency group is organised around shared need and wants the leader to look after it. People are seen as belonging together, and the emphasis is on the emotions and experiences that bind—on trust, loyalty, self-effacement, tradition. People are dependent and maturity is the capacity to show concern for those more needy than oneself. Group leaders pay attention to the many ways people need and depend on each other, specialising in the politics of sympathy and compassion and taking care not to put themselves too far ahead of the people they lead. The approach to leadership of the ALP before Gough Whitlam is an example of this. Ben Chifley's legendary humility as leader of federal Labor, his claim that he 'does not occupy the position of leader other than because I am one of the people in the movement', the emphasis in his speeches on the need to look after the weak, all make him an archetypal Group leader.

Where the Dependency group is formed around shared need, Bion's second group, Flight–Fight, is formed for survival in the face of common threats. It faces outward, ready for action, and the emphasis is on maintaining the internal cohesion and sense of shared purpose needed effectively to fight an external enemy. The Flight–Fight group's leader is the Strong leader, hardworking, tough and alert, proof against the temptations of pathos that might weaken the chances for the group's survival. He demands total loyalty from the group, using his strength not just to combat the enemy but to stare down any internal opposition.

The members of the Flight–Fight group are independent, carrying their supplies on their own sturdy backs. People are conceptualised as separate and independent, relating to each other through structured competition. Their natural desires set them in conflict with each other, and society or civilisation is necessary minimally to contain this conflict, more optimistically to channel it into useful human activity. This is Hobbes' individualism; it is also Freud's Oedipal theory in which the child's desire for the mother and rivalry with the father is the conflict from which the superego, society's internalised agent of repression, is born.

Bion's third group is the Pairing group. It is the hardest to grasp. Bion's Dependency and Flight–Fight groups, Little's Group and Strong leaders, map easily onto familiar cultural forms—hard and soft, masculine and feminine, protective and nurturing, dependence and independence, Maggie Thatcher's dry and wet. Pairing is different. As Bion describes it, a group will sometimes fall into the configuration of a pair, a twosome, in earnest, equal conversation. The group feels itself to be creative and senses the possibility of new things. Hope stirs and there's excitement in the air. This provides the context for Little's Inspiring leader, who is able to break through the habitual standoff between compassion and strength, and suggest that perhaps we can find political solutions which go beyond given social traditions and structures. It is the solution to the self–other dilemma which in some senses refuses to choose, holding self and other together in a mutual rapport, different but equal, the capacities of each enhanced by the other. Little is using Bion to give a psychological underpinning to Max Weber's category of charisma, arguing that the deus ex machina of the exceptional man, which Weber used to explain leaders who dramatically broke through the social structures of their time, is grounded in a widely shared form of relationship.

Little began developing his model of leadership in the 1970s, and he pegged his three types to three of the dominant Australian leaders of that time: Jim Cairns was the Group leader (as was Jimmy Carter), Malcolm Fraser the Strong leader (as were Maggie Thatcher and Ronald Reagan); and Whitlam (and Kennedy and Trudeau) were Inspiring, offering the vision and energy to break through the old structures to the new.

Little's triadic leadership typology has two great strengths. The first is that it is dynamic; the second, that it brings leaders and followers together in the same frame. No one way of solving the self–other dilemma is completely satisfactory. In emphasising certain human needs and capacities, it downplays others, casting the shadow of the emotions and psychological possibilities it excludes. This makes each leadership type inherently unstable, with its own characteristic ways of failing.

So the Strong leader can become rigid, demanding too much repression of individual initiative in the name of loyalty and stifling the new ideas that are needed to respond effectively to a changed external environment. Such was the fate of Malcolm Fraser's prime ministership, as he refused to listen to neoliberal ideas which challenged the settled assumptions of Australia's paternalistic and interventionist style of federal government. The Group leader's focus on the care of the weak can also stifle initiative, cutting down tall poppies, promoting the politics of envy, and punishing people who want to leave the group and get ahead. These are the standard accusations made by strong leadership against the left: the weakest will only be cared for if the group is strong; the group's survival cannot be beholden to its weakest members; the group's resources are necessarily limited, so it must not give in to the illusions of limitless compassion. In response, the Group leader sees a callousness in the Strong leader's refusal of sympathy, which threatens the polity's basic claims to humanity as it turns away vulnerable human beings appealing for succour and refuge.

These conflicting perspectives have been playing out in Australia since the *Tampa* crisis, when John Howard refused to accept refugees rescued from drowning by a Norwegian freighter. At base, this is a conflict over the limits and the compulsions of compassion for people outside the primary group—in this case, the nation. To call them asylum seekers is to recognise the legitimacy of their claim on our compassion; to call them illegal immigrants is to refuse it. In his response to the *Tampa* crisis Howard was a Strong leader par excellence, alert to the impact of their plea for help on the group's resources, imagining being flooded by limitless demands with order and rules collapsing into chaos.

Inspiring leaders, enlivened by hope and possibility, can also be self-absorbed and unworldly, with an exaggerated sense of their own and others' capacities to change, turning a deaf ear to the pleas for caution of those with much to lose. For Little, Whitlam was the paradigmatic Inspiring leader: he made his supporters believe that Australia could be a different, better place, and he still stands as a symbol of hope for many of them, but he came crashing down under the weight of his own hubris and inexperience, and seemed cold and irresponsible to those unmoved by his charms. This was true too of Keating, who rekindled something of Whitlam's vision of Labor as the party of modernising hope, but who showed little sympathy for those unexcited by change.

The structure is determinedly triadic. Each type exists in constant tension with the other two, warding off its rivals but also casting a shadow of the emotions it excludes. Little shows the shadow cast by each solution, and the way each shadow is a necessary consequence of that solution's strengths. In this he produces a dynamic political typology in which each solution can always only ever be temporary, as its structural failings cause inevitable mistakes of both over- and under-reaching and propel the momentum for change.

The second strength of Little's model is that it brings leaders and followers together into the same framework of interpretation. Leaders are not conceptualised as exceptional, operating in a world apart, with the electorate having the occasional opportunity to pass judgement. Nor are they seen as only judged on a rational basis in terms of their effectiveness or the benefits they deliver to their supporters. Rather, leaders and followers are seen as tied together in a shared and continuing moral and psychological drama. Little argues that the continuing fascination with the smallest sayings of our national leaders, the intensity of affect people feel for some leaders, draws deeply on people's experience of themselves in society. Leaders offer themselves to their publics not just on the basis of their policies and effectiveness, but on the basis of their personalities and the emotional style they will bring to governing the affairs of the nation. Little argues that leaders and followers find each other and that leaders appeal because they match their followers' characteristic solution to the self–other dilemma.

But there is more at work here than simple matching, like finding like. The leader plays out the possibilities of one solution in public, displaying the tensions between loyalty and ambition, the possibilities and limitations of power, the exhilarations and the costs of non-conformity, just how hard a heart can become, and so on. Followers react with satisfaction as they see the proud, overreaching leader fall, just as they knew he would; their disapproval increases as one cold, unsympathetic decision is followed by another, until finally the electorate recoils and turns to a leader who can restore their sense that they are kind decent people. Watching leaders and the stakes they play for confirms us in the habitual moral and emotional patterns of our daily lives.

This is politics as moral drama, as leaders' solutions to the self–other dilemma are played out publicly under intense pressure, and for the highest stakes, both personally and for the polity they lead. It is a theory which helps us to think about the pervasiveness of leadership in modern democracies, and the way leaders focus feelings about the polity, their capacity to inspire and to polarise. Little is arguing that the continuing fascination with the smallest sayings of our national leaders, the intensity of affect people feel for some leaders, draws deeply on people's experience of themselves in society.

His theory accommodates the responses of those who passionately reject a leader as well as of those who follow. Consider the longevity of Gough Whitlam's capacity to inspire, despite his governments' descent into chaos; or the excessiveness of the Howard haters. This cannot be explained by any actual harm that Howard's policies have done to the haters, but is rather the expression of their profound alienation from the emotional and psychological mood Howard brought to the government of the nation. Moral dramas have villains as well as heroes, and Little's theory encompasses them both.

Little's leadership types are Ideal Types, abstractions used to help analyse actual leaders in complex historical circumstances. Particular leaders will be both more and less than their type. But most members of the public are not biographers or historians. They do not look closely at their leaders, analysing the evidence and trying to understand the contradictions. They view the leader through the prism of their own experience, their own characteristic way of resolving the self–other dilemma, seeing what they are already attuned to see. Little's theory illuminates the pathways by which the private needs and experiences of a multitude of individuals are transformed into the public symbolic formations which leaders become.

---

* This essay draws on the following works by Graham Little: 'Leaders and Followers: A Psychosocial Prospectus', *Melbourne Journal of Politics*, 12, 1980, pp. 3–29; 'Ambivalence, Dilemma, Paradox: The Nature and Significance of Leader–Follower Ties with Comments on the Leadership of Margaret Thatcher', *Political Psychology*, 3, 4, 1984, pp. 553–71; *Political Ensembles: A Psychosocial Approach to Politics and Leadership*, Oxford University Press, Melbourne, 1985; and *Strong Leadership: Thatcher, Reagan and an Eminent Person*, Oxford University Press, Melbourne, 1988

3 The Chook in the Australian Unconscious

Meanjin, *volume 45, number 2, 1986.*

> *The dark-haired girl said in the next*
> *Life she would choose to be a chook*
> —David Campbell, 'Words with a Black Orpington'

Much has been made of the desert as a symbol for the precariousness of European civilisation's hold over both the Australian continent and the minds of those who dwell here, but for most Australians it is not the desert but the chook which symbolises the precariousness of our social order. Scratching out an existence from unyielding ground, collapsing into a flap when danger threatens, the chook not the desert haunts our dreams. And no one has gone into the national parliament dressed as a desert, or even its ship, the camel. For the chook symbolises the forces, both inner and outer, which we fear we have not conquered, and it does so by being a uniquely Australian comic figure.

The word 'chook' is a symbol of our cultural difference. Where the British have hens and the Americans chickens we have chooks, though as one moves up the social scale and ambivalence about Australia's difference from England increases the word is heard less frequently. Private-school-educated people nervously refer to hens;

and when chooks were being discussed at an academic dinner party
I attended, a professor of lower-middle-class origins remarked with
surprised wistfulness, '"Chook"—that's not a word you often hear
around the university these days.'

Social status is often expressed by one's distance from nature;
the more nature is controlled, and the more of it one controls, the
higher one is in the human pecking order. So, from chooks in the
house, to chooks running free round the backyard, to chooks neatly
penned, to the pinnacle of respectability where one is free from the
fowl altogether. Chooks are dirtier than hens, so the word, along
with other images of dirt now banished, carries something of the
allure of instinctual pleasures renounced for the dubious benefits
of an upward mobility measured by one's distance from the dirt.
Partridge describes the word as an Australian and New Zealand
colloquialism derived from Irish and English dialect and current
from about the mid-nineteenth century, though the use of 'chook'
as a pejorative referring to women is given as Australian only.

In his books *Totemism* and its successor, *The Savage Mind*, Claude
Lévi-Strauss shows how human beliefs about and practices towards
animals, which anthropologists had called the institution of totemism,
are really systems of classification with which human societies think
about their own social relations. Speculating on the relationships
between human society and different species of animals, he suggests
that the bird world is the most perfect metaphor for human society
that the natural kingdom offers.

> Birds...can be permitted to resemble men for the very reason
> that they are so different. They are feathered, winged, oviparous
> and they are also physically separated from human society by the
> element in which it is their privilege to move. As a result of this

fact, they form a community which is independent of our own but, precisely because of this independence, appears to us like another society, homologous to that in which we live: birds love freedom; they build themselves homes in which they live a family life and nurture their young; they often engage in social relations with other members of their species; and they communicate with them by acoustic means recalling articulated language. Consequently everything objective conspires to make us think of the bird world as a metaphorical human society.

Lévi-Strauss sees the society of birds as representing humanity's achievements—its love of freedom, its language, its caring family life, its sociability. But chooks are ground-dwelling birds penned in our own backyards, made ridiculous by their lumbering efforts to grace the air with a flight that's more aspiration than achievement. They are birds slipped from their rightful element, an image not of human society's achieved harmony and completeness, but of the vulnerability of humans and their social forms to some of the less admirable characteristics of their nature. The pecking order, closely observed, is not a lovely institution; neither is the chook pen under threat an image of an ordered social world.

It is the chook's vulnerability that is perhaps the key to its role in the unconscious. In *The Teach Your Chicken to Fly Manual* (Kangaroo Press, 1983) Trevor Weekes describes them as 'the birds evolution forgot' and gives detailed instructions for the building of a machine to exercise the domestic fowl's flying muscles. This little book, with its meticulous pencil drawings of chooks in mechanical contraptions and photos to show the machine in operation with a white leghorn called Gregory Peck, is evidence of both the sadism inspired by the chook's comparatively flightless fate and the laughter we use to defend ourselves against the knowledge of that sadism. To visit the chook pen in the backyard is always to risk finding the devastation wrought by a marauding dog or fox—blood, feathers, dismembered chooks that couldn't fly away. The cruelty of nature's ethic of survival made manifest in suburbia; culture's fragile control over nature destroyed. Throw a rock on the chook-house roof, run a stick along its corrugated-iron sides, and you can recreate the blind panic of flightless birds trying to escape. Ned, in Olga Masters' novel *Loving Daughters* (1984), returned from World War One not quite right in the head, beats the chook-house wall with a lump of wood whenever he passes it, stirring the din and frantic flapping of the chooks within to an echo of his own growing madness. And in the headless chook running round the backyard there is an image of panic not even death can stop. This image is a vivid childhood memory for many Australians, particularly those older ones who witnessed chooks being chased and killed for the family table. Perhaps for many their earliest experience of violent death, its impact was the greater because of the capacity for violence towards small living creatures it revealed in their axe-wielding parents.

The plucked carcass of the chook bears a remarkable resemblance to a human baby, or rather to its corpse—the beginning and end of the human life cycle brought together in a single image. After a difficult day with a new baby and cooking a roast chook for tea, a friend of mine had a dream: he trussed the baby, pink and vulnerable, for the oven. So in the barrel routine on TV's *Hey Hey It's Saturday*, in which numbered balls are replaced by numbered frozen chooks, there is a transformation of the symbolic equivalence of babies and chook carcasses to the world of the frozen embryo. In this transformation we see further evidence of the symbolic power of chooks and the need to give it cultural expression even within the urban world's attenuated relationship with nature. The particularly strong disgust evoked by battery-hen farming is further witness to the chook's continuing power as an image of vulnerability.

In most cultures it is the male not the female domestic fowl which has been loaded with symbolic importance. The cock of European and Asian culture, with its pride, courage, aggression and splendid plumage, has been a rich source of images of masculinity. And cockfighting has been and still is, despite being banned in most countries, a popular male pastime. So although there are tales of the foolishness of the cock's pride, and talk of cocks gives great scope for sexual innuendo, the cock is only incidentally a comic figure. In Australia the cock scarcely figures; a hanger-on among the chooks, if he is singled out at all it is by the bowdlerised American word 'rooster'. Australia has replaced one of the central masculine symbols of the old world with a comic female figure, suggesting that it is female rather than male sexuality that is problematic in the Antipodes.

One must beware of too glib an interpretation, resist the temptation to speculate about drooping cocks and other signs of national impotence. As Clifford Geertz has shown in his celebrated essay 'Deep Play: Notes on the Balinese Cockfight' (1972), cultural symbols are never simple reflections of social life. Rather, they are parts of stories cultures tell themselves about themselves, and like all stories they could have been different. Australians' interest in chooks rather than cocks may have little to do with sex and more to do with their unease with nature; and of course human sexuality can both demonstrate and symbolise humanity's implication in nature, particularly female sexuality, with all it implies about the physicalness of our birth and the consequent inevitability of our death. For, as Lévi-Strauss has argued, women have generally been seen by human societies as closer to nature than men, their integration into culture more ambivalent.

Partridge notes that the use of 'chook' as a pejorative term for women is peculiarly Australian. When Reg Ansett called air hostesses 'old boilers', they went on strike till he apologised. Pejorative terms express annoyance, generally caused by the speaker's inability to get the person so described to do what is wanted. They are a response to another's intractability, a railing against the limits of one's power. Intractable women, intractable nature. Female sexuality is particularly problematic here because nature is so problematic, both for those who try to farm it and for the urban majority who try to ignore it.

If nature were not so problematic here we would still have hens. Later in the poem of David Campbell's cited at the beginning, a rural idyll is evoked, and like all rural idylls it refers to an English not an Australian landscape.

> And she said she would be a homestead hen
> With a nest under a damson plum
> In the windfall orchard back home.

Hens are at home in a cosy domesticated nature; always plump, never scrawny, they peck away in the orchards and solid-stone barns of prosperous farms, red and black and speckled against the green fields of England; never dirty-white mongrel chooks scrabbling between ramshackle corrugated-iron and wood buildings in dusty paddocks.

The chook is an image of the tenuous hold Australians have over the land, its stubborn intractability and our ridiculous vulnerability. Whenever the word 'chook' occurs in conversations, at first people smile in the sophisticated way people smile at childish things they have put behind them; but if the topic is pursued, most soon respond—with stories, memories, jokes, and with the conspiratorial pride of sharing a cultural touchstone, of playing for a while with the secret identification in most Australians' hearts between themselves and the chook.